SUPERMAN

WORLDS' ☆ FINEST

WITHDRAWN

BATMAN

VOLUME 6

THE SECRET HISTORY OF SUPERMAN AND BATMAN

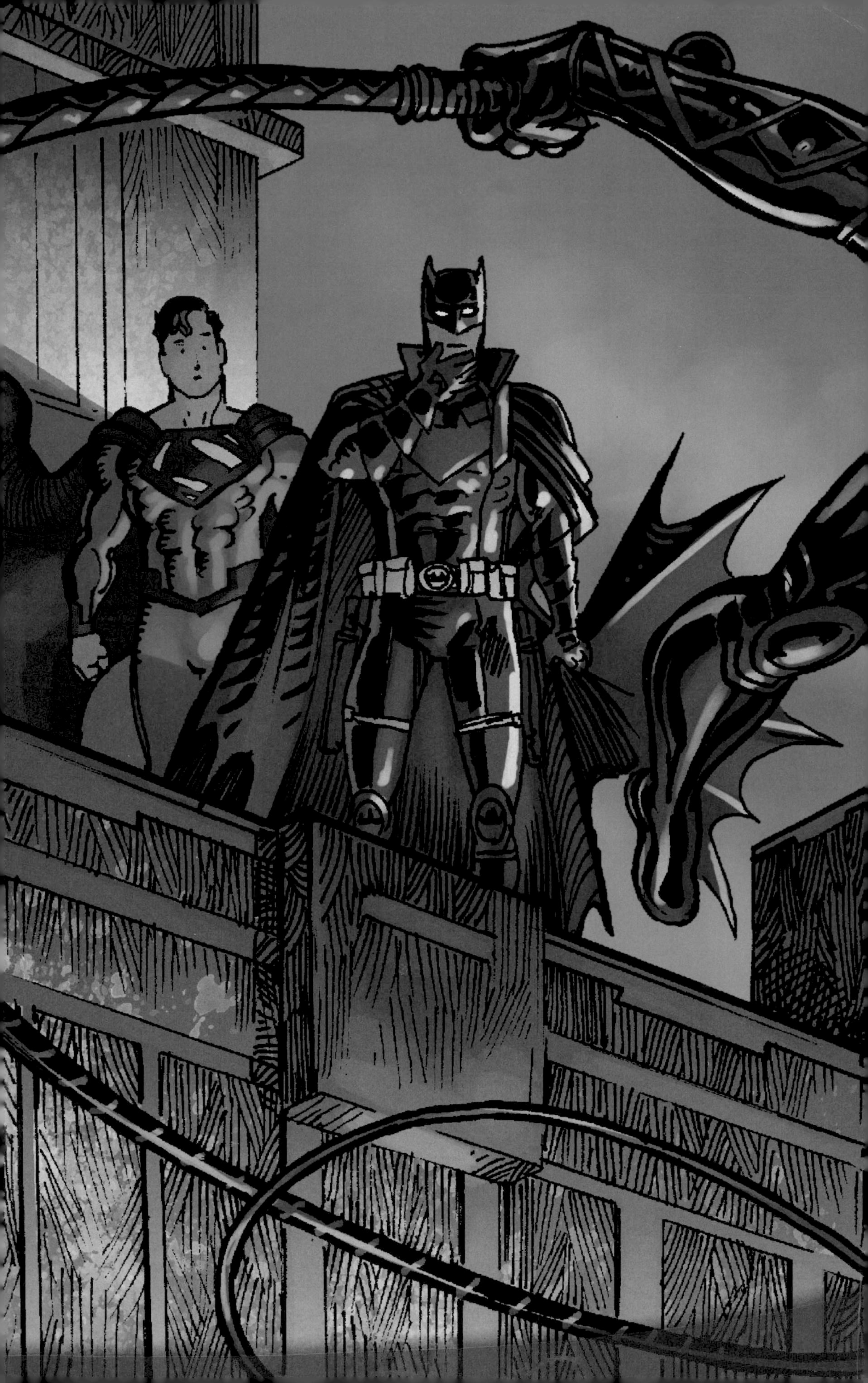

DC COMICS™

SUPERMAN™ WORLDS' FINEST™ BATMAN™

VOLUME 6 THE SECRET HISTORY OF SUPERMAN AND BATMAN

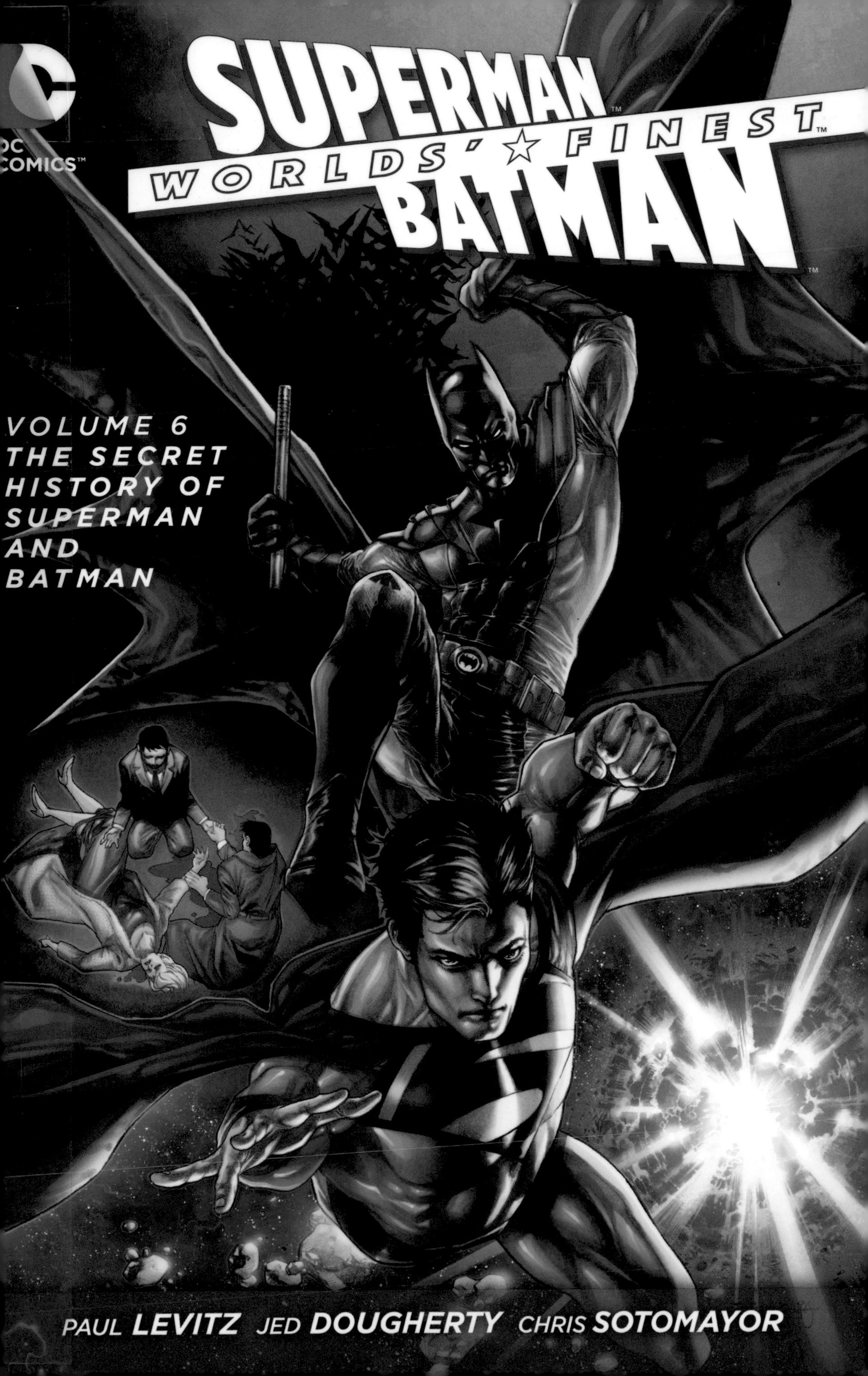

PAUL LEVITZ JED DOUGHERTY CHRIS SOTOMAYOR

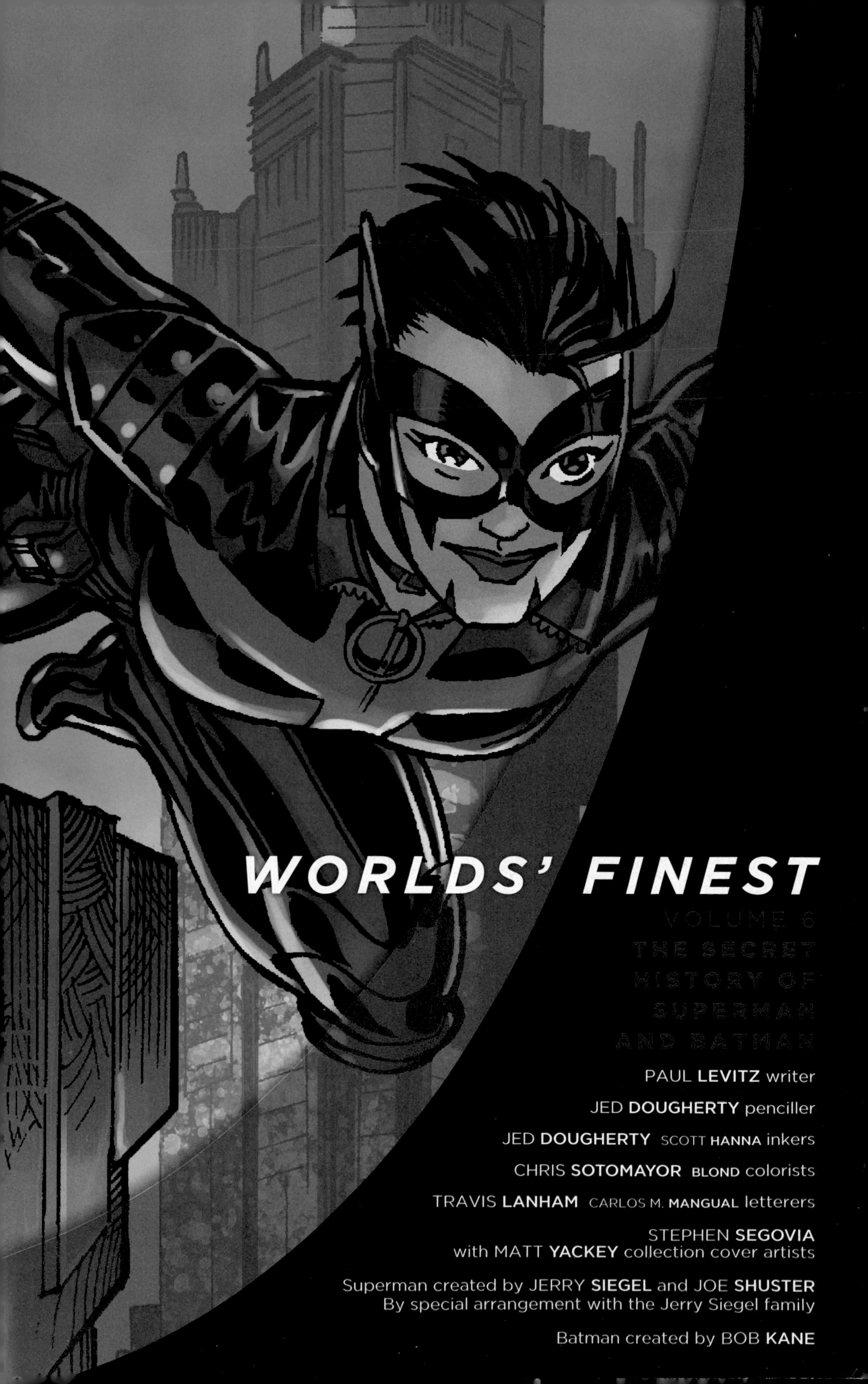

WORLDS' FINEST

VOLUME 6
THE SECRET HISTORY OF SUPERMAN AND BATMAN

PAUL **LEVITZ** writer

JED **DOUGHERTY** penciller

JED **DOUGHERTY** SCOTT **HANNA** inkers

CHRIS **SOTOMAYOR** **BLOND** colorists

TRAVIS **LANHAM** CARLOS M. **MANGUAL** letterers

STEPHEN **SEGOVIA**
with MATT **YACKEY** collection cover artists

Superman created by JERRY **SIEGEL** and JOE **SHUSTER**
By special arrangement with the Jerry Siegel family

Batman created by BOB **KANE**

RICKEY PURDIN RACHEL GLUCKSTERN Editors – Original Series DAVE WIELGOSZ Assistant Editor – Original Series
JEB WOODARD Group Editor – Collected Editions ROBIN WILDMAN Editor – Collected Edition ROBBIE BIEDERMAN Publication Design

BOB HARRAS Senior VP – Editor-in-Chief, DC Comics

DIANE NELSON President DAN DIDIO and JIM LEE Co-Publishers GEOFF JOHNS Chief Creative Officer
AMIT DESAI Senior VP – Marketing & Global Franchise Management NAIRI GARDINER Senior VP – Finance
SAM ADES VP – Digital Marketing BOBBIE CHASE VP – Talent Development
MARK CHIARELLO Senior VP – Art, Design & Collected Editions JOHN CUNNINGHAM VP – Content Strategy
ANNE DePIES VP – Strategy Planning & Reporting DON FALLETTI VP – Manufacturing Operations
LAWRENCE GANEM VP – Editorial Administration & Talent Relations ALISON GILL Senior VP – Manufacturing & Operations
HANK KANALZ Senior VP – Editorial Strategy & Administration JAY KOGAN VP – Legal Affairs
DEREK MADDALENA Senior VP – Sales & Business Development JACK MAHAN VP – Business Affairs
DAN MIRON VP – Sales Planning & Trade Development NICK NAPOLITANO VP – Manufacturing Administration
CAROL ROEDER VP – Marketing EDDIE SCANNELL VP – Mass Account & Digital Sales
COURTNEY SIMMONS Senior VP – Publicity & Communications JIM (SKI) SOKOLOWSKI VP – Comic Book Specialty & Newsstand Sales
SANDY YI Senior VP – Global Franchise Management

WORLDS' FINEST VOLUME 6: THE SECRET HISTORY OF SUPERMAN AND BATMAN

DC Comics, 4000 Warner Blvd., Burbank, CA 91522
A Warner Bros. Entertainment Company.
Printed by RR Donnelley, Salem, VA, USA. 10/30/15. First Printing.
ISBN: 978-1-4012-5776-7

Library of Congress Cataloging-in-Publication Data is available

PEFC Certified

Printed on paper from
sustainably managed
forests and controlled
sources

PEFC/29-31-75   www.pefc.org

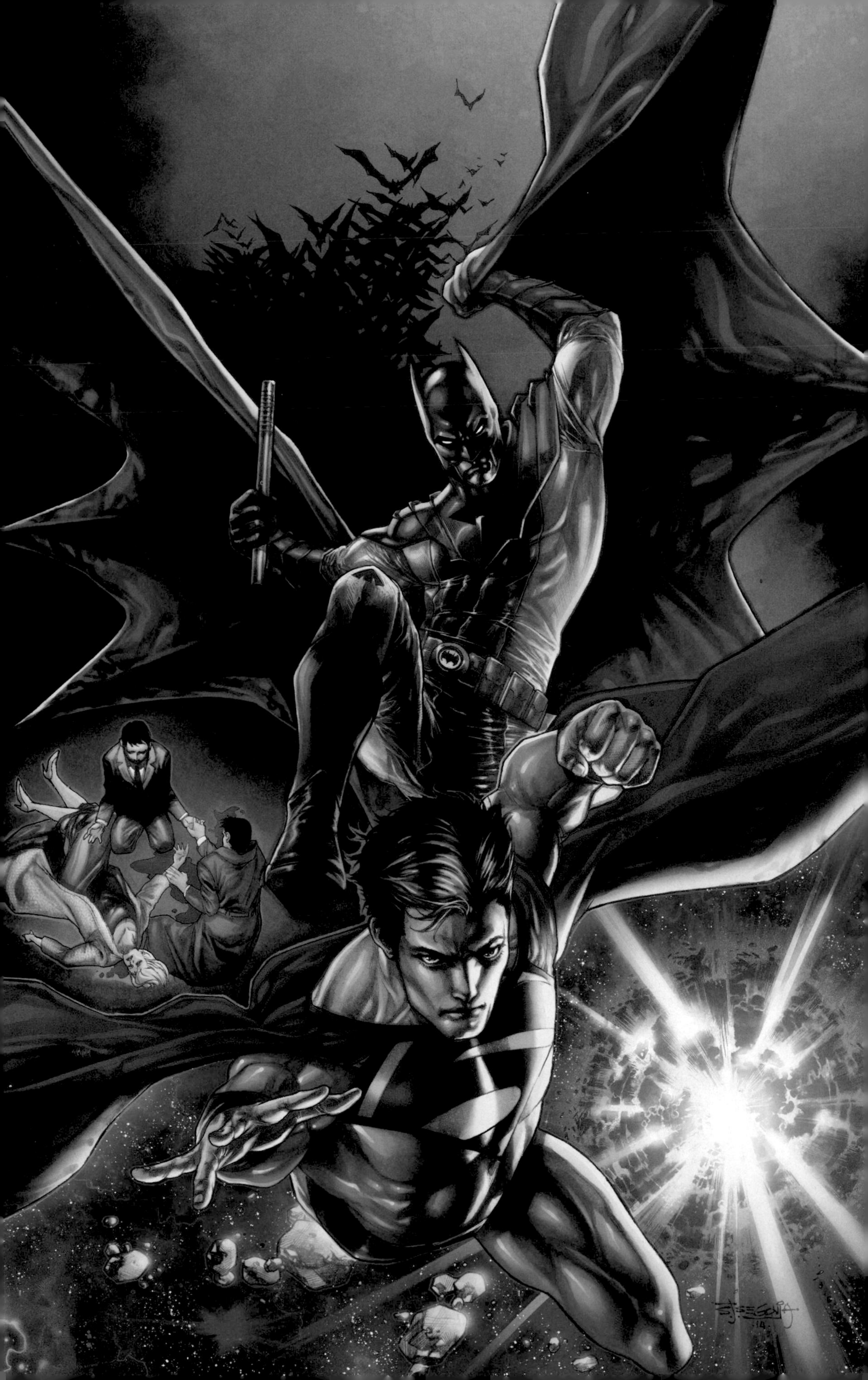

PART ONE: TEMPTATIONS

PAUL LEVITZ writer **JED DOUGHERTY** penciller **SCOTT HANNA** inker

BLOND colorist **CARLOS M. MANGUAL** letterer cover art by **STEPHEN SEGOVIA & MATT YACKEY**

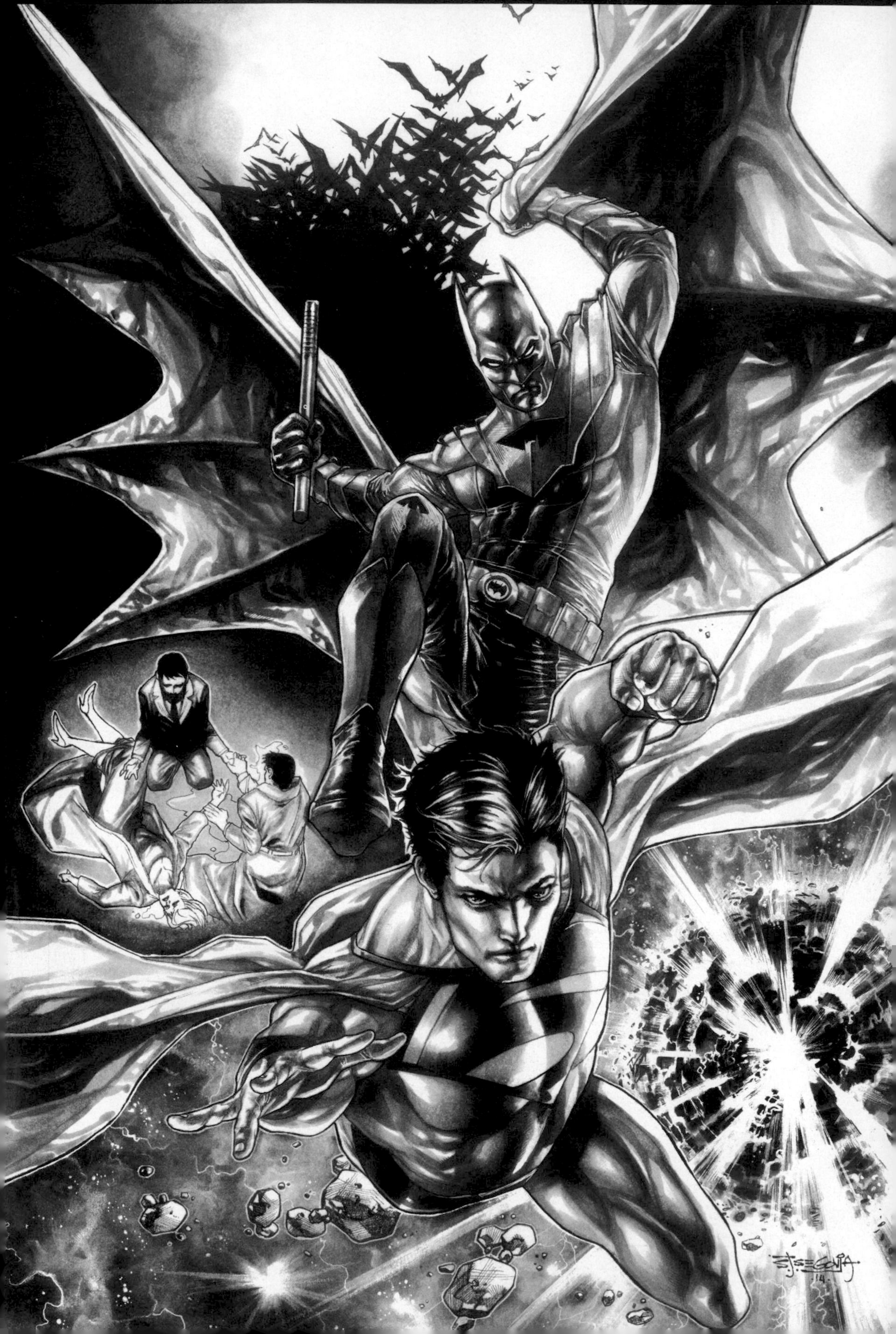

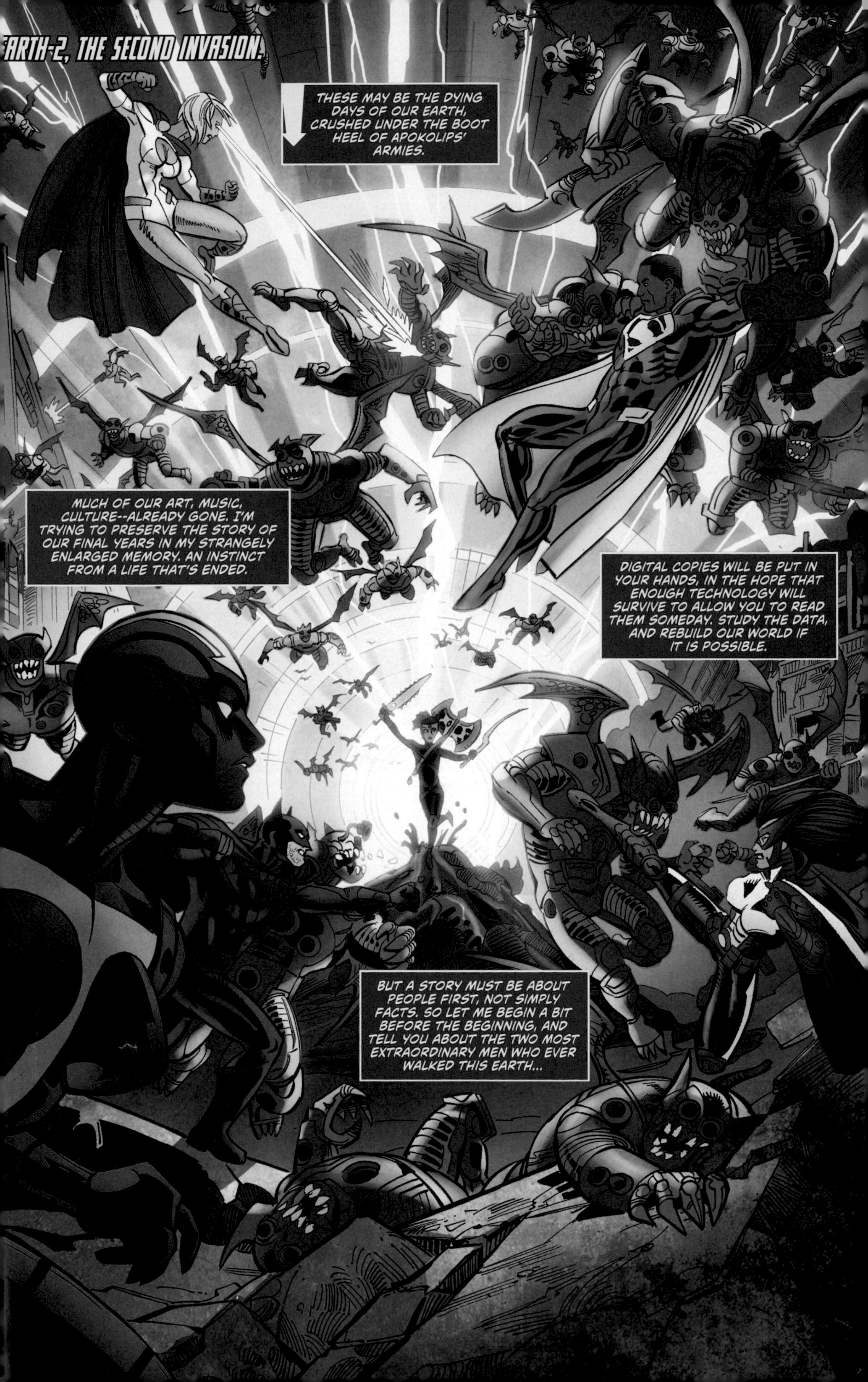
EARTH-2, THE SECOND INVASION:
THESE MAY BE THE DYING DAYS OF OUR EARTH, CRUSHED UNDER THE BOOT HEEL OF APOKOLIPS' ARMIES.
MUCH OF OUR ART, MUSIC, CULTURE--ALREADY GONE. I'M TRYING TO PRESERVE THE STORY OF OUR FINAL YEARS IN MY STRANGELY ENLARGED MEMORY. AN INSTINCT FROM A LIFE THAT'S ENDED.
DIGITAL COPIES WILL BE PUT IN YOUR HANDS, IN THE HOPE THAT ENOUGH TECHNOLOGY WILL SURVIVE TO ALLOW YOU TO READ THEM SOMEDAY. STUDY THE DATA, AND REBUILD OUR WORLD IF IT IS POSSIBLE.
BUT A STORY MUST BE ABOUT PEOPLE FIRST, NOT SIMPLY FACTS. SO LET ME BEGIN A BIT BEFORE THE BEGINNING, AND TELL YOU ABOUT THE TWO MOST EXTRAORDINARY MEN WHO EVER WALKED THIS EARTH...

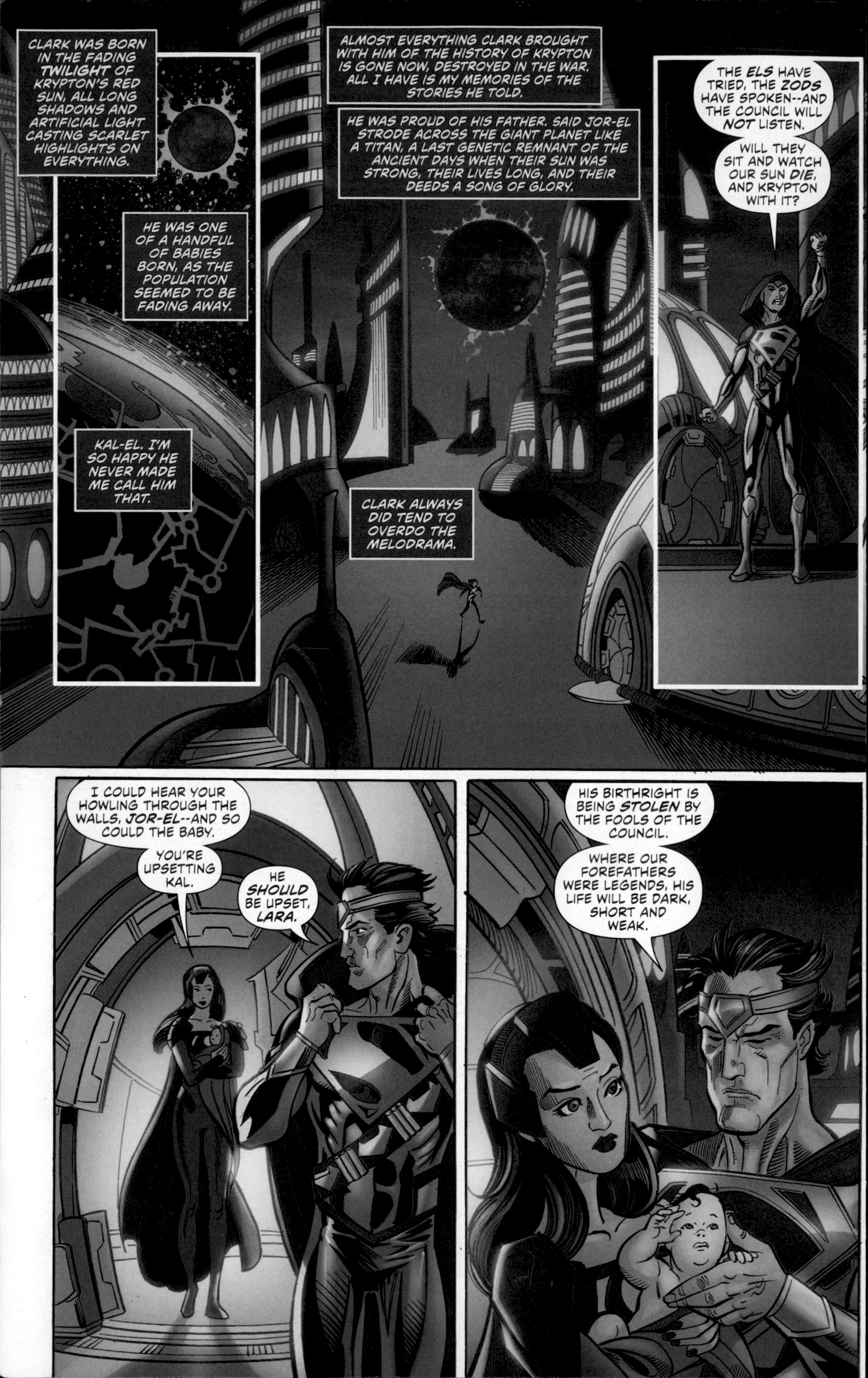

CLARK WAS BORN IN THE FADING TWILIGHT OF KRYPTON'S RED SUN, ALL LONG SHADOWS AND ARTIFICIAL LIGHT CASTING SCARLET HIGHLIGHTS ON EVERYTHING.
HE WAS ONE OF A HANDFUL OF BABIES BORN, AS THE POPULATION SEEMED TO BE FADING AWAY.
KAL-EL. I'M SO HAPPY HE NEVER MADE ME CALL HIM THAT.
ALMOST EVERYTHING CLARK BROUGHT WITH HIM OF THE HISTORY OF KRYPTON IS GONE NOW, DESTROYED IN THE WAR. ALL I HAVE IS MY MEMORIES OF THE STORIES HE TOLD.
HE WAS PROUD OF HIS FATHER. SAID JOR-EL STRODE ACROSS THE GIANT PLANET LIKE A TITAN, A LAST GENETIC REMNANT OF THE ANCIENT DAYS WHEN THEIR SUN WAS STRONG, THEIR LIVES LONG, AND THEIR DEEDS A SONG OF GLORY.
CLARK ALWAYS DID TEND TO OVERDO THE MELODRAMA.
THE ELS HAVE TRIED, THE ZODS HAVE SPOKEN--AND THE COUNCIL WILL NOT LISTEN.
WILL THEY SIT AND WATCH OUR SUN DIE, AND KRYPTON WITH IT?
I COULD HEAR YOUR HOWLING THROUGH THE WALLS, JOR-EL--AND SO COULD THE BABY.
YOU'RE UPSETTING KAL.
HE SHOULD BE UPSET, LARA.
HIS BIRTHRIGHT IS BEING STOLEN BY THE FOOLS OF THE COUNCIL.
WHERE OUR FOREFATHERS WERE LEGENDS, HIS LIFE WILL BE DARK, SHORT AND WEAK.

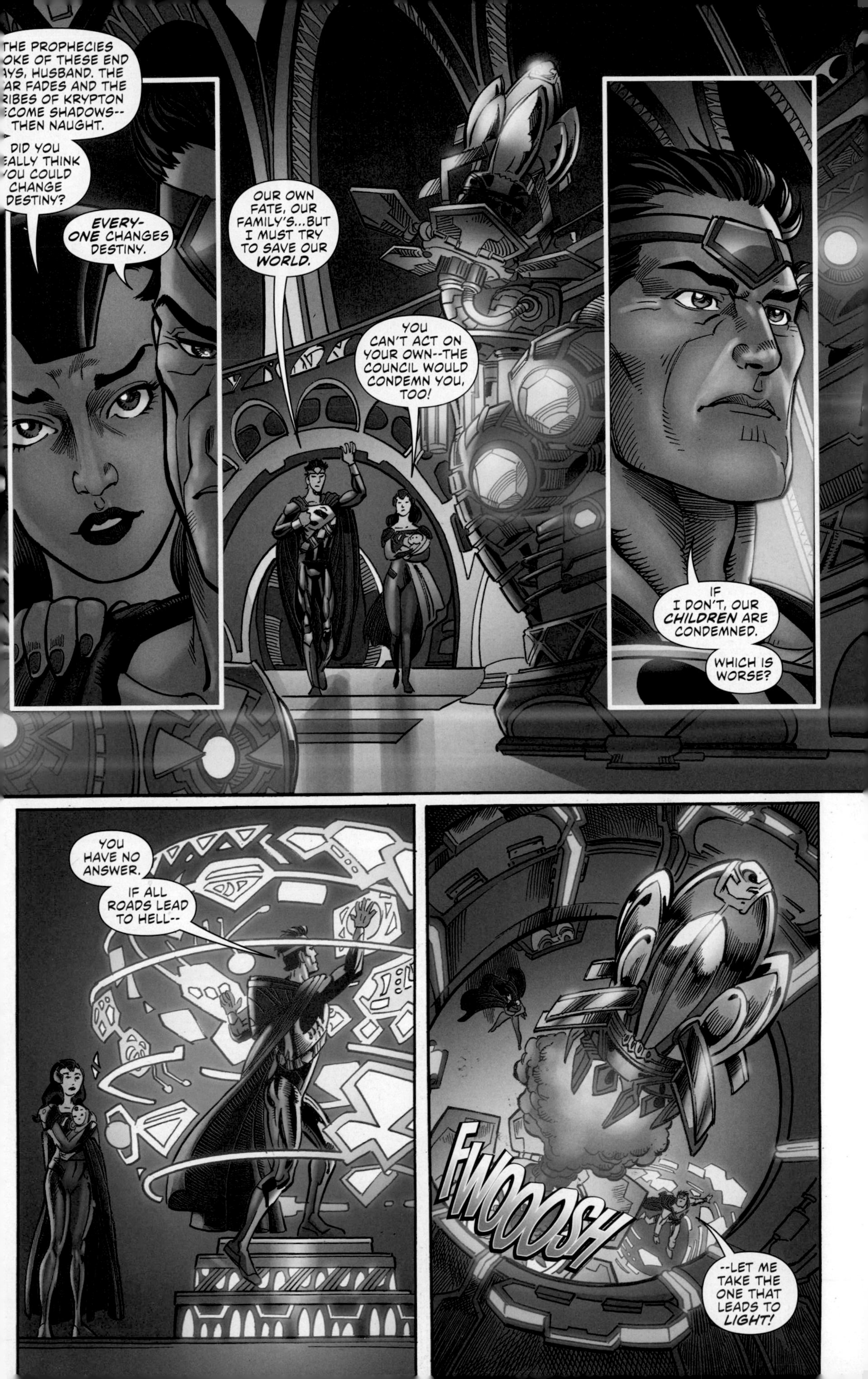
THE PROPHECIES OKE OF THESE END AYS, HUSBAND. THE AR FADES AND THE RIBES OF KRYPTON ECOME SHADOWS-- THEN NAUGHT.
DID YOU EALLY THINK YOU COULD CHANGE DESTINY?
EVERY-ONE CHANGES DESTINY.
OUR OWN FATE, OUR FAMILY'S...BUT I MUST TRY TO SAVE OUR WORLD.
YOU CAN'T ACT ON YOUR OWN--THE COUNCIL WOULD CONDEMN YOU, TOO!
IF I DON'T, OUR CHILDREN ARE CONDEMNED.
WHICH IS WORSE?
YOU HAVE NO ANSWER.
IF ALL ROADS LEAD TO HELL--
FWOOOSH
--LET ME TAKE THE ONE THAT LEADS TO LIGHT!

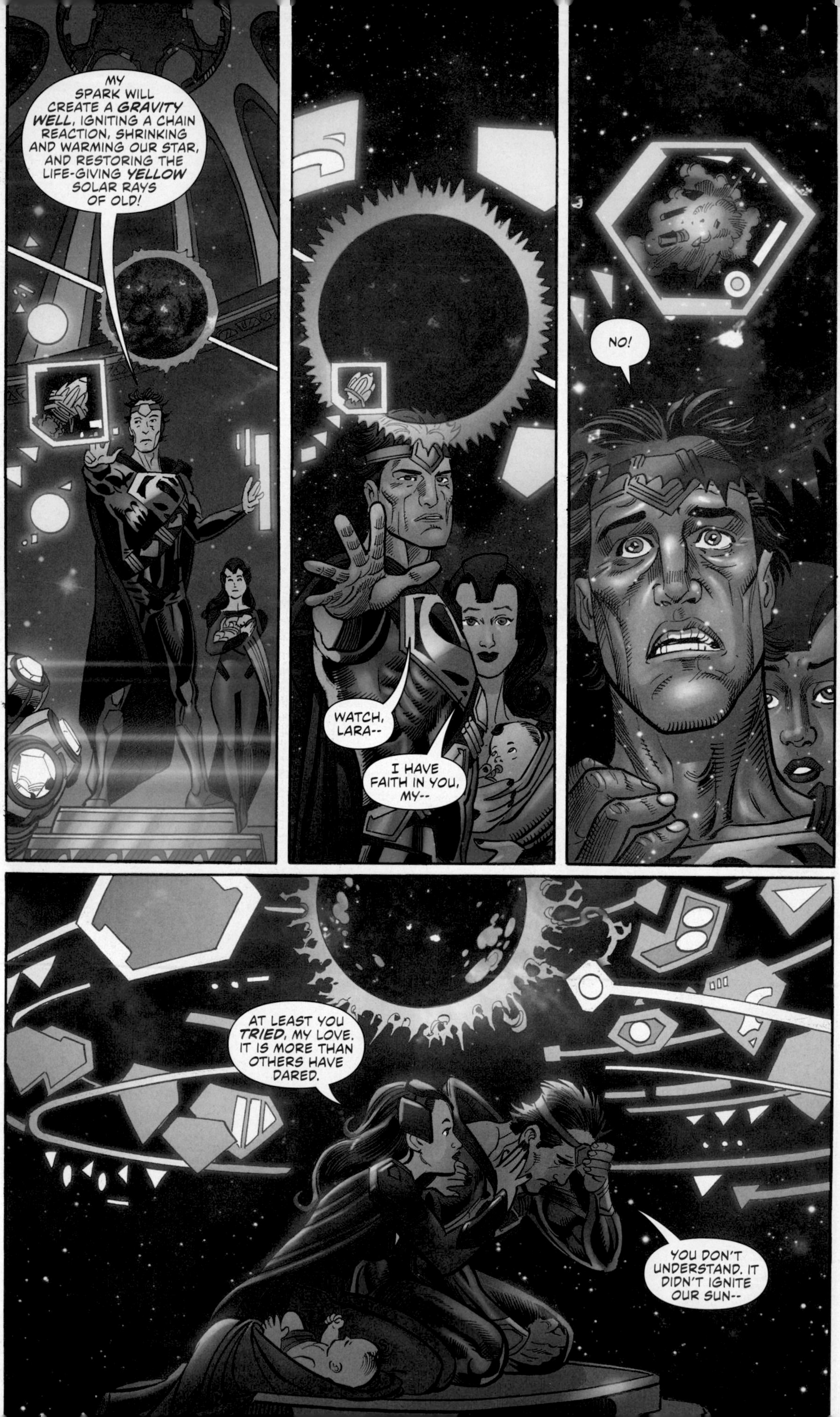
MY SPARK WILL CREATE A GRAVITY WELL, IGNITING A CHAIN REACTION, SHRINKING AND WARMING OUR STAR, AND RESTORING THE LIFE-GIVING YELLOW SOLAR RAYS OF OLD!
WATCH, LARA--
I HAVE FAITH IN YOU, MY--
NO!
AT LEAST YOU TRIED, MY LOVE. IT IS MORE THAN OTHERS HAVE DARED.
YOU DON'T UNDERSTAND. IT DIDN'T IGNITE OUR SUN--

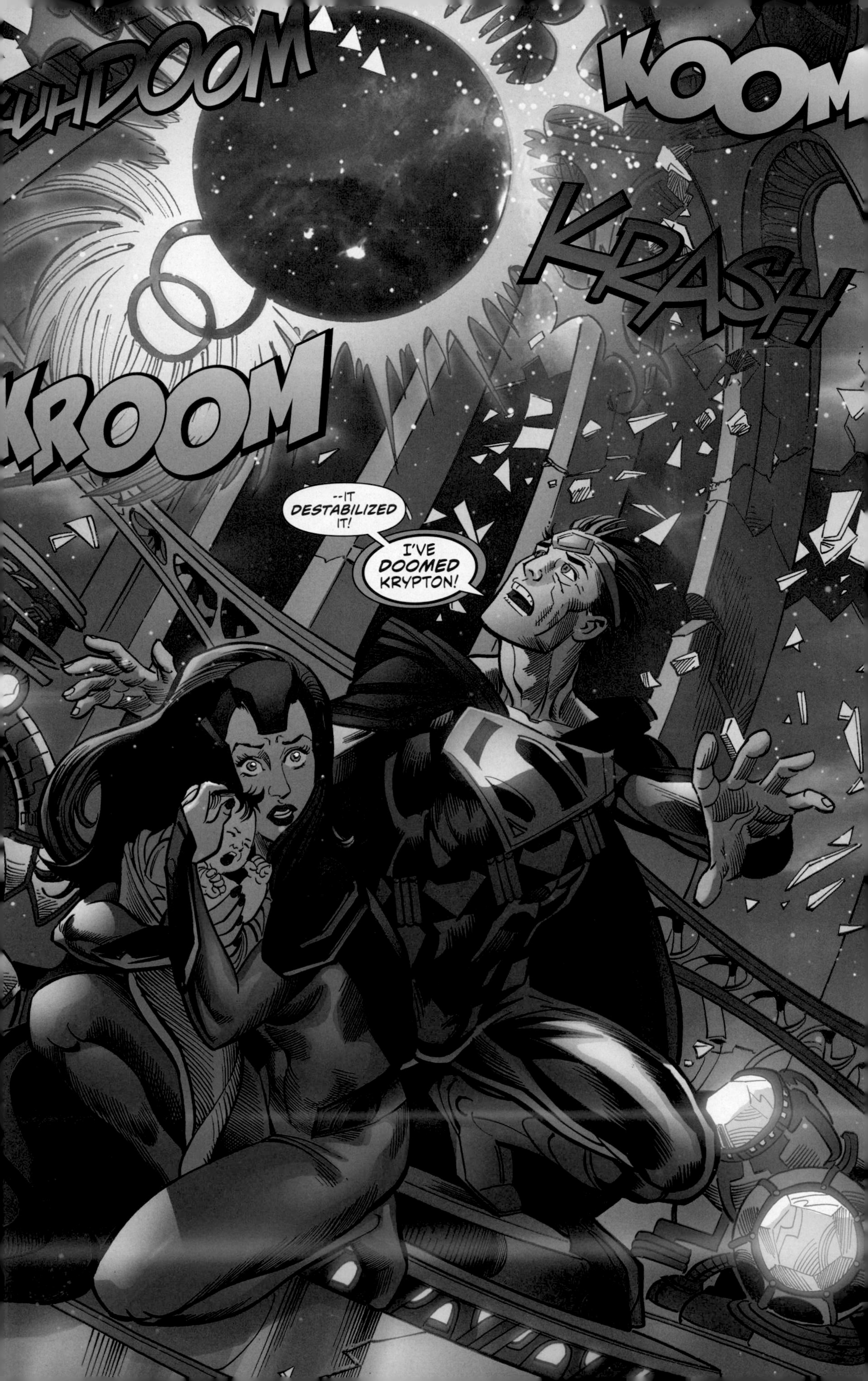

UHDOOM
KOOM
KRASH
KROOM
--IT DESTABILIZED IT!
I'VE DOOMED KRYPTON!

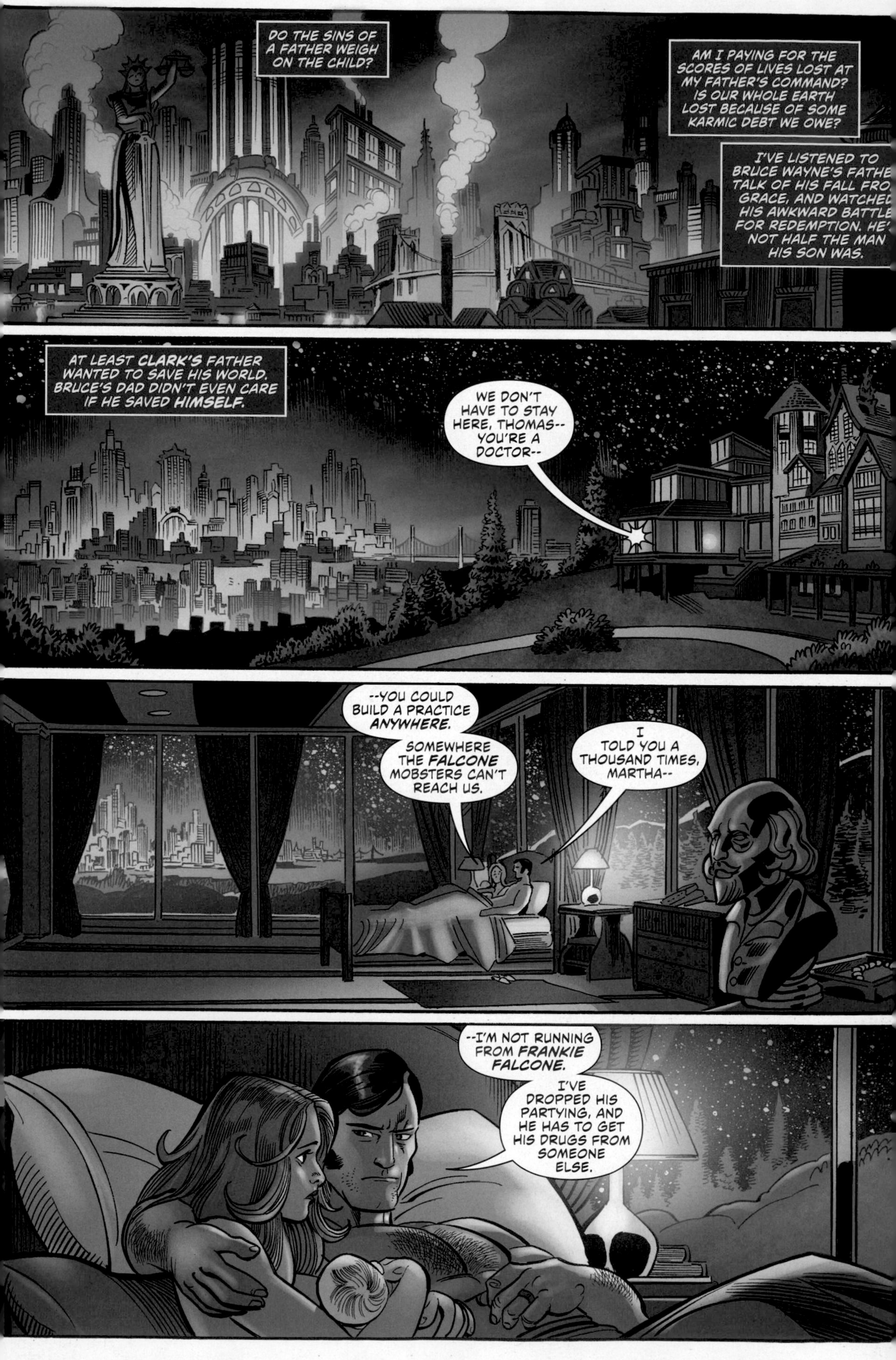

DO THE SINS OF A FATHER WEIGH ON THE CHILD?
AM I PAYING FOR THE SCORES OF LIVES LOST AT MY FATHER'S COMMAND? IS OUR WHOLE EARTH LOST BECAUSE OF SOME KARMIC DEBT WE OWE?
I'VE LISTENED TO BRUCE WAYNE'S FATHE TALK OF HIS FALL FRO GRACE, AND WATCHED HIS AWKWARD BATTL FOR REDEMPTION. HE' NOT HALF THE MAN HIS SON WAS.
AT LEAST CLARK'S FATHER WANTED TO SAVE HIS WORLD. BRUCE'S DAD DIDN'T EVEN CARE IF HE SAVED HIMSELF.
WE DON'T HAVE TO STAY HERE, THOMAS-- YOU'RE A DOCTOR--
--YOU COULD BUILD A PRACTICE ANYWHERE.
SOMEWHERE THE FALCONE MOBSTERS CAN'T REACH US.
I TOLD YOU A THOUSAND TIMES, MARTHA--
--I'M NOT RUNNING FROM FRANKIE FALCONE.
I'VE DROPPED HIS PARTYING, AND HE HAS TO GET HIS DRUGS FROM SOMEONE ELSE.

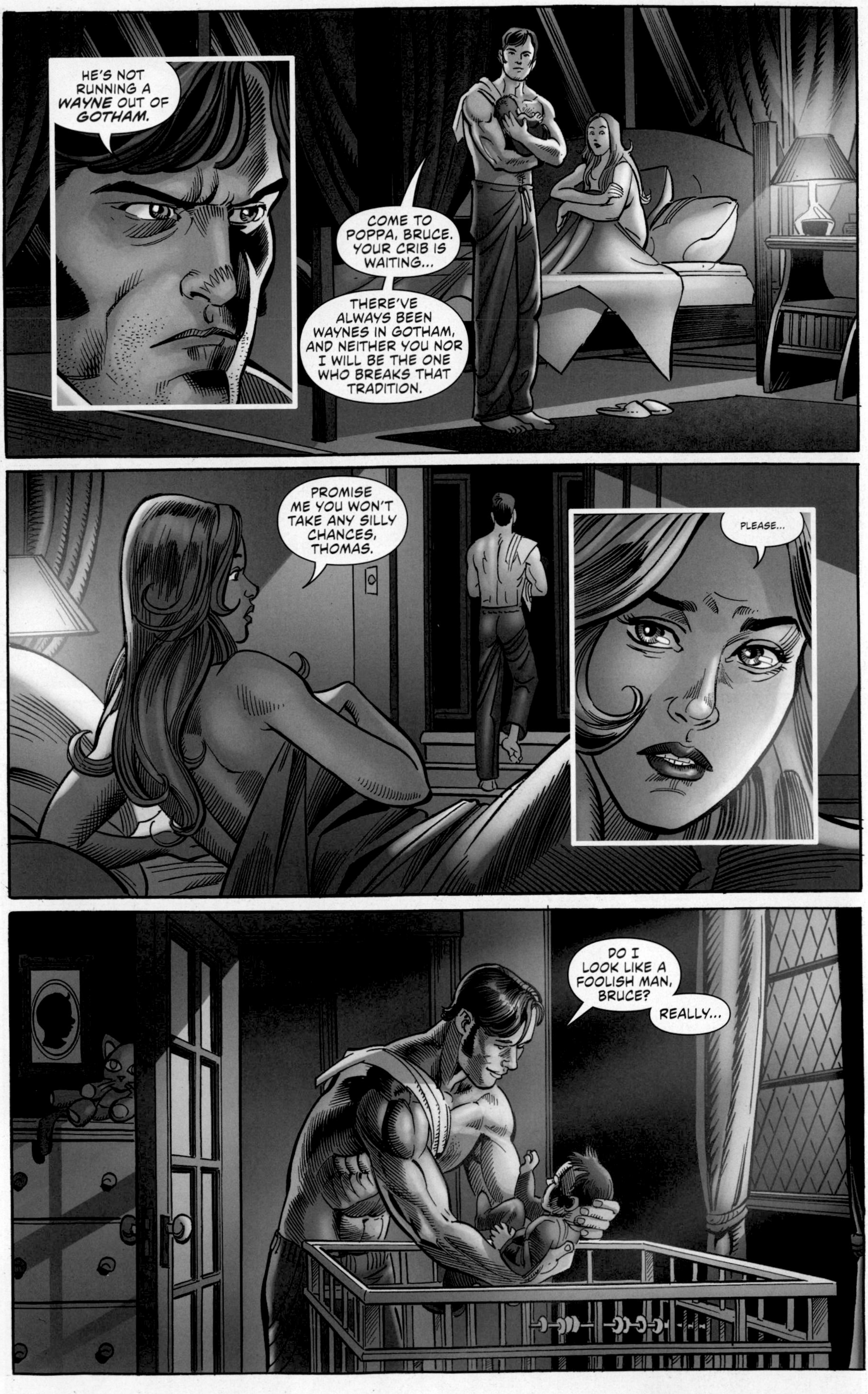
HE'S NOT RUNNING A WAYNE OUT OF GOTHAM.
COME TO POPPA, BRUCE. YOUR CRIB IS WAITING...
THERE'VE ALWAYS BEEN WAYNES IN GOTHAM, AND NEITHER YOU NOR I WILL BE THE ONE WHO BREAKS THAT TRADITION.
PROMISE ME YOU WON'T TAKE ANY SILLY CHANCES, THOMAS.
PLEASE...
DO I LOOK LIKE A FOOLISH MAN, BRUCE?
REALLY...

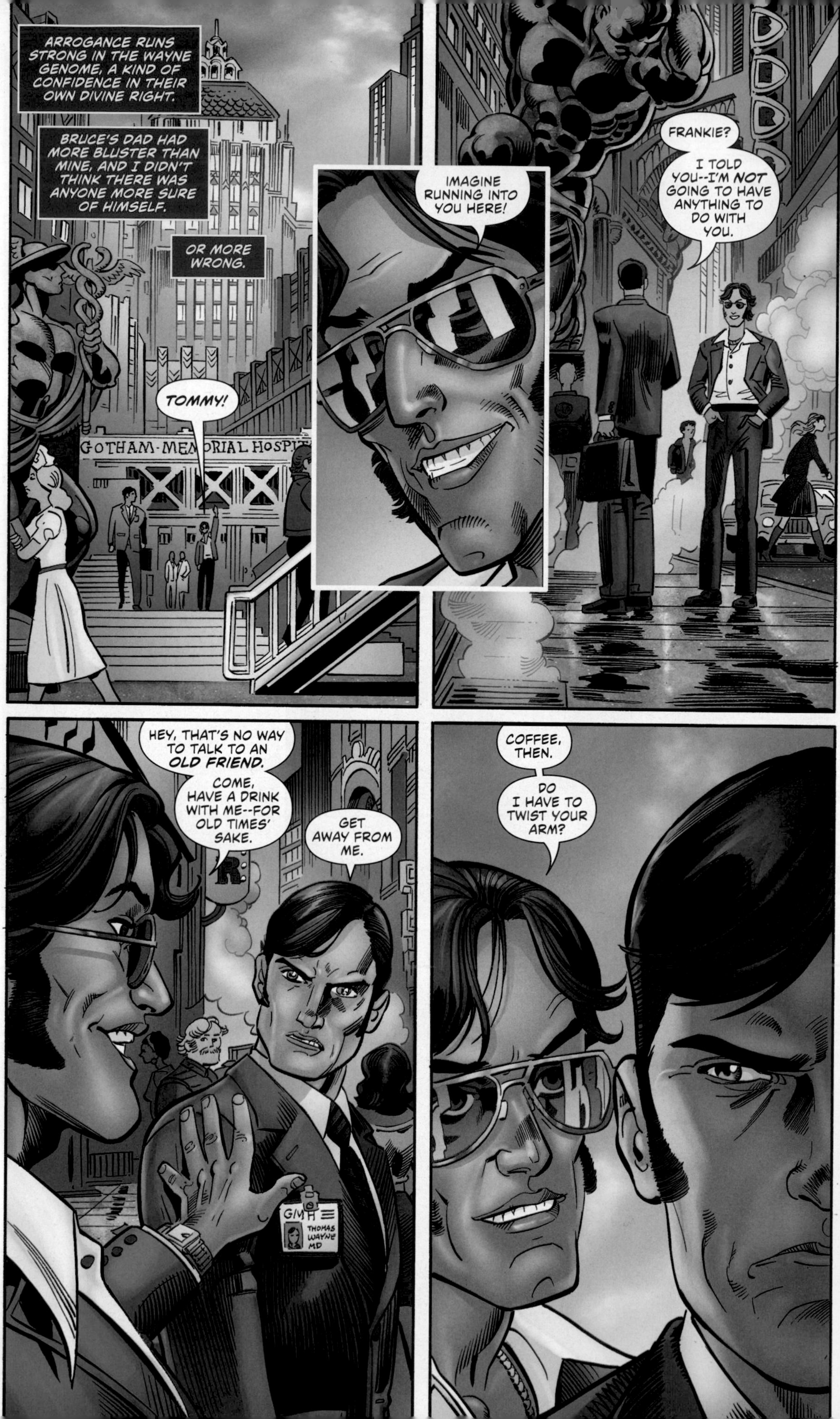
ARROGANCE RUNS STRONG IN THE WAYNE GENOME, A KIND OF CONFIDENCE IN THEIR OWN DIVINE RIGHT.
BRUCE'S DAD HAD MORE BLUSTER THAN MINE, AND I DIDN'T THINK THERE WAS ANYONE MORE SURE OF HIMSELF.
OR MORE WRONG.
TOMMY!
GOTHAM-MEMORIAL HOSPI
IMAGINE RUNNING INTO YOU HERE!
FRANKIE?
I TOLD YOU--I'M NOT GOING TO HAVE ANYTHING TO DO WITH YOU.
HEY, THAT'S NO WAY TO TALK TO AN OLD FRIEND.
COME, HAVE A DRINK WITH ME--FOR OLD TIMES' SAKE.
GET AWAY FROM ME.
GMH
THOMAS WAYNE MD
COFFEE, THEN.
DO I HAVE TO TWIST YOUR ARM?

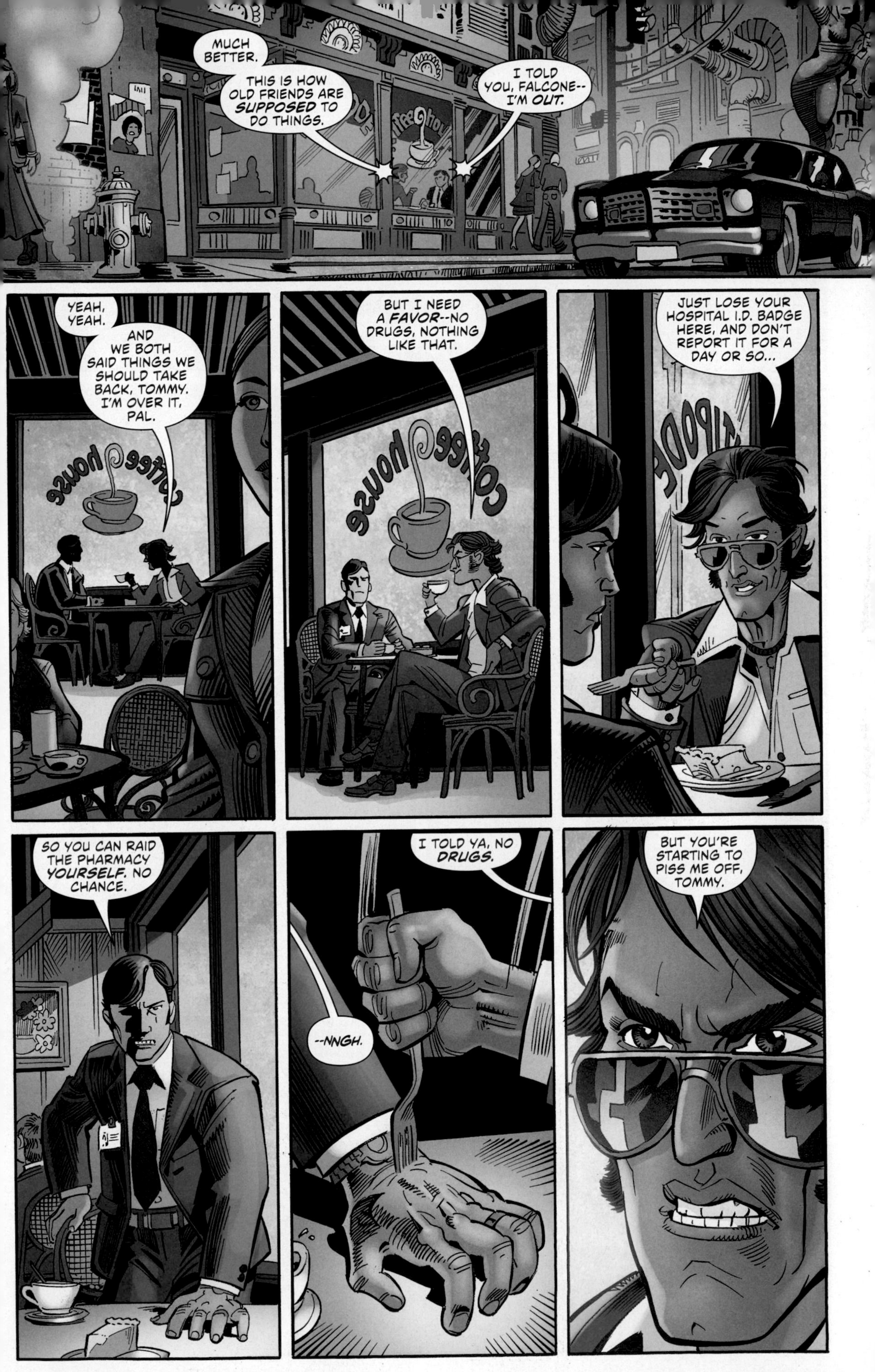
MUCH BETTER.
THIS IS HOW OLD FRIENDS ARE SUPPOSED TO DO THINGS.
I TOLD YOU, FALCONE-- I'M OUT.
YEAH, YEAH.
AND WE BOTH SAID THINGS WE SHOULD TAKE BACK, TOMMY. I'M OVER IT, PAL.
BUT I NEED A FAVOR--NO DRUGS, NOTHING LIKE THAT.
JUST LOSE YOUR HOSPITAL I.D. BADGE HERE, AND DON'T REPORT IT FOR A DAY OR SO...
SO YOU CAN RAID THE PHARMACY YOURSELF. NO CHANCE.
I TOLD YA, NO DRUGS.
--NNGH.
BUT YOU'RE STARTING TO PISS ME OFF, TOMMY.

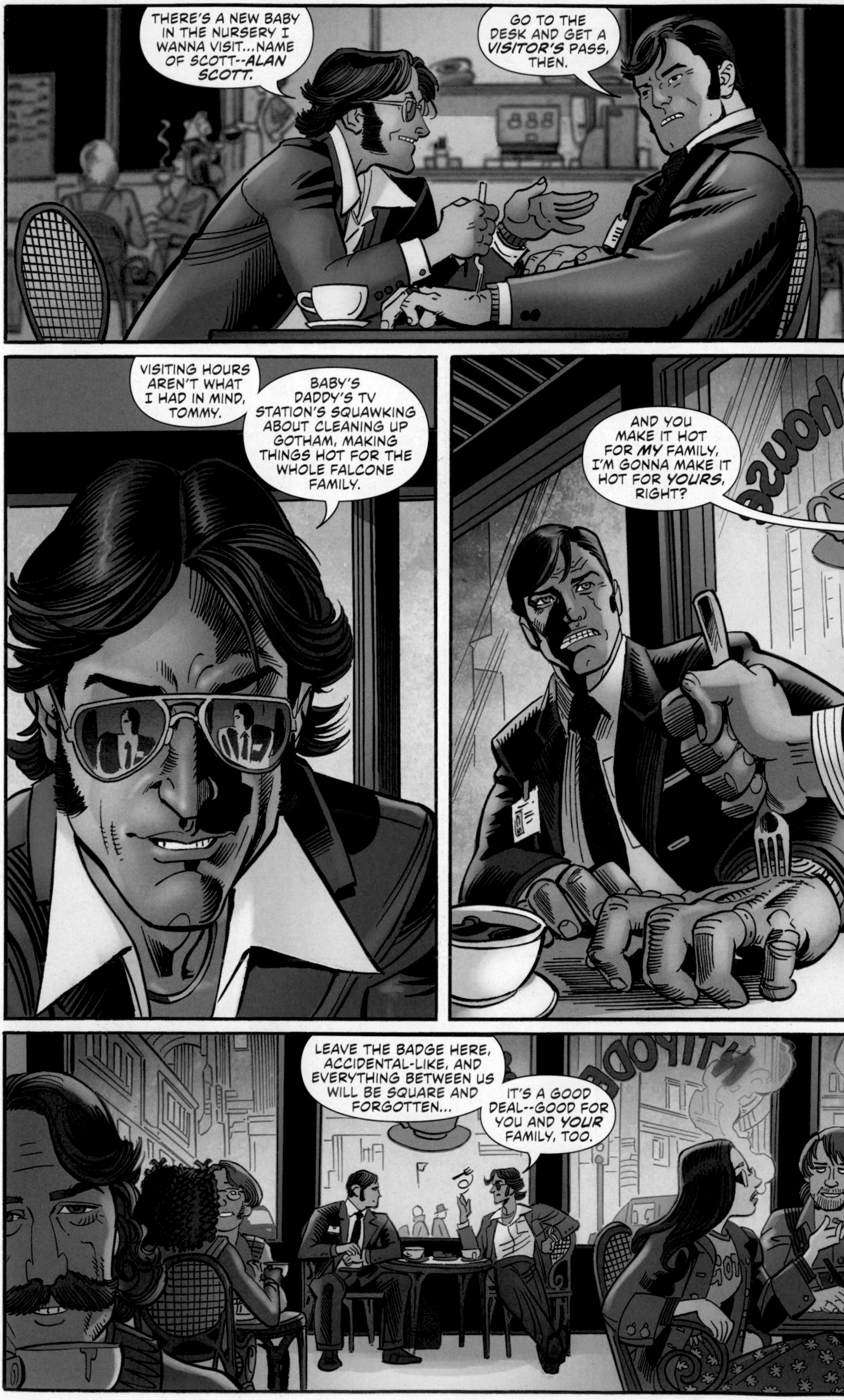
THERE'S A NEW BABY IN THE NURSERY I WANNA VISIT...NAME OF SCOTT--ALAN SCOTT.
GO TO THE DESK AND GET A VISITOR'S PASS, THEN.
VISITING HOURS AREN'T WHAT I HAD IN MIND, TOMMY.
BABY'S DADDY'S TV STATION'S SQUAWKING ABOUT CLEANING UP GOTHAM, MAKING THINGS HOT FOR THE WHOLE FALCONE FAMILY.
AND YOU MAKE IT HOT FOR MY FAMILY, I'M GONNA MAKE IT HOT FOR YOURS, RIGHT?
LEAVE THE BADGE HERE, ACCIDENTAL-LIKE, AND EVERYTHING BETWEEN US WILL BE SQUARE AND FORGOTTEN...
IT'S A GOOD DEAL--GOOD FOR YOU AND YOUR FAMILY, TOO.

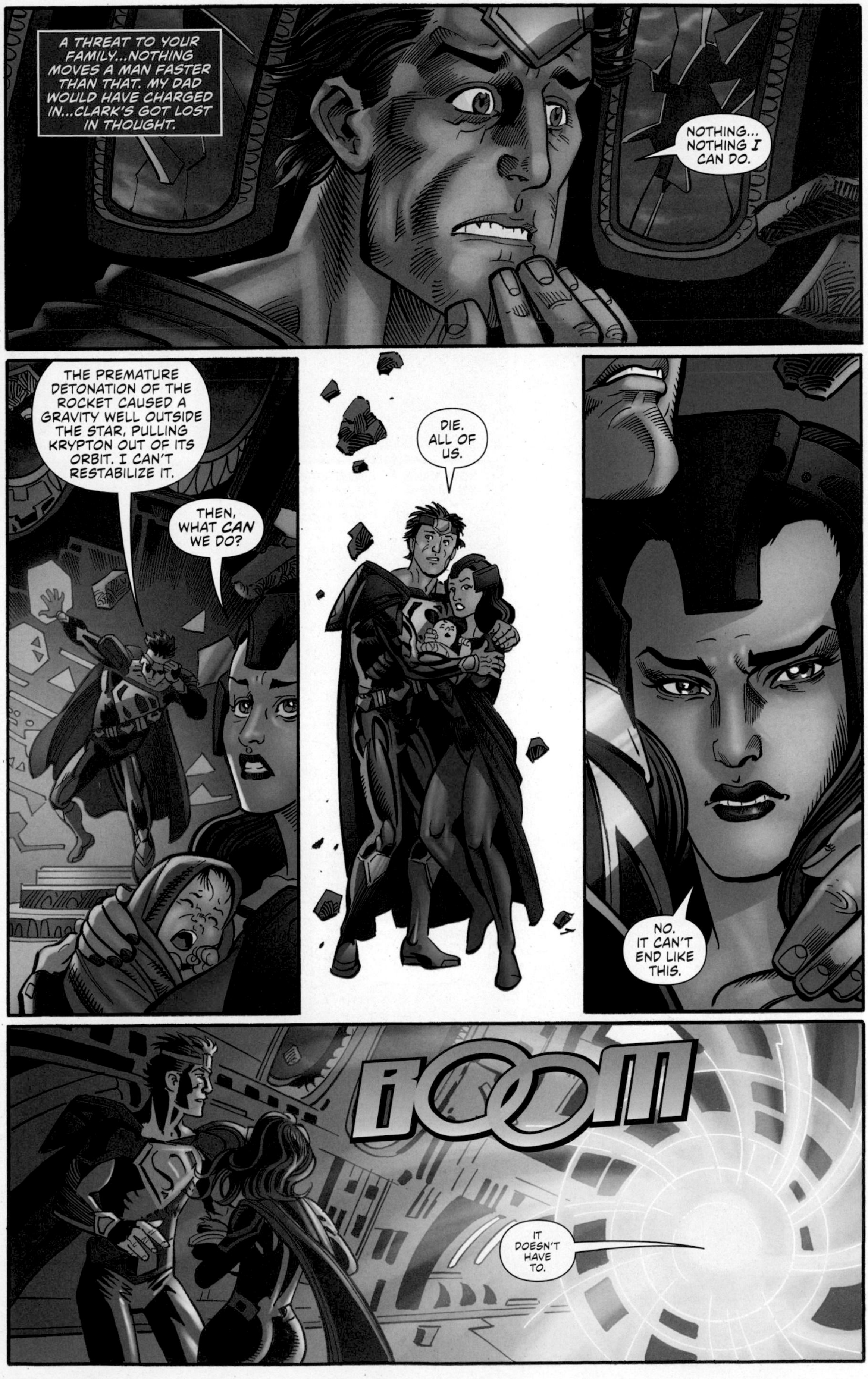
A THREAT TO YOUR FAMILY...NOTHING MOVES A MAN FASTER THAN THAT. MY DAD WOULD HAVE CHARGED IN...CLARK'S GOT LOST IN THOUGHT.
NOTHING... NOTHING I CAN DO.
THE PREMATURE DETONATION OF THE ROCKET CAUSED A GRAVITY WELL OUTSIDE THE STAR, PULLING KRYPTON OUT OF ITS ORBIT. I CAN'T RESTABILIZE IT.
THEN, WHAT CAN WE DO?
DIE. ALL OF US.
NO. IT CAN'T END LIKE THIS.
BOOM
IT DOESN'T HAVE TO.

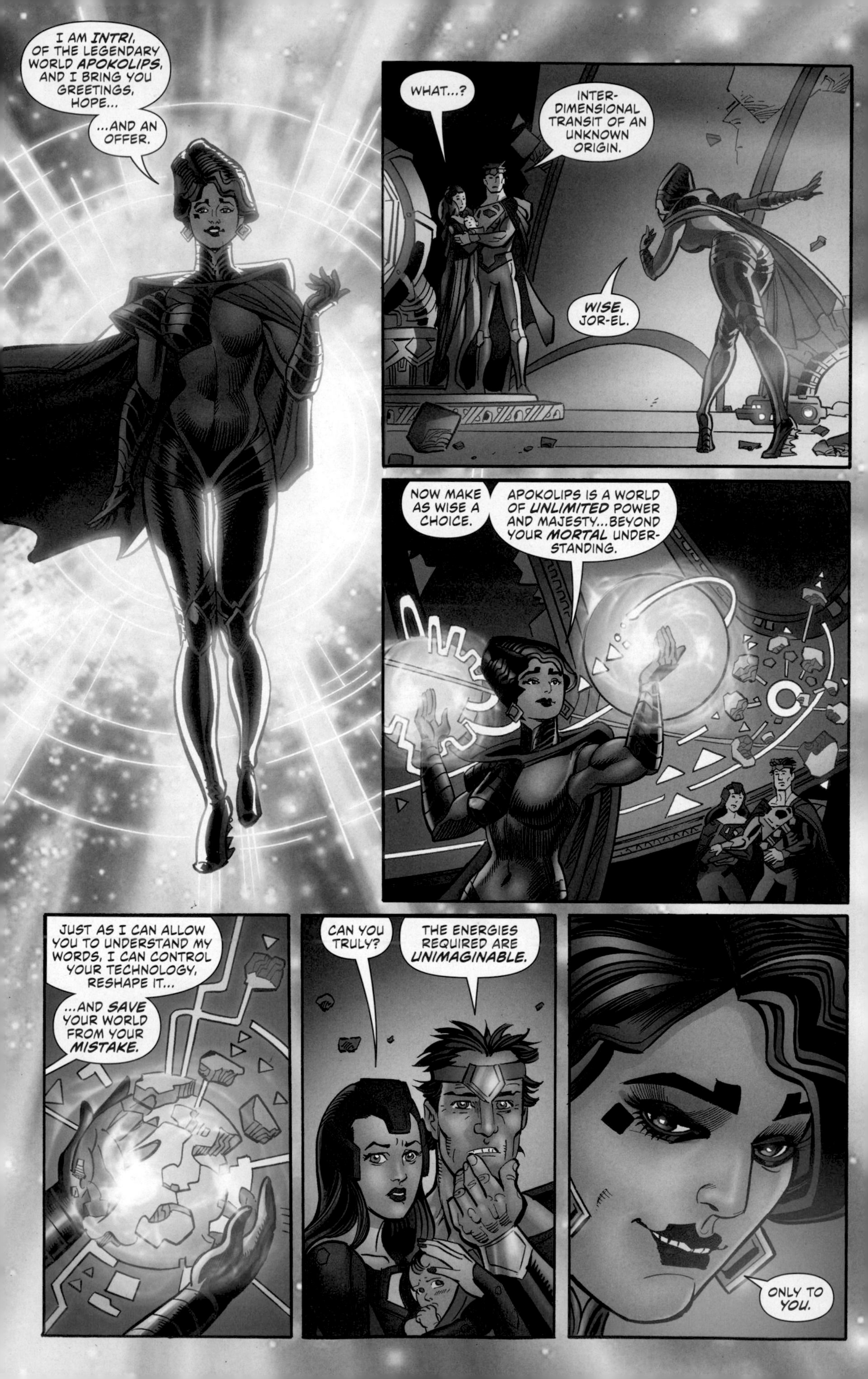
I AM INTRI, OF THE LEGENDARY WORLD APOKOLIPS, AND I BRING YOU GREETINGS, HOPE...
...AND AN OFFER.
WHAT...?
INTER-DIMENSIONAL TRANSIT OF AN UNKNOWN ORIGIN.
WISE, JOR-EL.
NOW MAKE AS WISE A CHOICE.
APOKOLIPS IS A WORLD OF UNLIMITED POWER AND MAJESTY...BEYOND YOUR MORTAL UNDER-STANDING.
JUST AS I CAN ALLOW YOU TO UNDERSTAND MY WORDS, I CAN CONTROL YOUR TECHNOLOGY, RESHAPE IT...
...AND SAVE YOUR WORLD FROM YOUR MISTAKE.
CAN YOU TRULY?
THE ENERGIES REQUIRED ARE UNIMAGINABLE.
ONLY TO YOU.

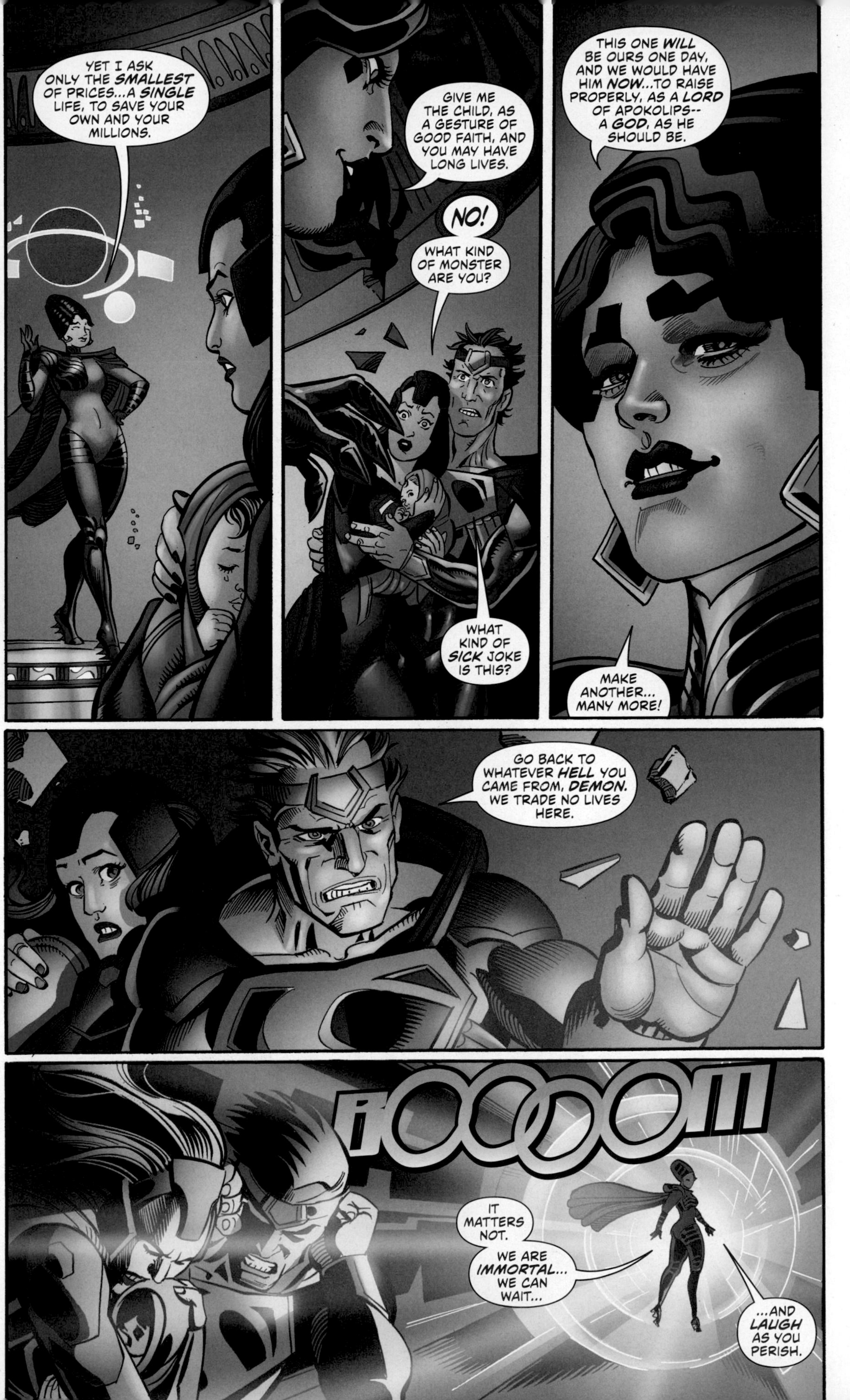
YET I ASK ONLY THE SMALLEST OF PRICES...A SINGLE LIFE, TO SAVE YOUR OWN AND YOUR MILLIONS.
GIVE ME THE CHILD, AS A GESTURE OF GOOD FAITH, AND YOU MAY HAVE LONG LIVES.
NO!
WHAT KIND OF MONSTER ARE YOU?
WHAT KIND OF SICK JOKE IS THIS?
THIS ONE WILL BE OURS ONE DAY, AND WE WOULD HAVE HIM NOW...TO RAISE PROPERLY, AS A LORD OF APOKOLIPS-- A GOD, AS HE SHOULD BE.
MAKE ANOTHER... MANY MORE!
GO BACK TO WHATEVER HELL YOU CAME FROM, DEMON. WE TRADE NO LIVES HERE.
BOOOOM
IT MATTERS NOT.
WE ARE IMMORTAL... WE CAN WAIT...
...AND LAUGH AS YOU PERISH.

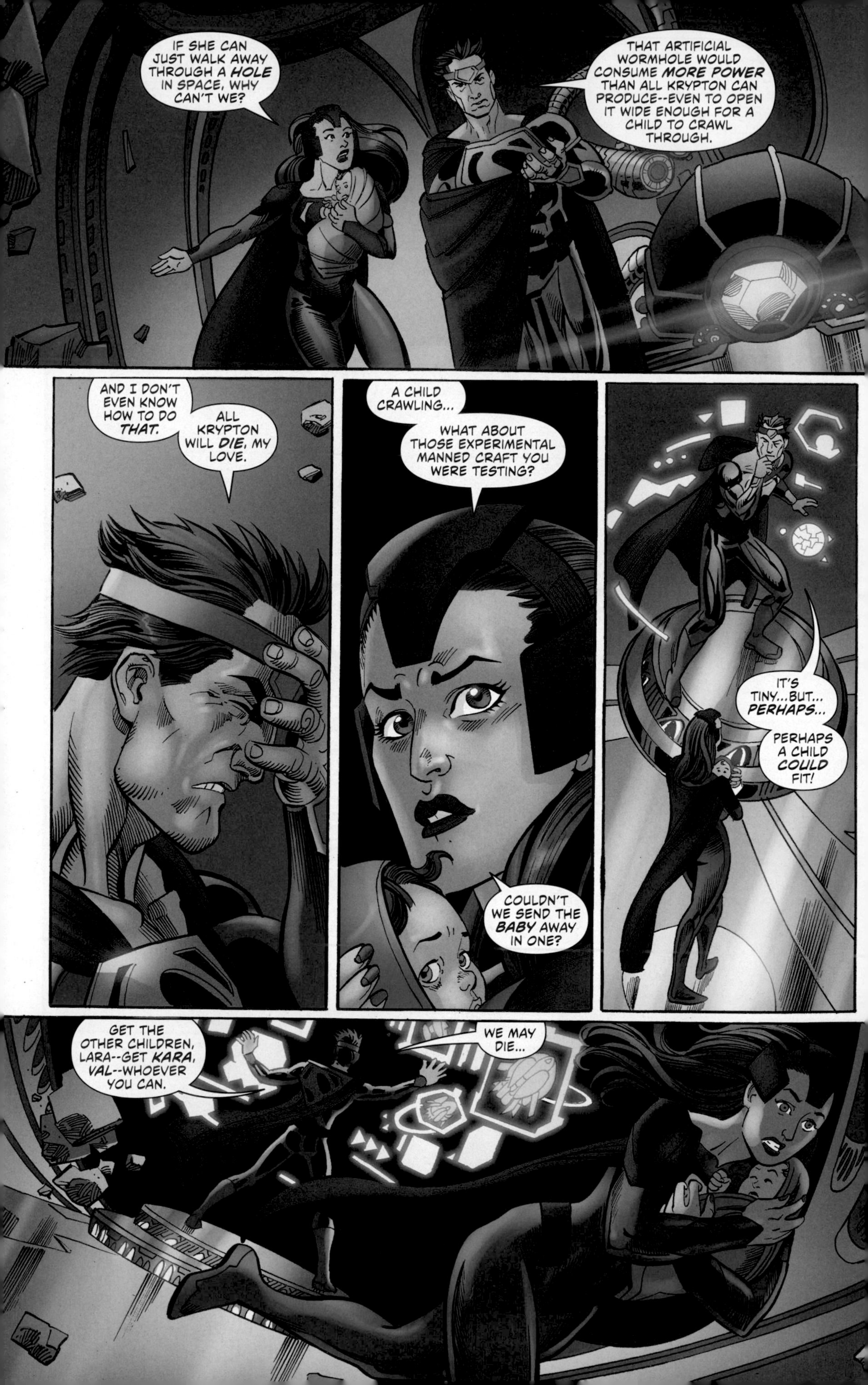
IF SHE CAN JUST WALK AWAY THROUGH A *HOLE* IN SPACE, WHY CAN'T WE?
THAT ARTIFICIAL WORMHOLE WOULD CONSUME *MORE POWER* THAN ALL KRYPTON CAN PRODUCE--EVEN TO OPEN IT WIDE ENOUGH FOR A CHILD TO CRAWL THROUGH.
AND I DON'T EVEN KNOW HOW TO DO *THAT.*
ALL KRYPTON WILL *DIE*, MY LOVE.
A CHILD CRAWLING...
WHAT ABOUT THOSE EXPERIMENTAL MANNED CRAFT YOU WERE TESTING?
COULDN'T WE SEND THE *BABY* AWAY IN ONE?
IT'S TINY...BUT... *PERHAPS*...
PERHAPS A CHILD *COULD* FIT!
GET THE OTHER CHILDREN, LARA--GET *KARA*, *VAL*--WHOEVER YOU CAN.
WE MAY DIE...

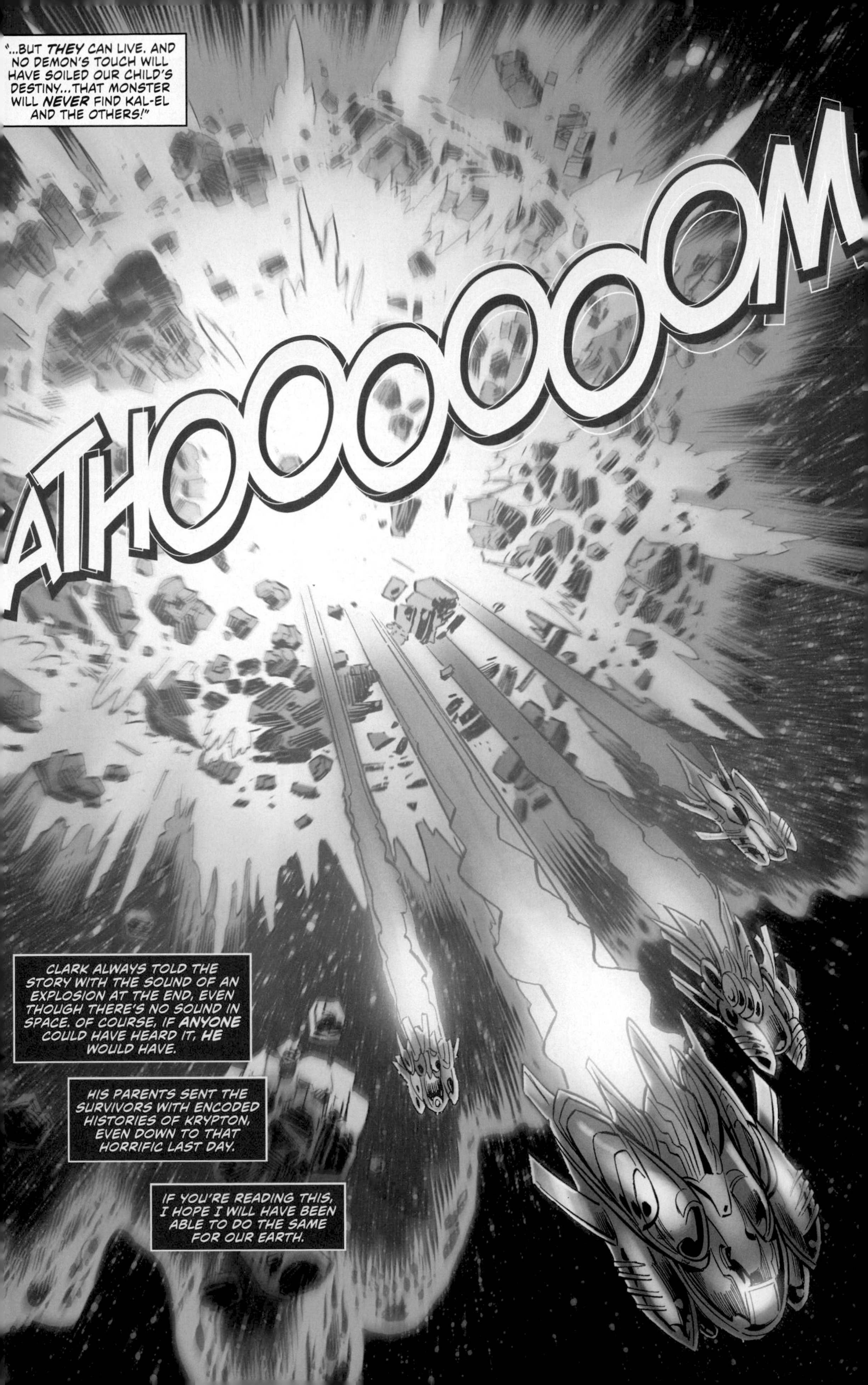
"...BUT THEY CAN LIVE. AND NO DEMON'S TOUCH WILL HAVE SOILED OUR CHILD'S DESTINY...THAT MONSTER WILL NEVER FIND KAL-EL AND THE OTHERS!"
AHOOOOOOOM
CLARK ALWAYS TOLD THE STORY WITH THE SOUND OF AN EXPLOSION AT THE END, EVEN THOUGH THERE'S NO SOUND IN SPACE. OF COURSE, IF ANYONE COULD HAVE HEARD IT, HE WOULD HAVE.
HIS PARENTS SENT THE SURVIVORS WITH ENCODED HISTORIES OF KRYPTON, EVEN DOWN TO THAT HORRIFIC LAST DAY.
IF YOU'RE READING THIS, I HOPE I WILL HAVE BEEN ABLE TO DO THE SAME FOR OUR EARTH.

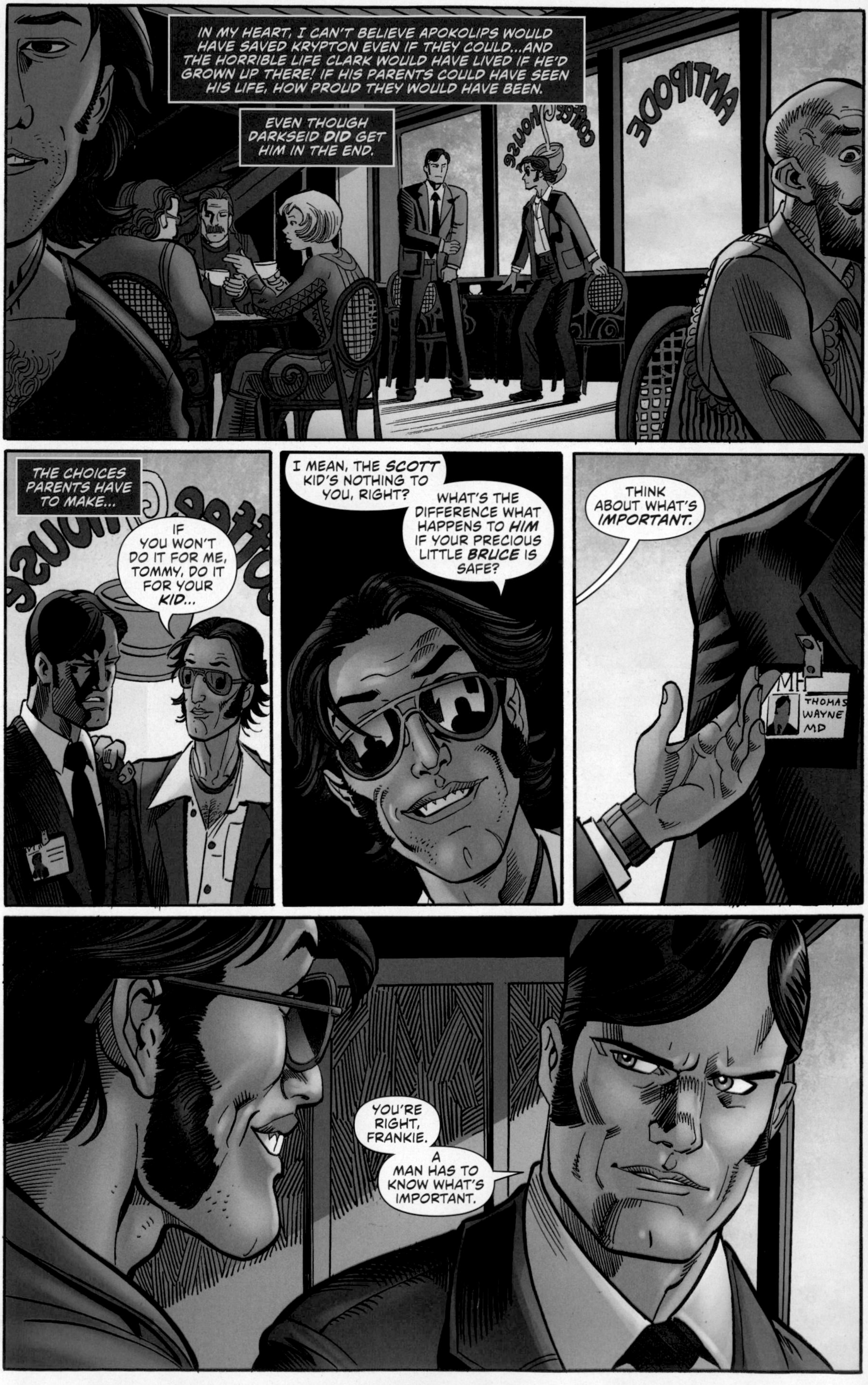

IN MY HEART, I CAN'T BELIEVE APOKOLIPS WOULD HAVE SAVED KRYPTON EVEN IF THEY COULD...AND THE HORRIBLE LIFE CLARK WOULD HAVE LIVED IF HE'D GROWN UP THERE! IF HIS PARENTS COULD HAVE SEEN HIS LIFE, HOW PROUD THEY WOULD HAVE BEEN.
EVEN THOUGH DARKSEID DID GET HIM IN THE END.
ANTIPODE
COFFEE HOUSE
THE CHOICES PARENTS HAVE TO MAKE...
IF YOU WON'T DO IT FOR ME, TOMMY, DO IT FOR YOUR KID...
I MEAN, THE SCOTT KID'S NOTHING TO YOU, RIGHT?
WHAT'S THE DIFFERENCE WHAT HAPPENS TO HIM IF YOUR PRECIOUS LITTLE BRUCE IS SAFE?
THINK ABOUT WHAT'S IMPORTANT.
THOMAS WAYNE MD
YOU'RE RIGHT, FRANKIE.
A MAN HAS TO KNOW WHAT'S IMPORTANT.

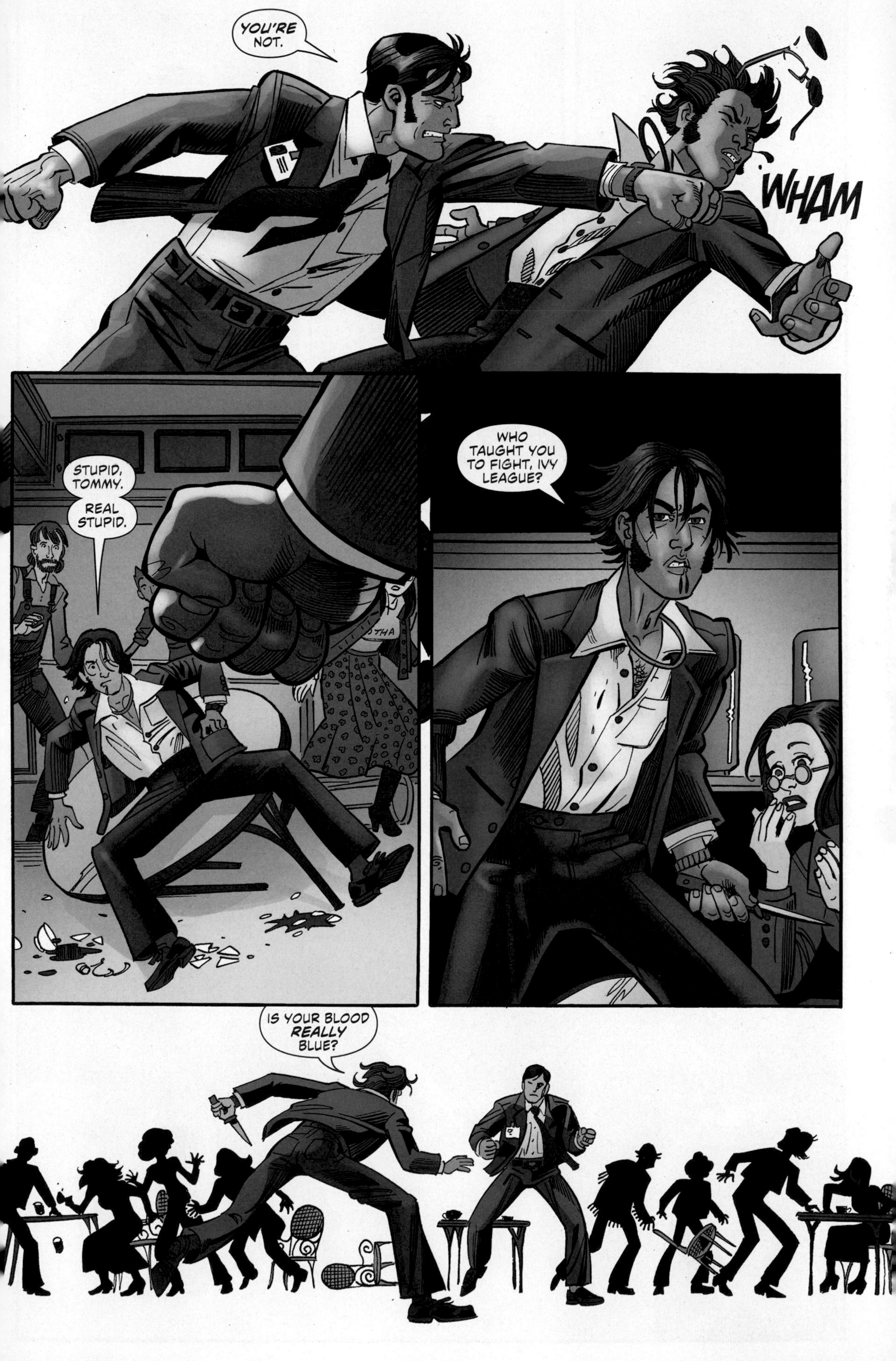
YOU'RE NOT.
WHAM
STUPID, TOMMY.
REAL STUPID.
WHO TAUGHT YOU TO FIGHT, IVY LEAGUE?
IS YOUR BLOOD REALLY BLUE?

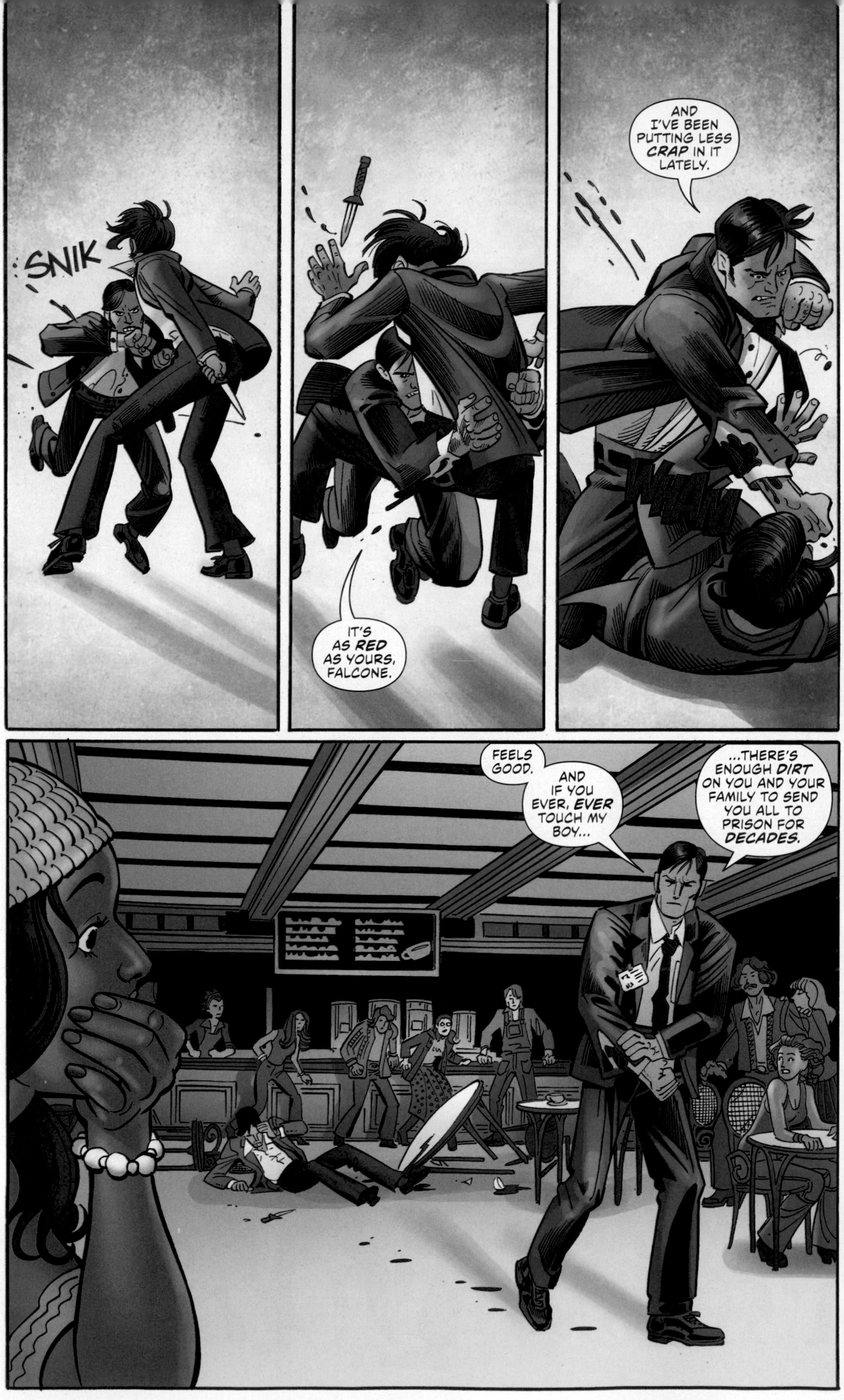
SNIK
IT'S AS RED AS YOURS, FALCONE.
AND I'VE BEEN PUTTING LESS CRAP IN IT LATELY.
WHAM
FEELS GOOD.
AND IF YOU EVER, EVER TOUCH MY BOY...
...THERE'S ENOUGH DIRT ON YOU AND YOUR FAMILY TO SEND YOU ALL TO PRISON FOR DECADES.

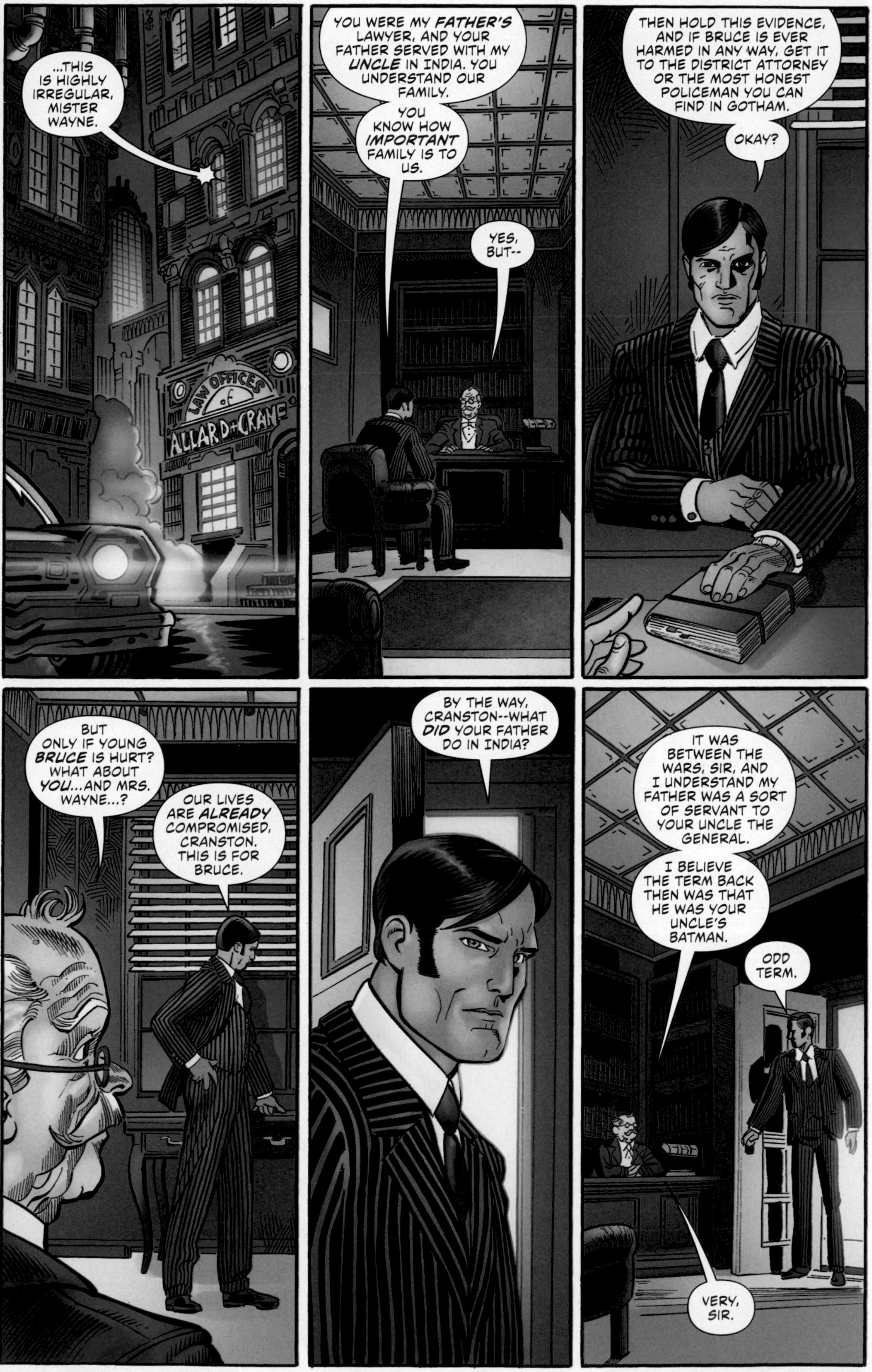
...THIS IS HIGHLY IRREGULAR, MISTER WAYNE.
LAW OFFICES of ALLARD + CRAN
YOU WERE MY FATHER'S LAWYER, AND YOUR FATHER SERVED WITH MY UNCLE IN INDIA. YOU UNDERSTAND OUR FAMILY.
YOU KNOW HOW IMPORTANT FAMILY IS TO US.
YES, BUT--
THEN HOLD THIS EVIDENCE, AND IF BRUCE IS EVER HARMED IN ANY WAY, GET IT TO THE DISTRICT ATTORNEY OR THE MOST HONEST POLICEMAN YOU CAN FIND IN GOTHAM.
OKAY?
BUT ONLY IF YOUNG BRUCE IS HURT? WHAT ABOUT YOU...AND MRS. WAYNE...?
OUR LIVES ARE ALREADY COMPROMISED, CRANSTON. THIS IS FOR BRUCE.
BY THE WAY, CRANSTON--WHAT DID YOUR FATHER DO IN INDIA?
IT WAS BETWEEN THE WARS, SIR, AND I UNDERSTAND MY FATHER WAS A SORT OF SERVANT TO YOUR UNCLE THE GENERAL.
I BELIEVE THE TERM BACK THEN WAS THAT HE WAS YOUR UNCLE'S BATMAN.
ODD TERM.
VERY, SIR.

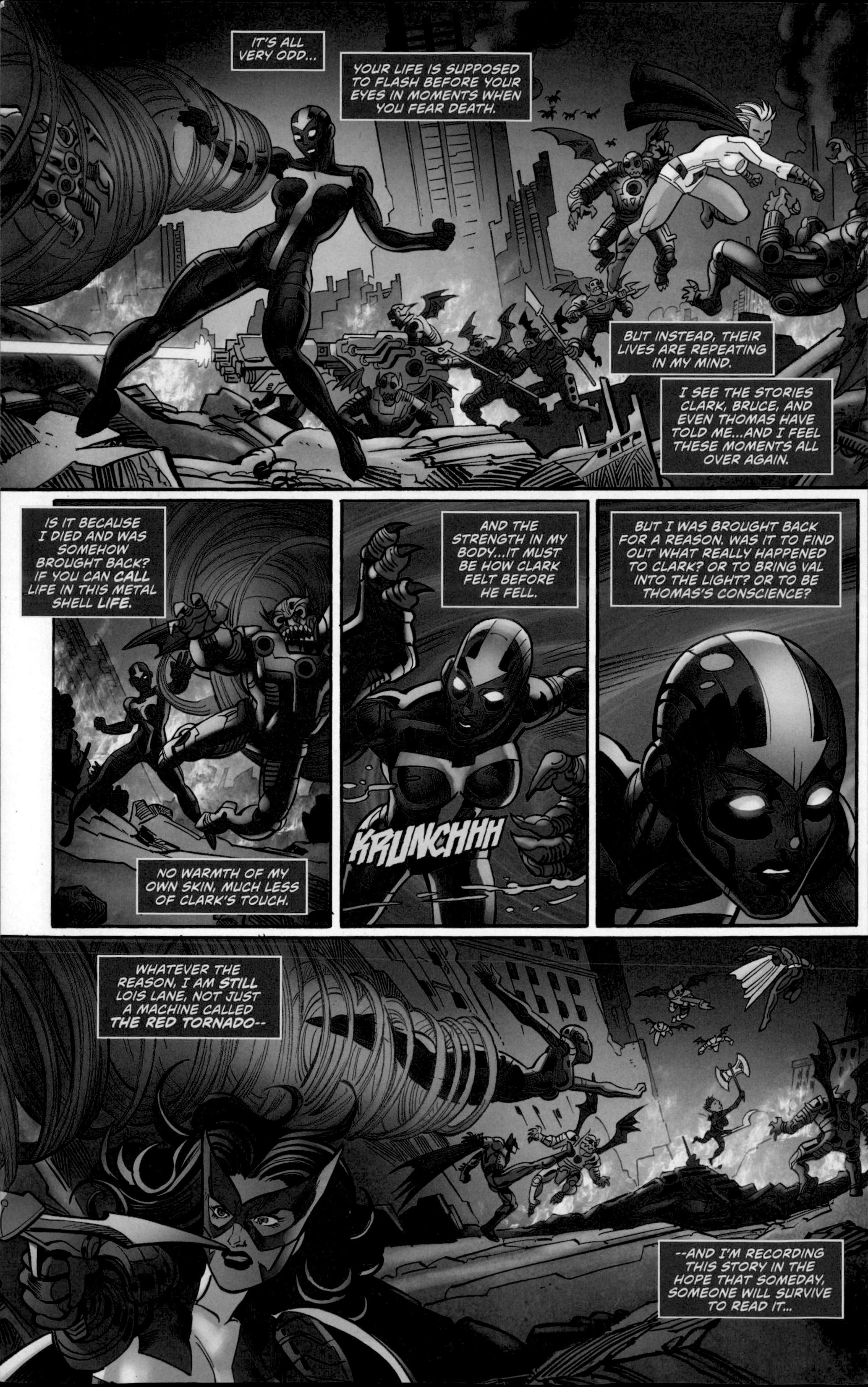
IT'S ALL VERY ODD...
YOUR LIFE IS SUPPOSED TO FLASH BEFORE YOUR EYES IN MOMENTS WHEN YOU FEAR DEATH.
BUT INSTEAD, THEIR LIVES ARE REPEATING IN MY MIND.
I SEE THE STORIES CLARK, BRUCE, AND EVEN THOMAS HAVE TOLD ME...AND I FEEL THESE MOMENTS ALL OVER AGAIN.
IS IT BECAUSE I DIED AND WAS SOMEHOW BROUGHT BACK? IF YOU CAN CALL LIFE IN THIS METAL SHELL LIFE.
NO WARMTH OF MY OWN SKIN, MUCH LESS OF CLARK'S TOUCH.
AND THE STRENGTH IN MY BODY...IT MUST BE HOW CLARK FELT BEFORE HE FELL.
KRUNCHHH
BUT I WAS BROUGHT BACK FOR A REASON. WAS IT TO FIND OUT WHAT REALLY HAPPENED TO CLARK? OR TO BRING VAL INTO THE LIGHT? OR TO BE THOMAS'S CONSCIENCE?
WHATEVER THE REASON, I AM STILL LOIS LANE, NOT JUST A MACHINE CALLED THE RED TORNADO--
--AND I'M RECORDING THIS STORY IN THE HOPE THAT SOMEDAY, SOMEONE WILL SURVIVE TO READ IT...

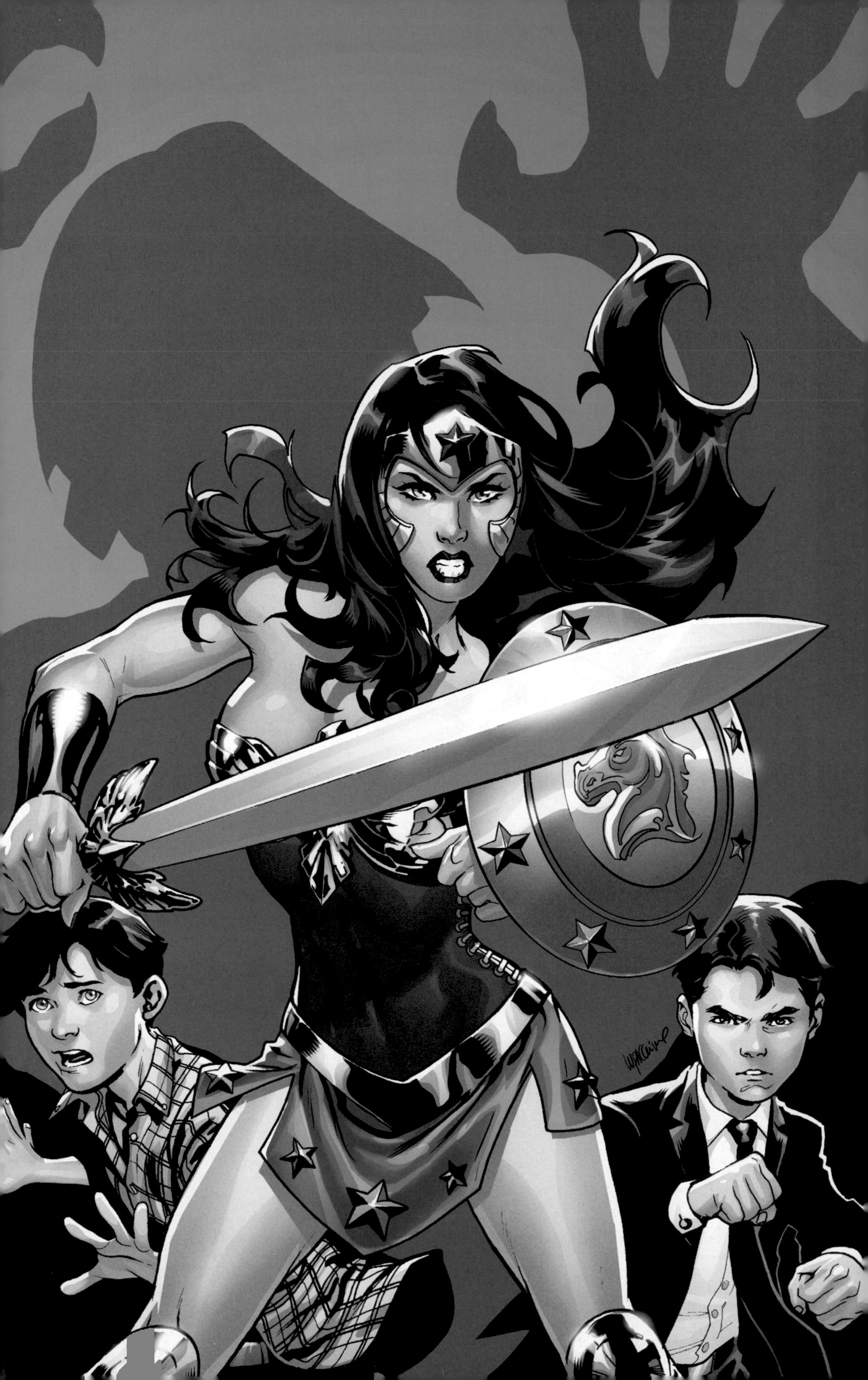

PART TWO: PRESENTIMENTS

PAUL LEVITZ writer JED DOUGHERTY artist BLOND colorist

TRAVIS LANHAM letterer cover art by EMANUELA LUPACCHINO & HI-FI

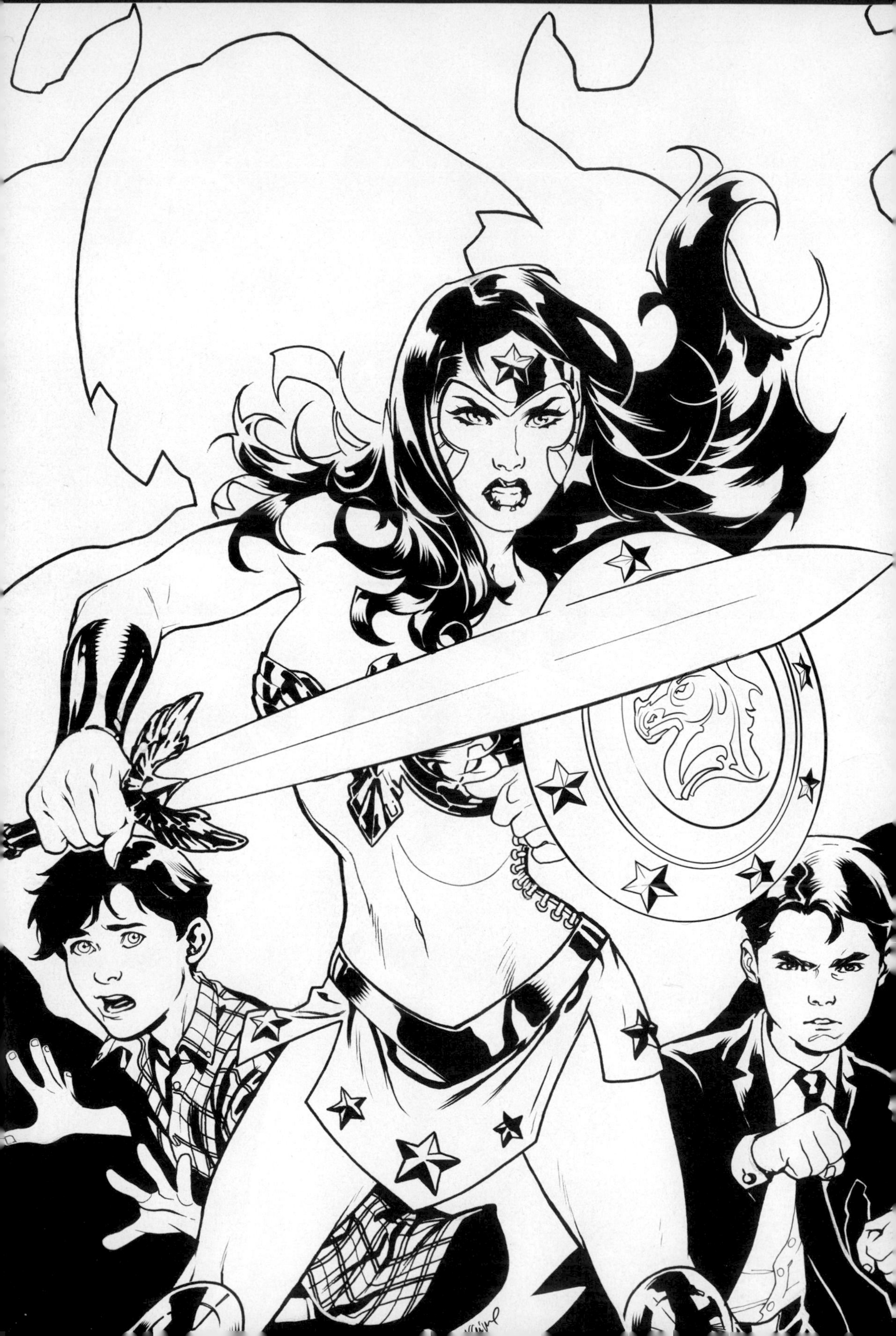

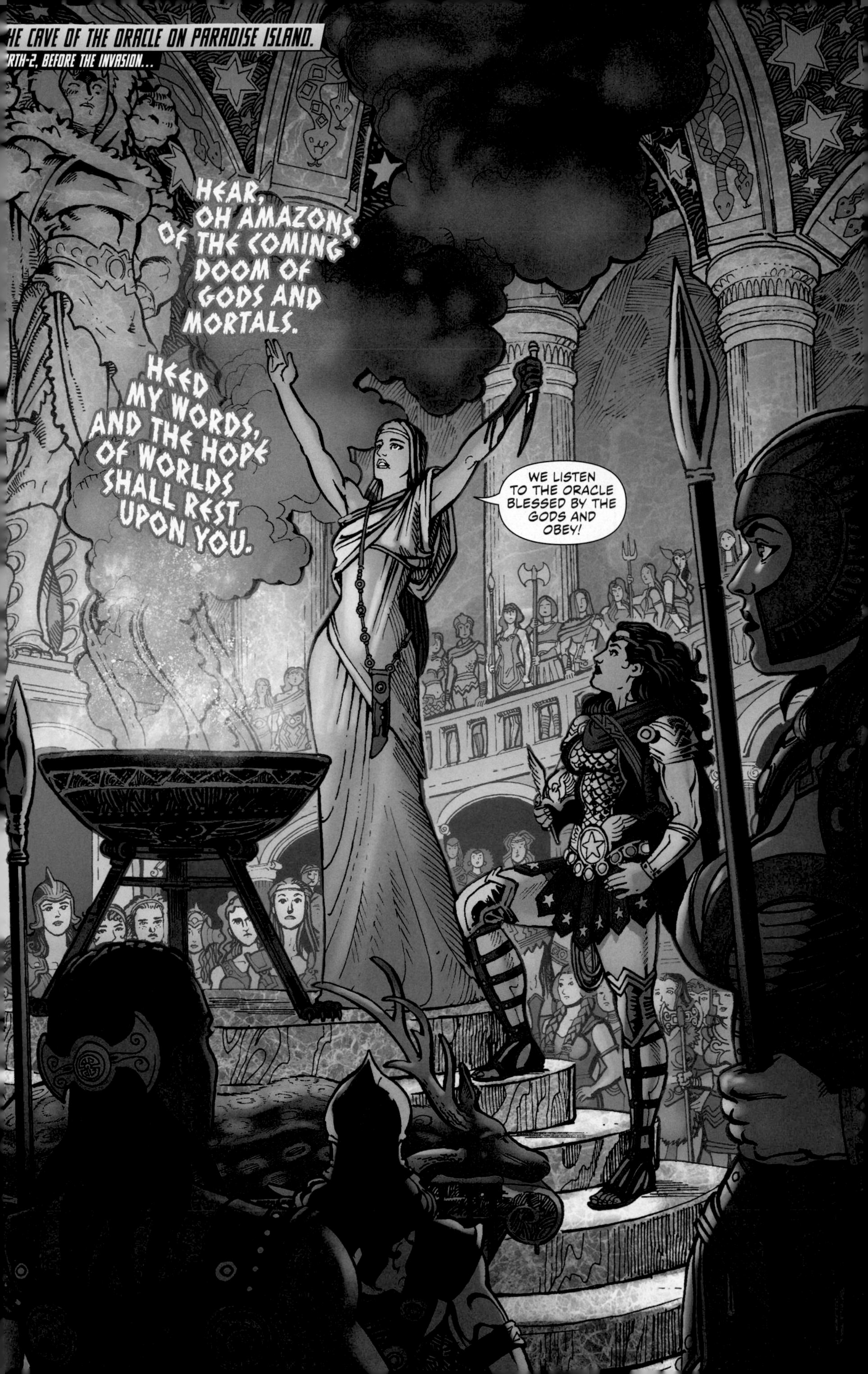
HE CAVE OF THE ORACLE ON PARADISE ISLAND.
RTH-2, BEFORE THE INVASION...
HEAR, OH AMAZONS, OF THE COMING DOOM OF GODS AND MORTALS.
HEED MY WORDS, AND THE HOPE OF WORLDS SHALL REST UPON YOU.
WE LISTEN TO THE ORACLE BLESSED BY THE GODS AND OBEY!

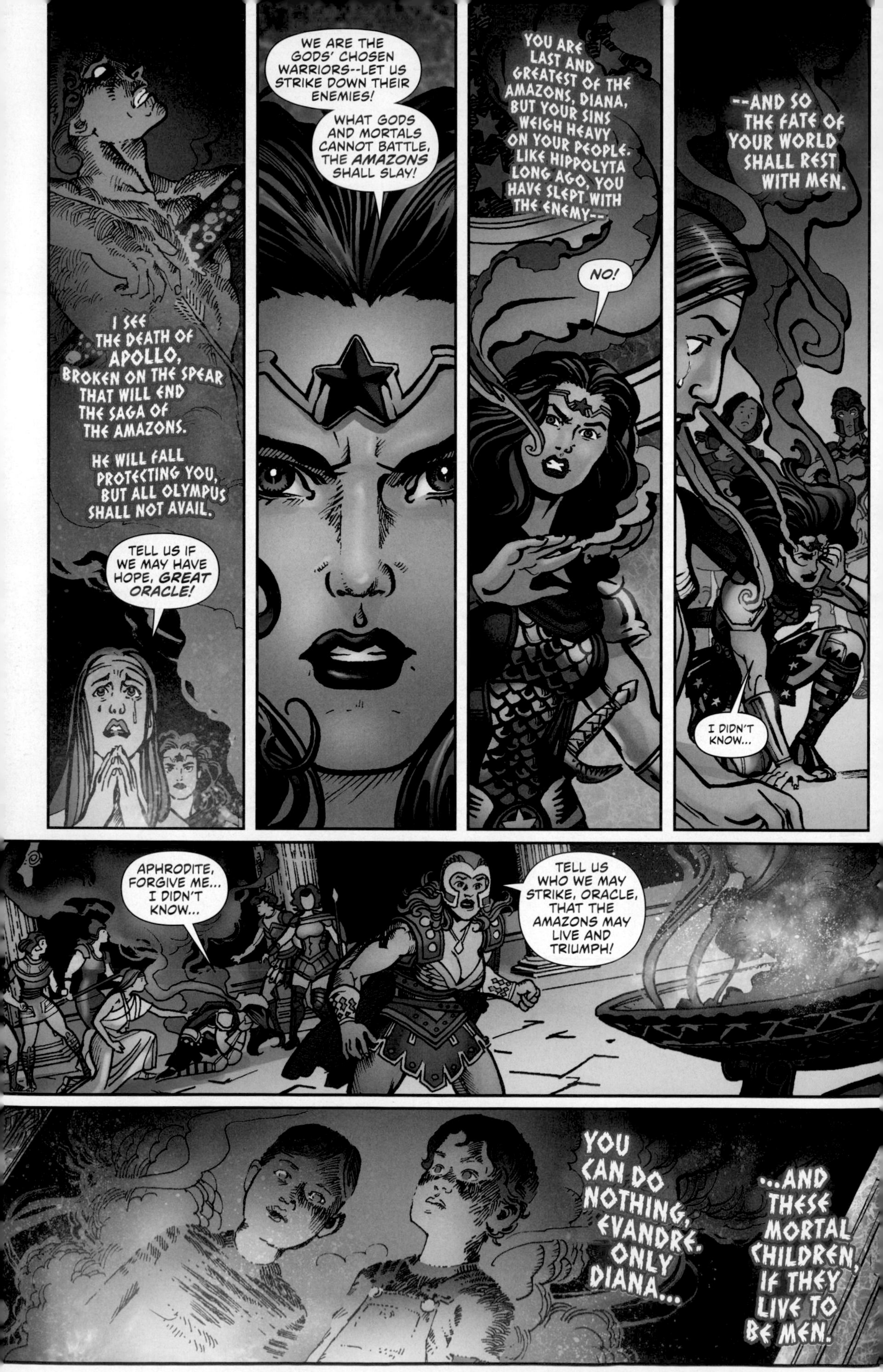

I SEE THE DEATH OF APOLLO, BROKEN ON THE SPEAR THAT WILL END THE SAGA OF THE AMAZONS.
HE WILL FALL PROTECTING YOU, BUT ALL OLYMPUS SHALL NOT AVAIL.
TELL US IF WE MAY HAVE HOPE, GREAT ORACLE!
WE ARE THE GODS' CHOSEN WARRIORS--LET US STRIKE DOWN THEIR ENEMIES!
WHAT GODS AND MORTALS CANNOT BATTLE, THE AMAZONS SHALL SLAY!
YOU ARE LAST AND GREATEST OF THE AMAZONS, DIANA, BUT YOUR SINS WEIGH HEAVY ON YOUR PEOPLE. LIKE HIPPOLYTA LONG AGO, YOU HAVE SLEPT WITH THE ENEMY--
NO!
--AND SO THE FATE OF YOUR WORLD SHALL REST WITH MEN.
I DIDN'T KNOW...
APHRODITE, FORGIVE ME... I DIDN'T KNOW...
TELL US WHO WE MAY STRIKE, ORACLE, THAT THE AMAZONS MAY LIVE AND TRIUMPH!
YOU CAN DO NOTHING, EVANDRE. ONLY DIANA...
...AND THESE MORTAL CHILDREN, IF THEY LIVE TO BE MEN.

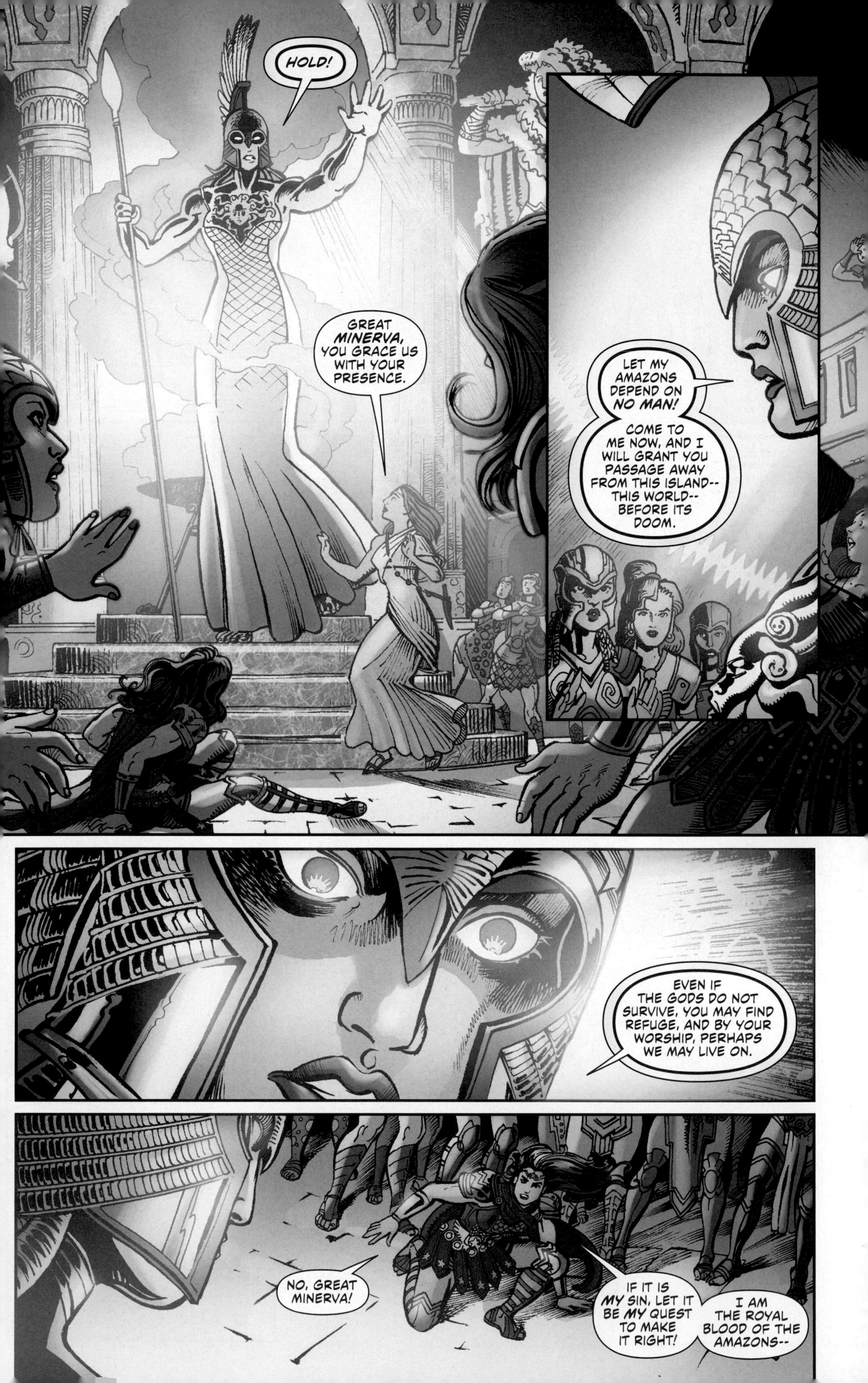
HOLD!
GREAT MINERVA, YOU GRACE US WITH YOUR PRESENCE.
LET MY AMAZONS DEPEND ON NO MAN!
COME TO ME NOW, AND I WILL GRANT YOU PASSAGE AWAY FROM THIS ISLAND-- THIS WORLD-- BEFORE ITS DOOM.
EVEN IF THE GODS DO NOT SURVIVE, YOU MAY FIND REFUGE, AND BY YOUR WORSHIP, PERHAPS WE MAY LIVE ON.
NO, GREAT MINERVA!
IF IT IS MY SIN, LET IT BE MY QUEST TO MAKE IT RIGHT!
I AM THE ROYAL BLOOD OF THE AMAZONS--

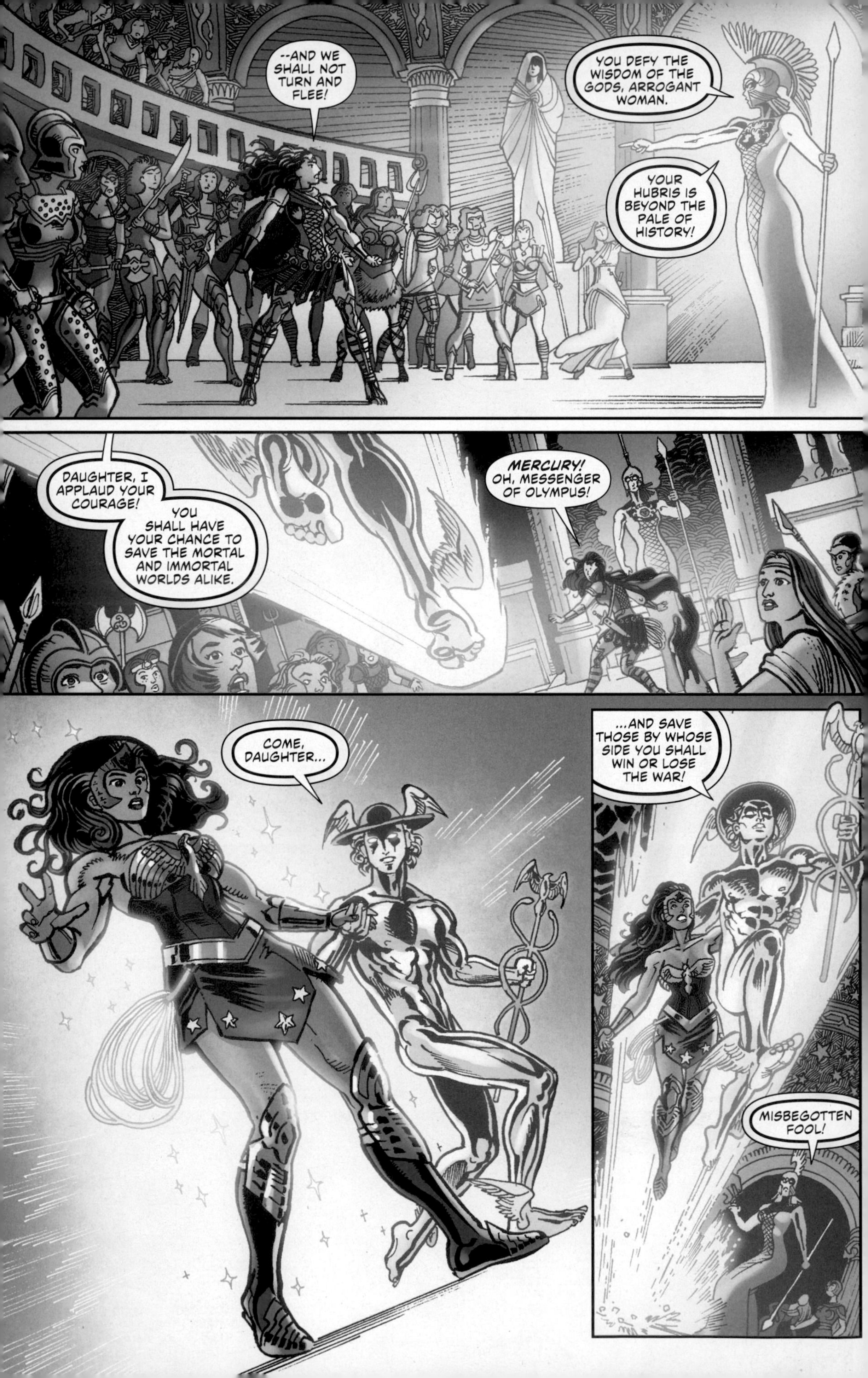
--AND WE SHALL NOT TURN AND FLEE!
YOU DEFY THE WISDOM OF THE GODS, ARROGANT WOMAN.
YOUR HUBRIS IS BEYOND THE PALE OF HISTORY!
DAUGHTER, I APPLAUD YOUR COURAGE!
YOU SHALL HAVE YOUR CHANCE TO SAVE THE MORTAL AND IMMORTAL WORLDS ALIKE.
MERCURY! OH, MESSENGER OF OLYMPUS!
COME, DAUGHTER...
...AND SAVE THOSE BY WHOSE SIDE YOU SHALL WIN OR LOSE THE WAR!
MISBEGOTTEN FOOL!

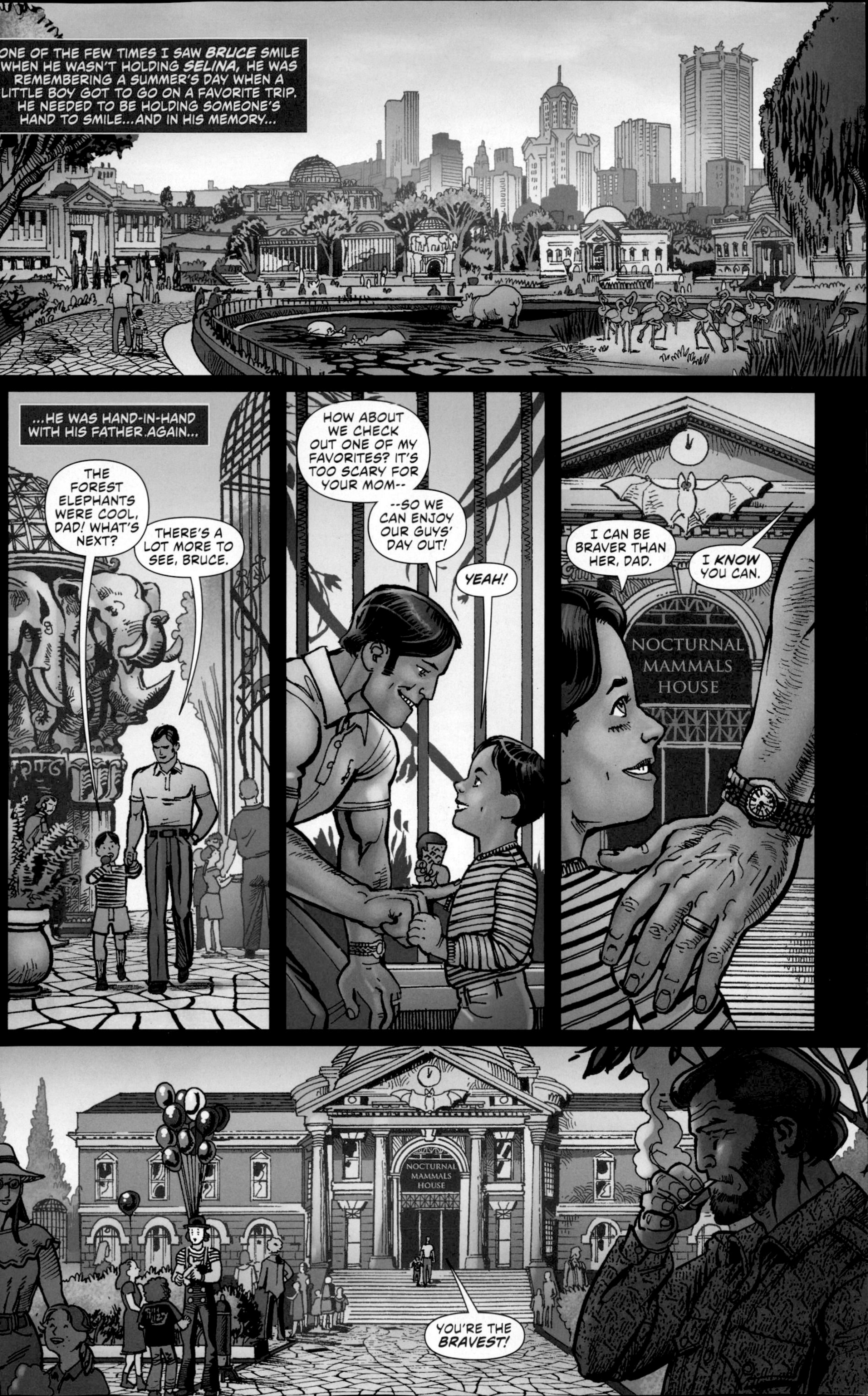
ONE OF THE FEW TIMES I SAW BRUCE SMILE WHEN HE WASN'T HOLDING SELINA, HE WAS REMEMBERING A SUMMER'S DAY WHEN A LITTLE BOY GOT TO GO ON A FAVORITE TRIP. HE NEEDED TO BE HOLDING SOMEONE'S HAND TO SMILE...AND IN HIS MEMORY...
...HE WAS HAND-IN-HAND WITH HIS FATHER AGAIN...
THE FOREST ELEPHANTS WERE COOL, DAD! WHAT'S NEXT?
THERE'S A LOT MORE TO SEE, BRUCE.
HOW ABOUT WE CHECK OUT ONE OF MY FAVORITES? IT'S TOO SCARY FOR YOUR MOM--
--SO WE CAN ENJOY OUR GUYS' DAY OUT!
YEAH!
NOCTURNAL MAMMALS HOUSE
I CAN BE BRAVER THAN HER, DAD.
I KNOW YOU CAN.
NOCTURNAL MAMMALS HOUSE
YOU'RE THE BRAVEST!

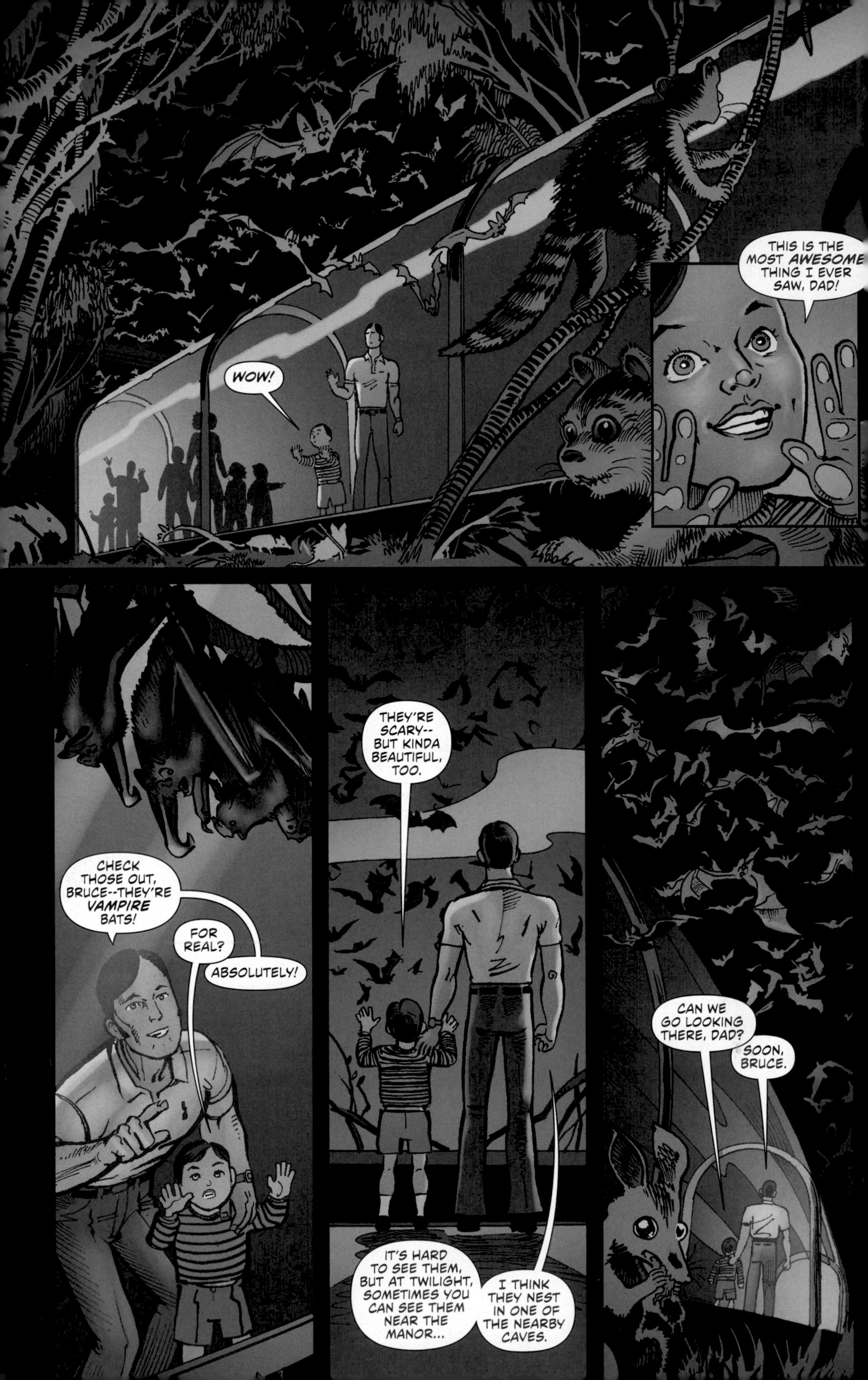
WOW!
THIS IS THE MOST AWESOME THING I EVER SAW, DAD!
CHECK THOSE OUT, BRUCE--THEY'RE VAMPIRE BATS!
FOR REAL?
ABSOLUTELY!
THEY'RE SCARY-- BUT KINDA BEAUTIFUL, TOO.
IT'S HARD TO SEE THEM, BUT AT TWILIGHT, SOMETIMES YOU CAN SEE THEM NEAR THE MANOR...
I THINK THEY NEST IN ONE OF THE NEARBY CAVES.
CAN WE GO LOOKING THERE, DAD?
SOON, BRUCE.

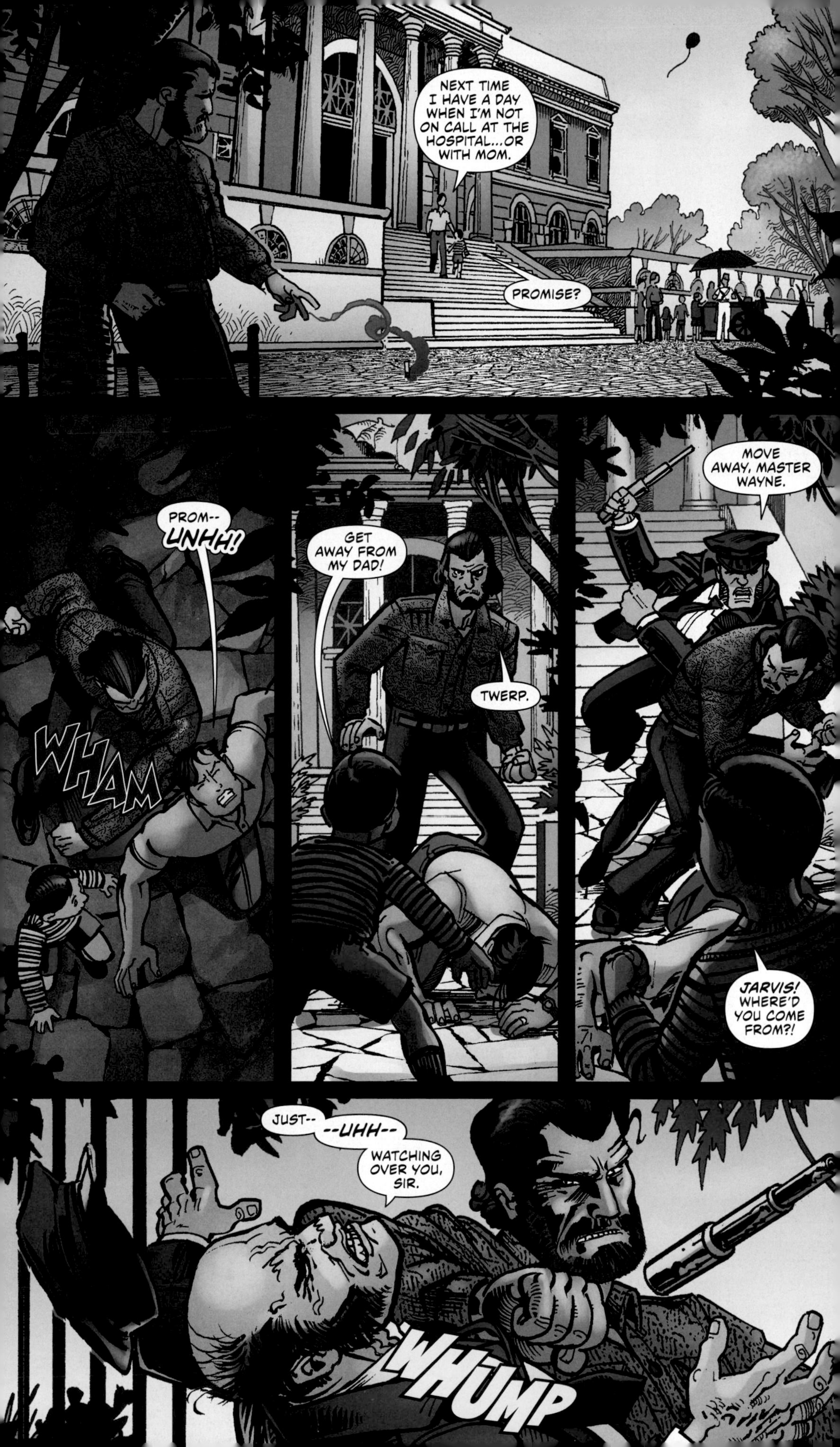
NEXT TIME I HAVE A DAY WHEN I'M NOT ON CALL AT THE HOSPITAL...OR WITH MOM.
PROMISE?
PROM-- UNHH!
WHAM
GET AWAY FROM MY DAD!
TWERP.
MOVE AWAY, MASTER WAYNE.
JARVIS! WHERE'D YOU COME FROM?!
JUST--
--UHH--
WATCHING OVER YOU, SIR.
WHUMP

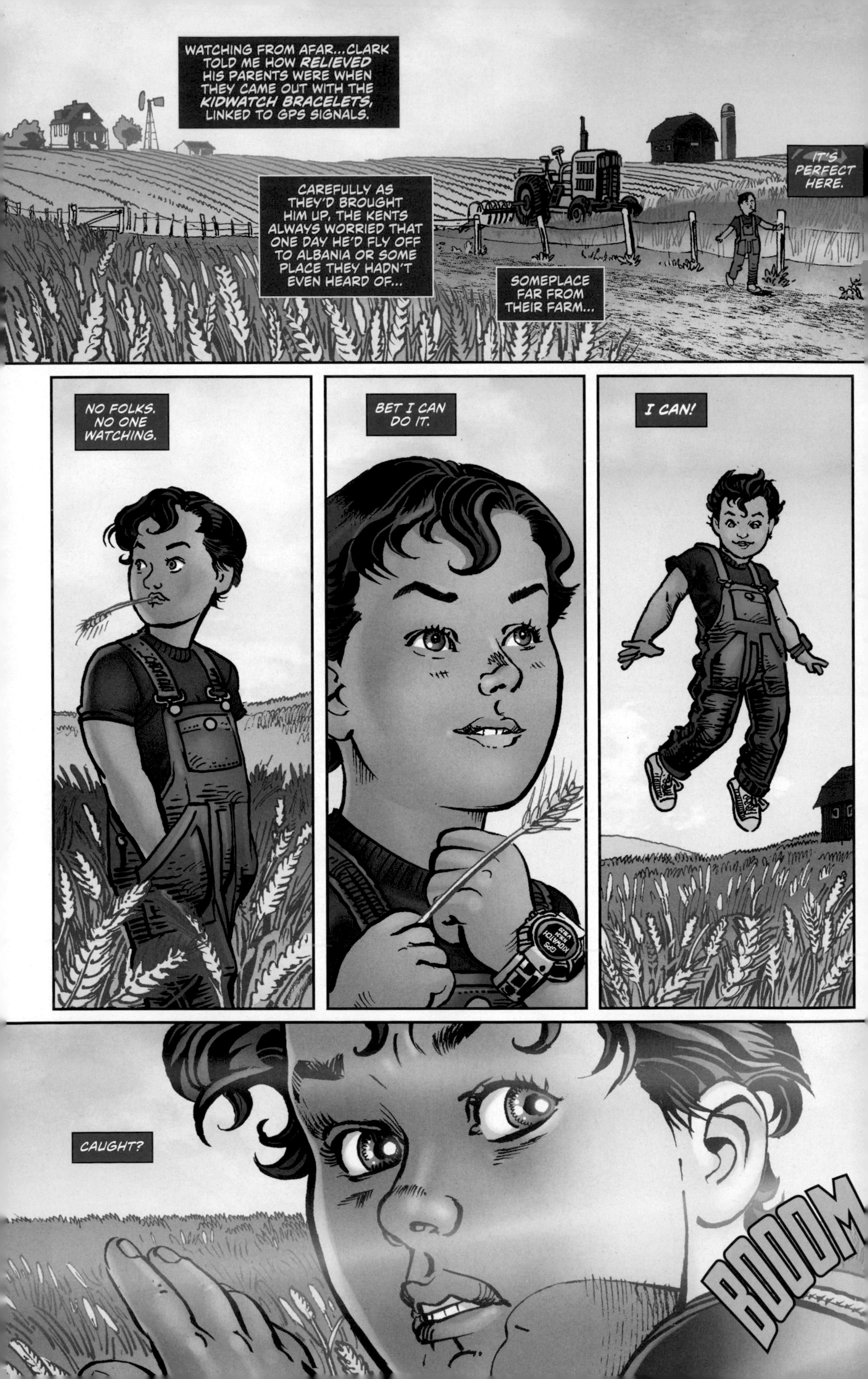

WATCHING FROM AFAR...CLARK TOLD ME HOW *RELIEVED* HIS PARENTS WERE WHEN THEY CAME OUT WITH THE *KIDWATCH BRACELETS,* LINKED TO GPS SIGNALS.
CAREFULLY AS THEY'D BROUGHT HIM UP, THE KENTS ALWAYS WORRIED THAT ONE DAY HE'D FLY OFF TO ALBANIA OR SOME PLACE THEY HADN'T EVEN HEARD OF...
SOMEPLACE FAR FROM THEIR FARM...
IT'S PERFECT HERE.
NO FOLKS. NO ONE WATCHING.
BET I CAN DO IT.
GPS
KIDWATCH
I CAN!
CAUGHT?
BOOOM

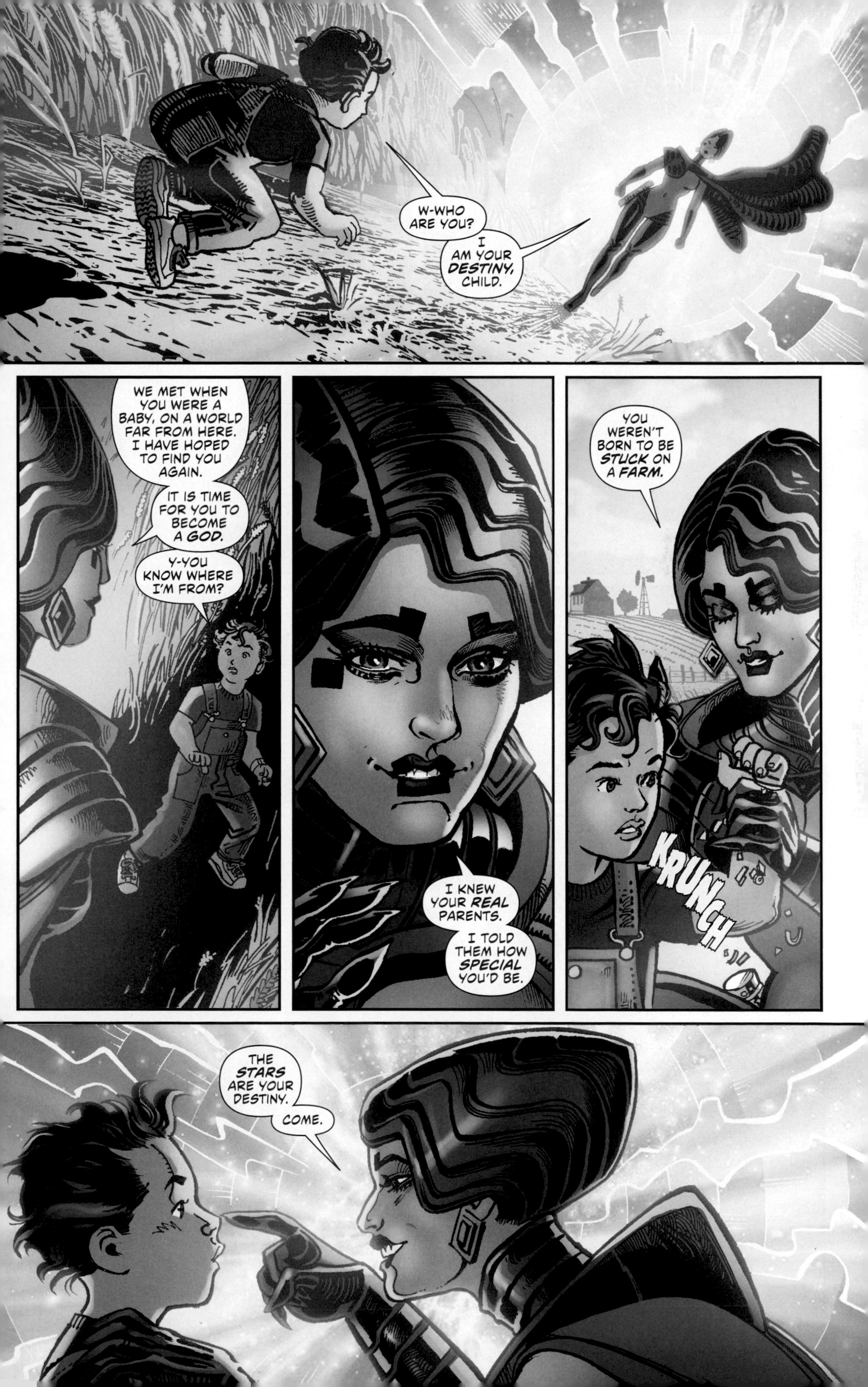
W-WHO ARE YOU?
I AM YOUR DESTINY, CHILD.
WE MET WHEN YOU WERE A BABY, ON A WORLD FAR FROM HERE. I HAVE HOPED TO FIND YOU AGAIN.
IT IS TIME FOR YOU TO BECOME A GOD.
Y-YOU KNOW WHERE I'M FROM?
I KNEW YOUR REAL PARENTS.
I TOLD THEM HOW SPECIAL YOU'D BE.
YOU WEREN'T BORN TO BE STUCK ON A FARM.
KRUNCH
THE STARS ARE YOUR DESTINY.
COME.

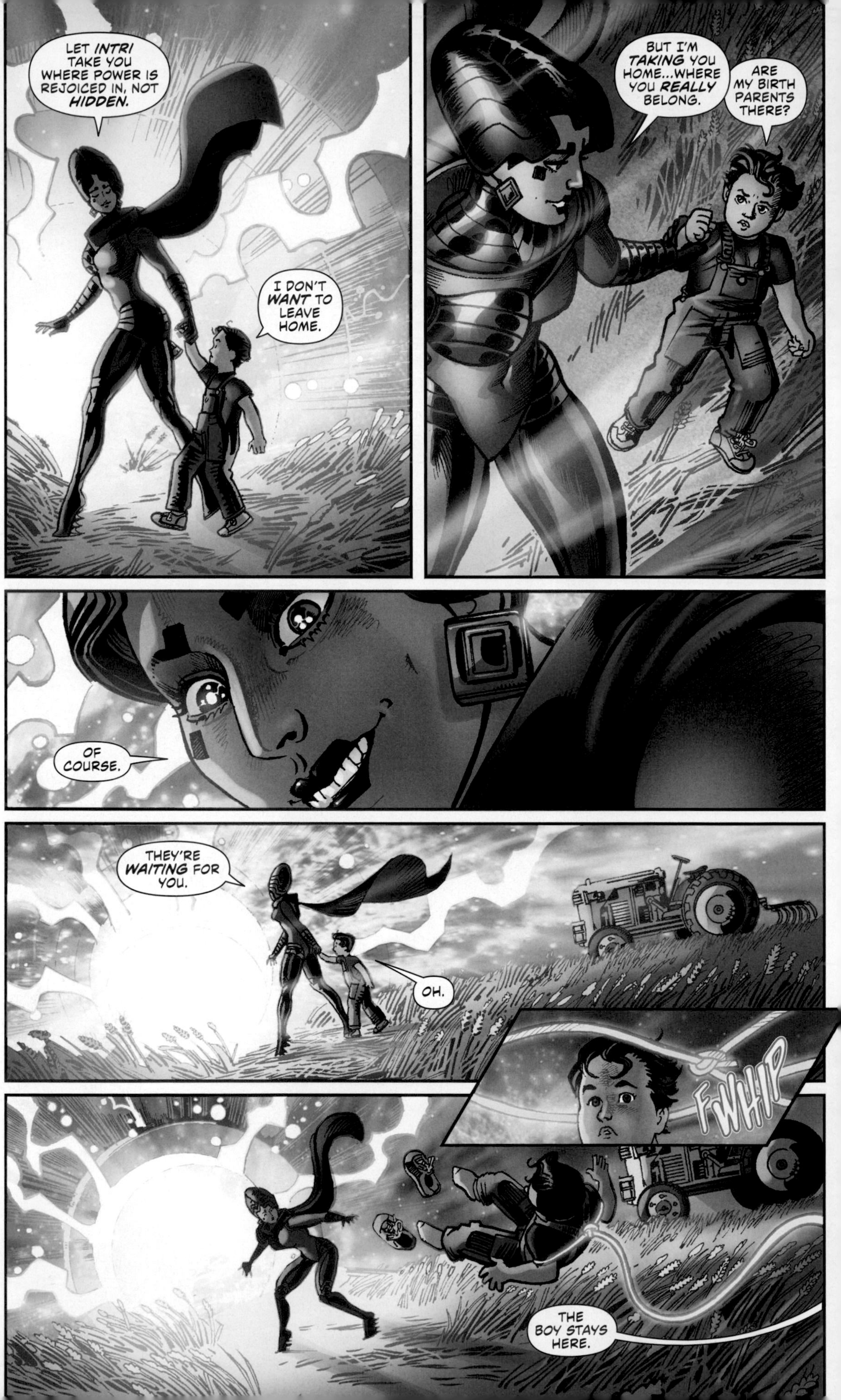
LET INTRI TAKE YOU WHERE POWER IS REJOICED IN, NOT HIDDEN.
I DON'T WANT TO LEAVE HOME.
BUT I'M TAKING YOU HOME...WHERE YOU REALLY BELONG.
ARE MY BIRTH PARENTS THERE?
OF COURSE.
THEY'RE WAITING FOR YOU.
OH.
FWHIP
THE BOY STAYS HERE.

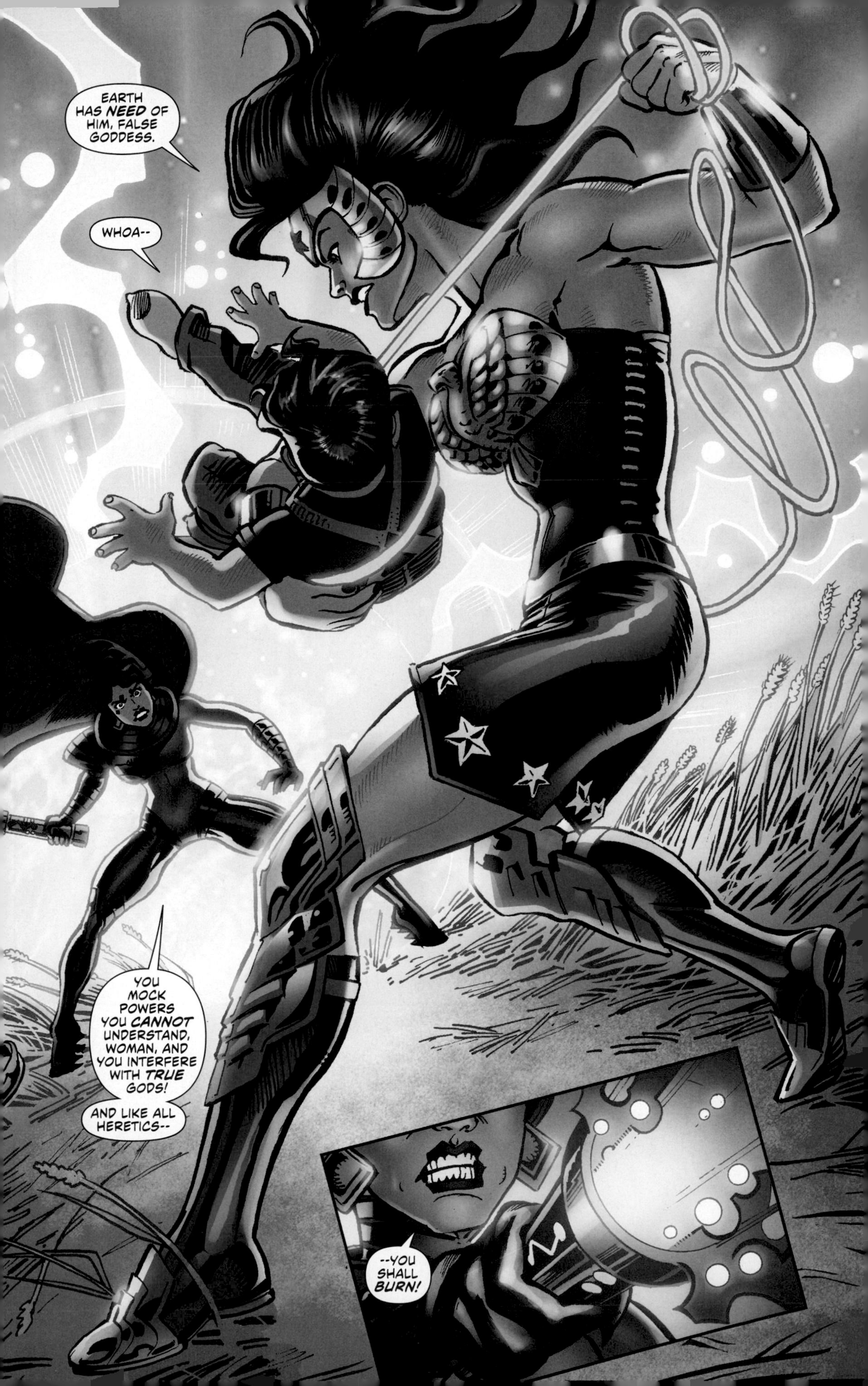
EARTH HAS NEED OF HIM, FALSE GODDESS.
WHOA--
YOU MOCK POWERS YOU CANNOT UNDERSTAND, WOMAN, AND YOU INTERFERE WITH TRUE GODS!
AND LIKE ALL HERETICS--
--YOU SHALL BURN!

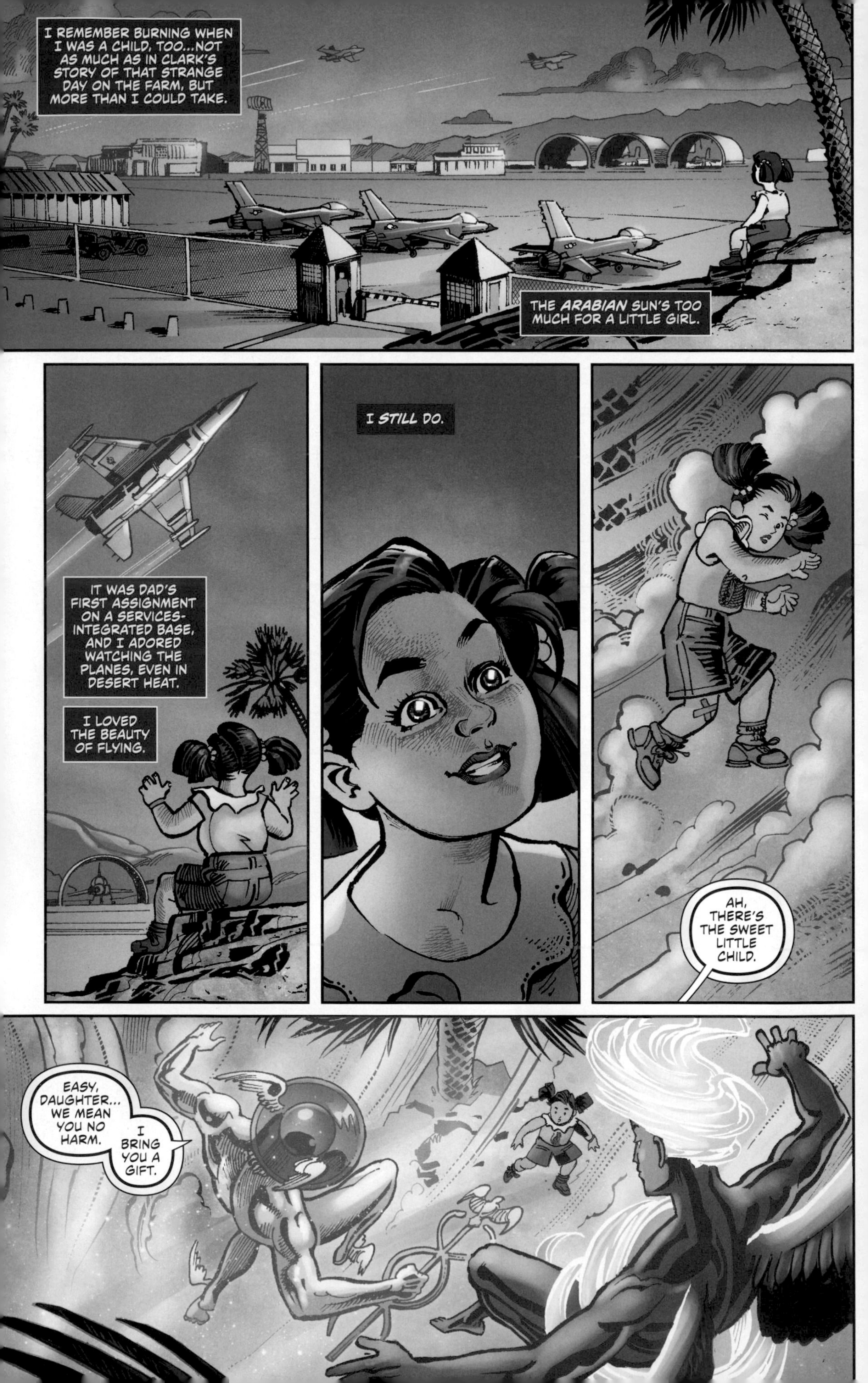
I REMEMBER BURNING WHEN I WAS A CHILD, TOO...NOT AS MUCH AS IN CLARK'S STORY OF THAT STRANGE DAY ON THE FARM, BUT MORE THAN I COULD TAKE.
THE *ARABIAN* SUN'S TOO MUCH FOR A LITTLE GIRL.
IT WAS DAD'S FIRST ASSIGNMENT ON A SERVICES-INTEGRATED BASE, AND I ADORED WATCHING THE PLANES, EVEN IN DESERT HEAT.
I LOVED THE BEAUTY OF FLYING.
I *STILL* DO.
AH, THERE'S THE SWEET LITTLE CHILD.
EASY, DAUGHTER... WE MEAN YOU NO HARM.
I BRING YOU A GIFT.

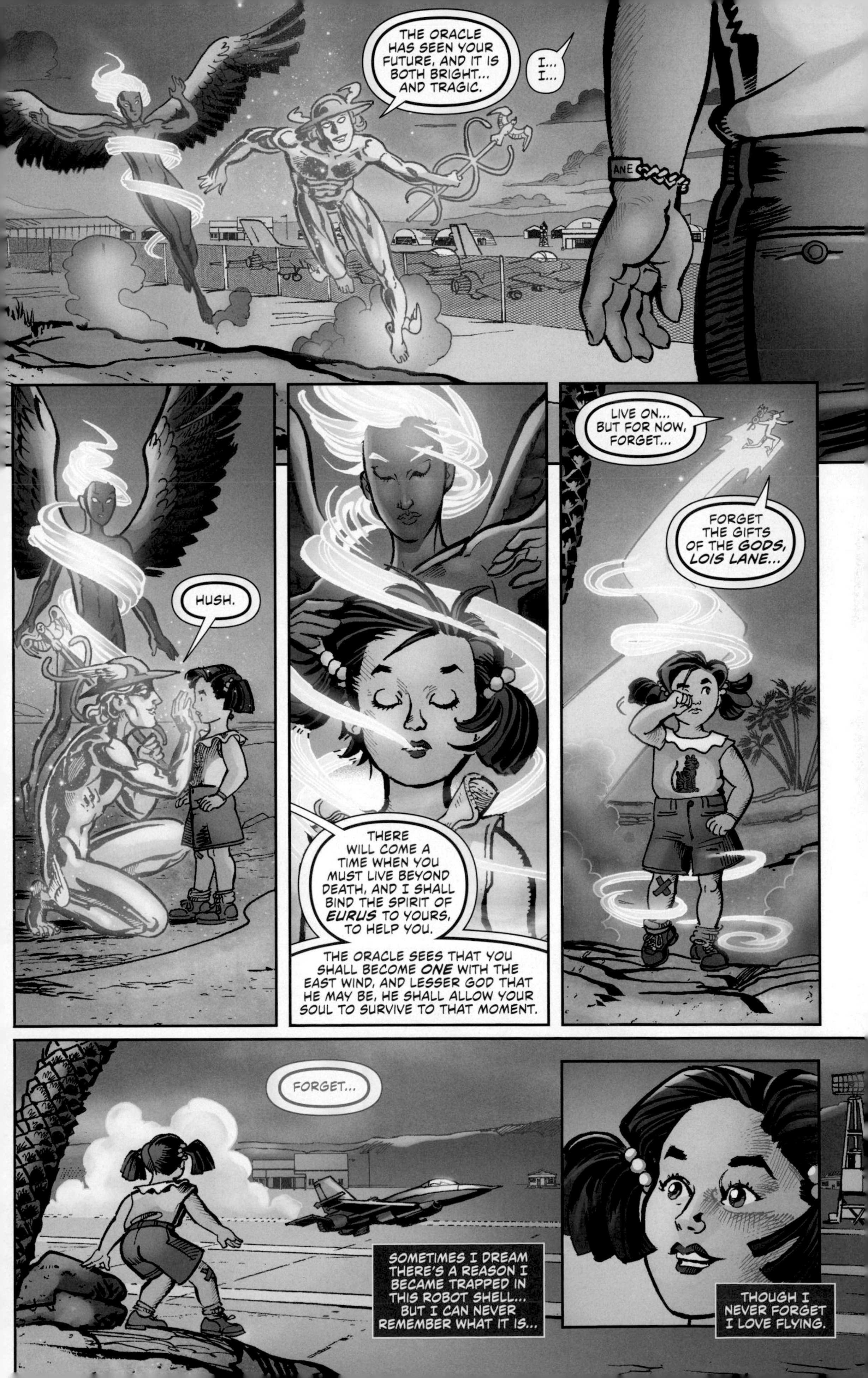

THE ORACLE HAS SEEN YOUR FUTURE, AND IT IS BOTH BRIGHT... AND TRAGIC.
I... I...
ANE
HUSH.
THERE WILL COME A TIME WHEN YOU MUST LIVE BEYOND DEATH, AND I SHALL BIND THE SPIRIT OF EURUS TO YOURS, TO HELP YOU.
THE ORACLE SEES THAT YOU SHALL BECOME ONE WITH THE EAST WIND, AND LESSER GOD THAT HE MAY BE, HE SHALL ALLOW YOUR SOUL TO SURVIVE TO THAT MOMENT.
LIVE ON... BUT FOR NOW, FORGET...
FORGET THE GIFTS OF THE GODS, LOIS LANE...
FORGET...
SOMETIMES I DREAM THERE'S A REASON I BECAME TRAPPED IN THIS ROBOT SHELL... BUT I CAN NEVER REMEMBER WHAT IT IS...
THOUGH I NEVER FORGET I LOVE FLYING.

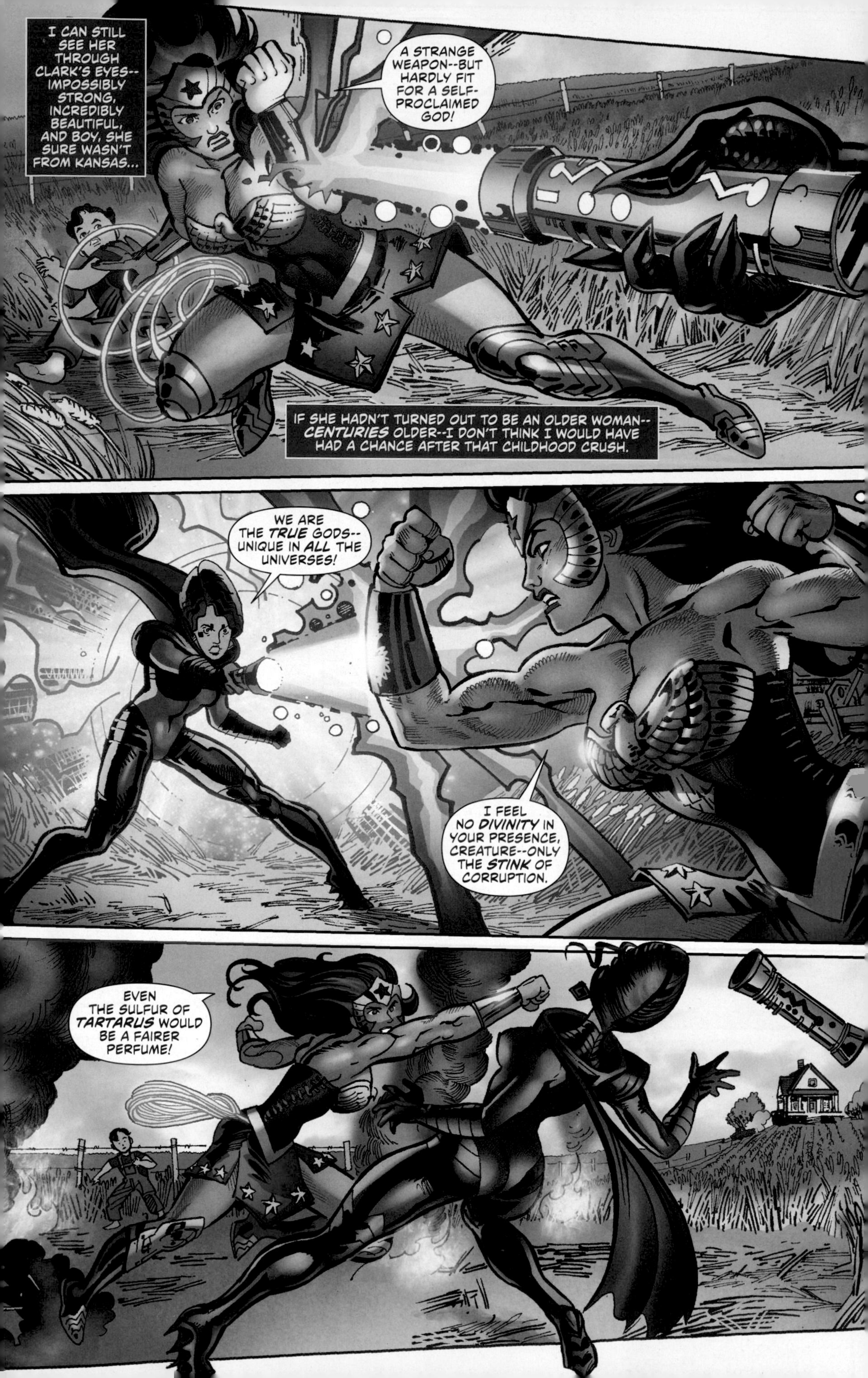
I CAN STILL SEE HER THROUGH CLARK'S EYES-- IMPOSSIBLY STRONG, INCREDIBLY BEAUTIFUL, AND BOY, SHE SURE WASN'T FROM KANSAS...
A STRANGE WEAPON--BUT HARDLY FIT FOR A SELF-PROCLAIMED GOD!
IF SHE HADN'T TURNED OUT TO BE AN OLDER WOMAN-- CENTURIES OLDER--I DON'T THINK I WOULD HAVE HAD A CHANCE AFTER THAT CHILDHOOD CRUSH.
WE ARE THE TRUE GODS-- UNIQUE IN ALL THE UNIVERSES!
I FEEL NO DIVINITY IN YOUR PRESENCE, CREATURE--ONLY THE STINK OF CORRUPTION.
EVEN THE SULFUR OF TARTARUS WOULD BE A FAIRER PERFUME!

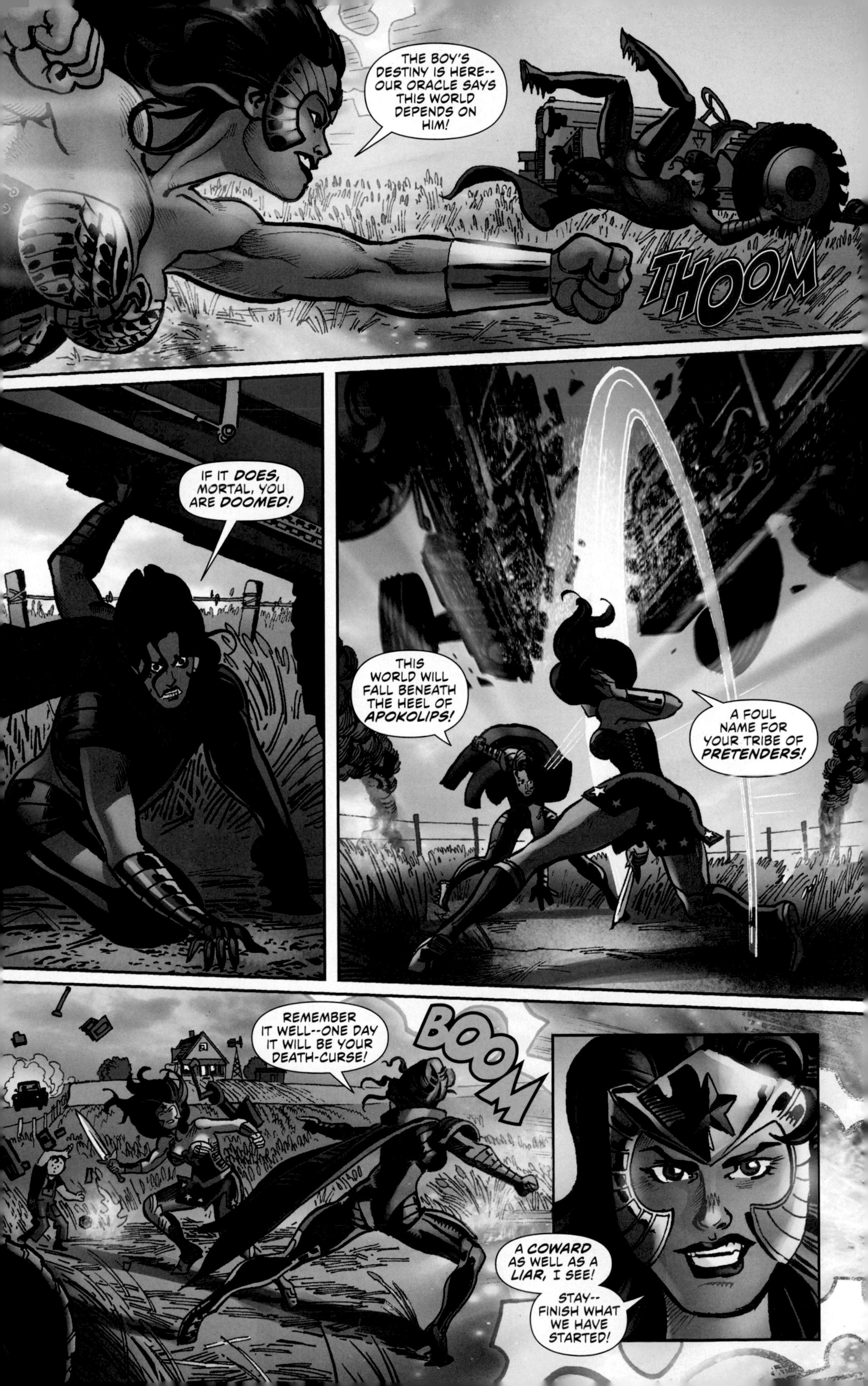
THE BOY'S DESTINY IS HERE-- OUR ORACLE SAYS THIS WORLD DEPENDS ON HIM!
THOOM
IF IT DOES, MORTAL, YOU ARE DOOMED!
THIS WORLD WILL FALL BENEATH THE HEEL OF APOKOLIPS!
A FOUL NAME FOR YOUR TRIBE OF PRETENDERS!
REMEMBER IT WELL--ONE DAY IT WILL BE YOUR DEATH-CURSE!
BOOM
A COWARD AS WELL AS A LIAR, I SEE!
STAY-- FINISH WHAT WE HAVE STARTED!

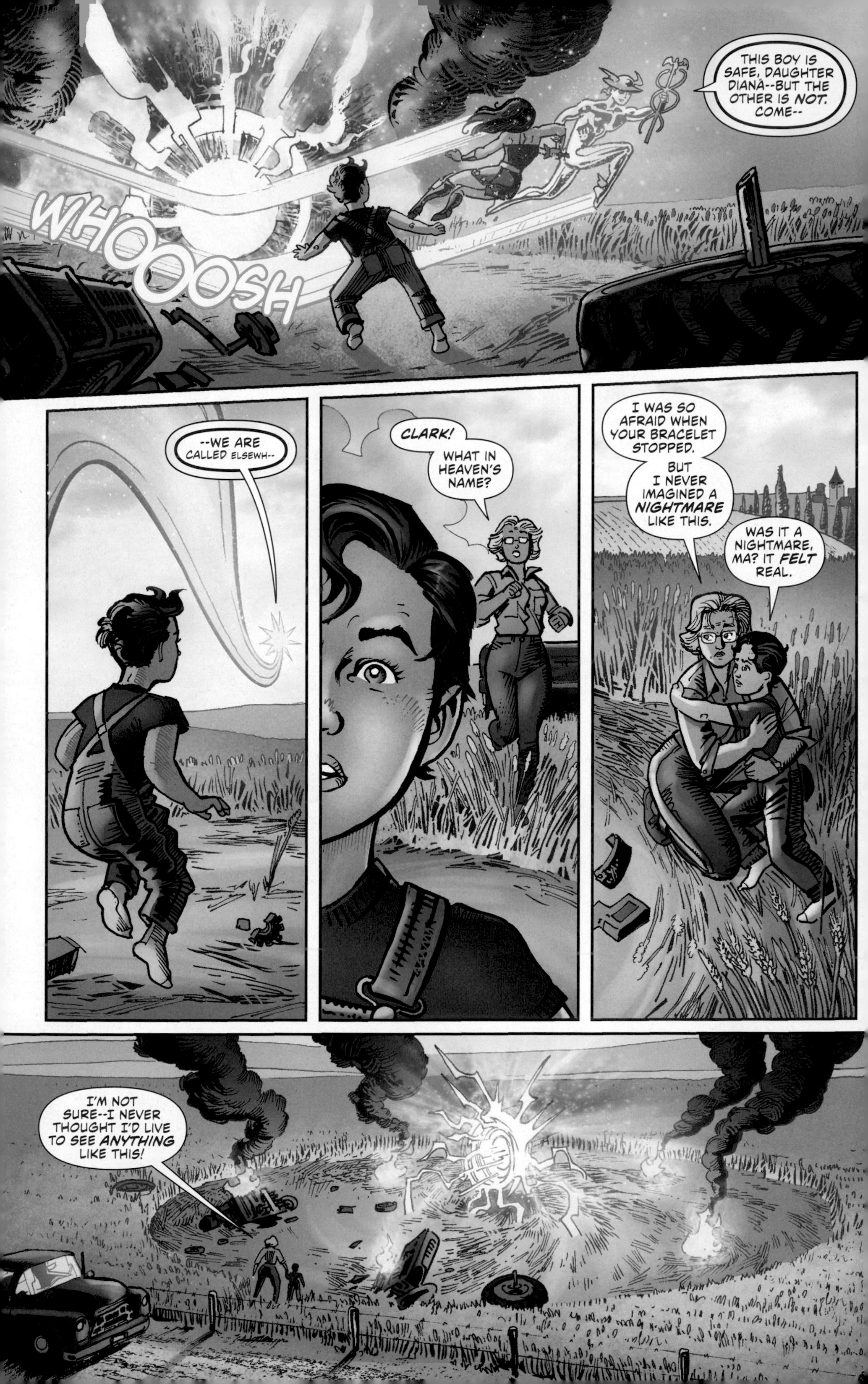
THIS BOY IS SAFE, DAUGHTER DIANA--BUT THE OTHER IS NOT. COME--
WHOOOSH
--WE ARE CALLED ELSEWH--
CLARK!
WHAT IN HEAVEN'S NAME?
I WAS SO AFRAID WHEN YOUR BRACELET STOPPED.
BUT I NEVER IMAGINED A NIGHTMARE LIKE THIS.
WAS IT A NIGHTMARE, MA? IT FELT REAL.
I'M NOT SURE--I NEVER THOUGHT I'D LIVE TO SEE ANYTHING LIKE THIS!

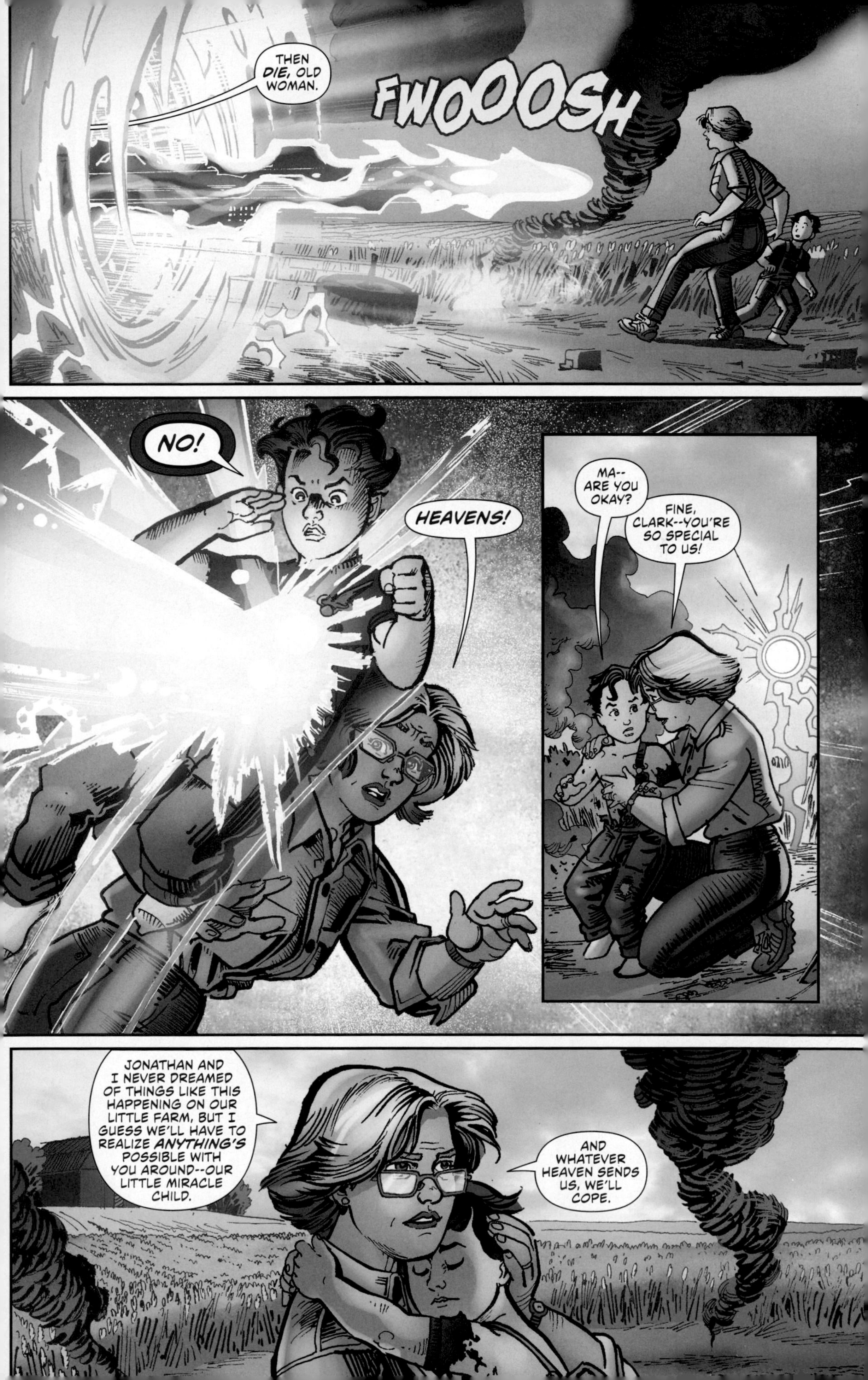
THEN DIE, OLD WOMAN.
FWOOOSH
NO!
HEAVENS!
MA-- ARE YOU OKAY?
FINE, CLARK--YOU'RE SO SPECIAL TO US!
JONATHAN AND I NEVER DREAMED OF THINGS LIKE THIS HAPPENING ON OUR LITTLE FARM, BUT I GUESS WE'LL HAVE TO REALIZE ANYTHING'S POSSIBLE WITH YOU AROUND--OUR LITTLE MIRACLE CHILD.
AND WHATEVER HEAVEN SENDS US, WE'LL COPE.

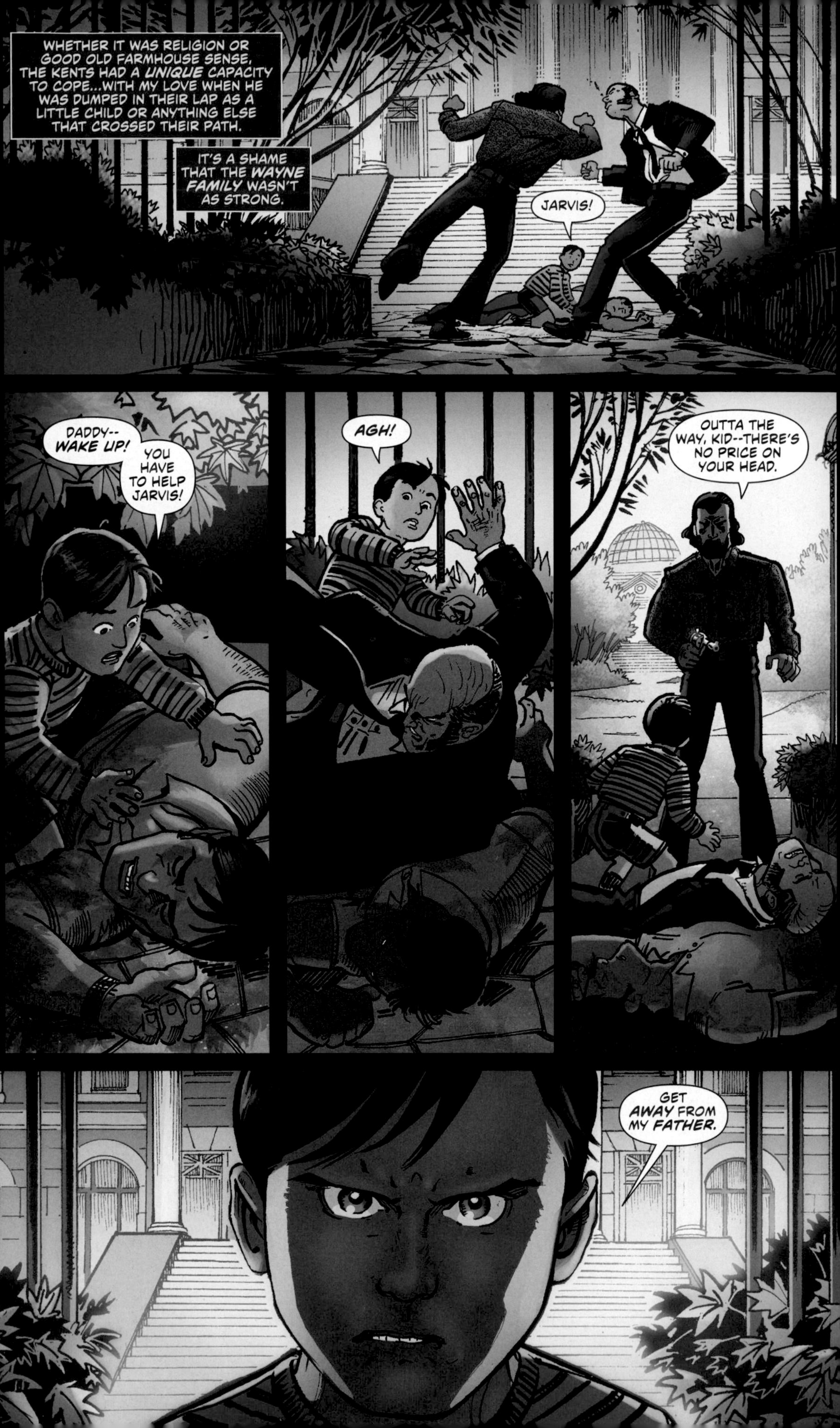
WHETHER IT WAS RELIGION OR GOOD OLD FARMHOUSE SENSE, THE KENTS HAD A UNIQUE CAPACITY TO COPE...WITH MY LOVE WHEN HE WAS DUMPED IN THEIR LAP AS A LITTLE CHILD OR ANYTHING ELSE THAT CROSSED THEIR PATH.
IT'S A SHAME THAT THE WAYNE FAMILY WASN'T AS STRONG.
JARVIS!
DADDY-- WAKE UP!
YOU HAVE TO HELP JARVIS!
AGH!
OUTTA THE WAY, KID--THERE'S NO PRICE ON YOUR HEAD.
GET AWAY FROM MY FATHER.

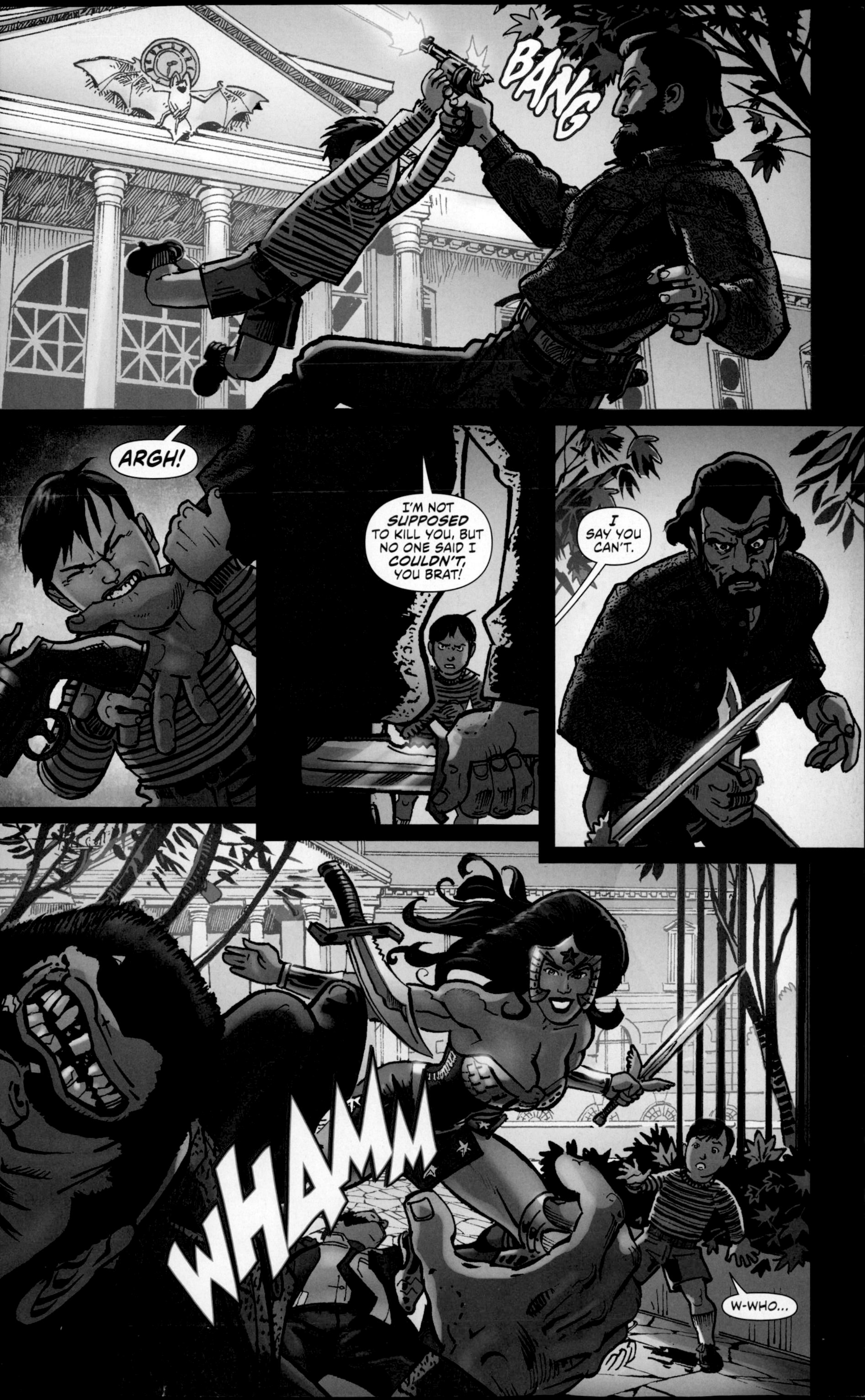
BANG
ARGH!
I'M NOT SUPPOSED TO KILL YOU, BUT NO ONE SAID I COULDN'T, YOU BRAT!
I SAY YOU CAN'T.
WHAMM
W-WHO...

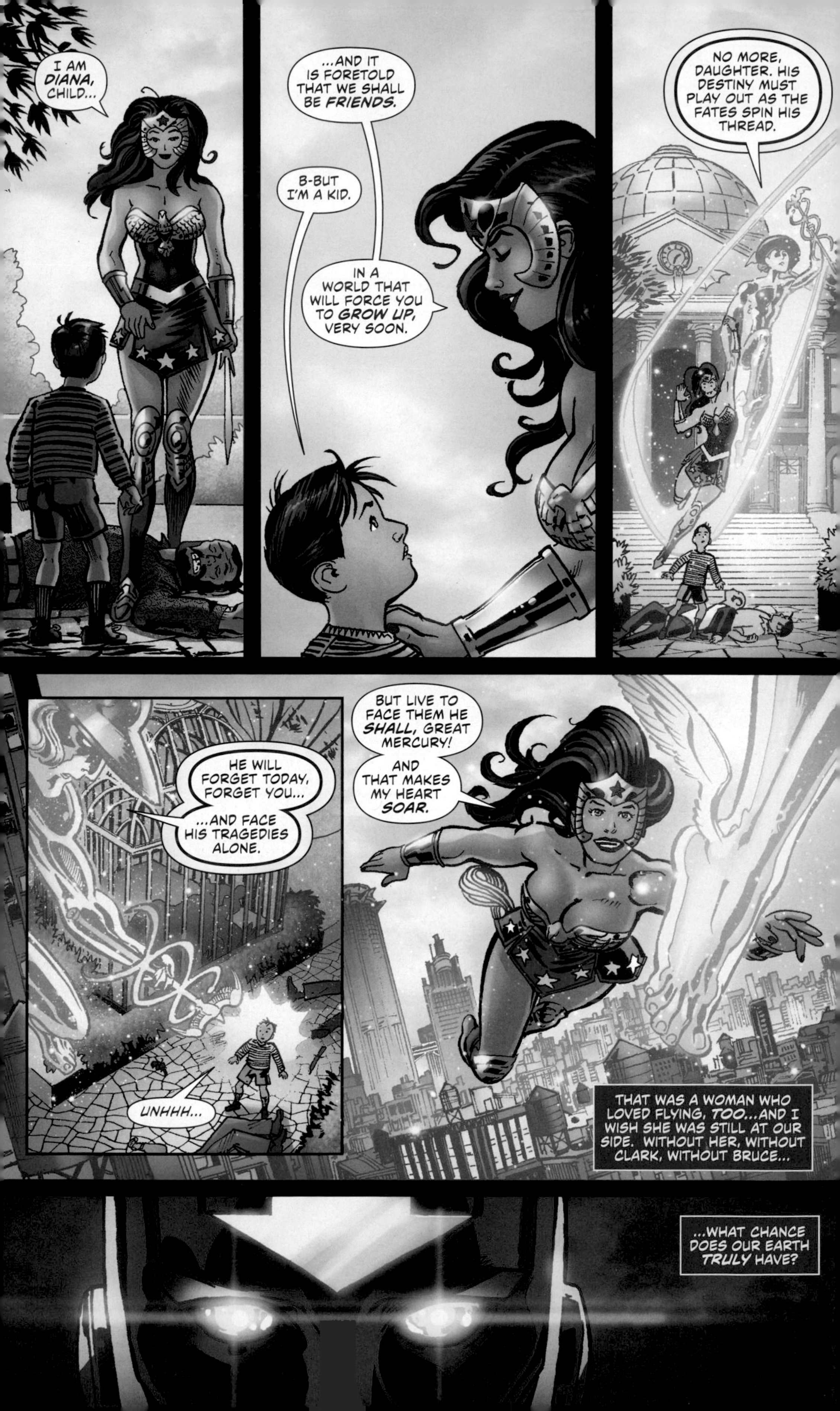
I AM DIANA, CHILD...
...AND IT IS FORETOLD THAT WE SHALL BE FRIENDS.
B-BUT I'M A KID.
IN A WORLD THAT WILL FORCE YOU TO GROW UP, VERY SOON.
NO MORE, DAUGHTER. HIS DESTINY MUST PLAY OUT AS THE FATES SPIN HIS THREAD.
HE WILL FORGET TODAY, FORGET YOU...
...AND FACE HIS TRAGEDIES ALONE.
UNHHH...
BUT LIVE TO FACE THEM HE SHALL, GREAT MERCURY!
AND THAT MAKES MY HEART SOAR.
THAT WAS A WOMAN WHO LOVED FLYING, TOO...AND I WISH SHE WAS STILL AT OUR SIDE. WITHOUT HER, WITHOUT CLARK, WITHOUT BRUCE...
...WHAT CHANCE DOES OUR EARTH TRULY HAVE?

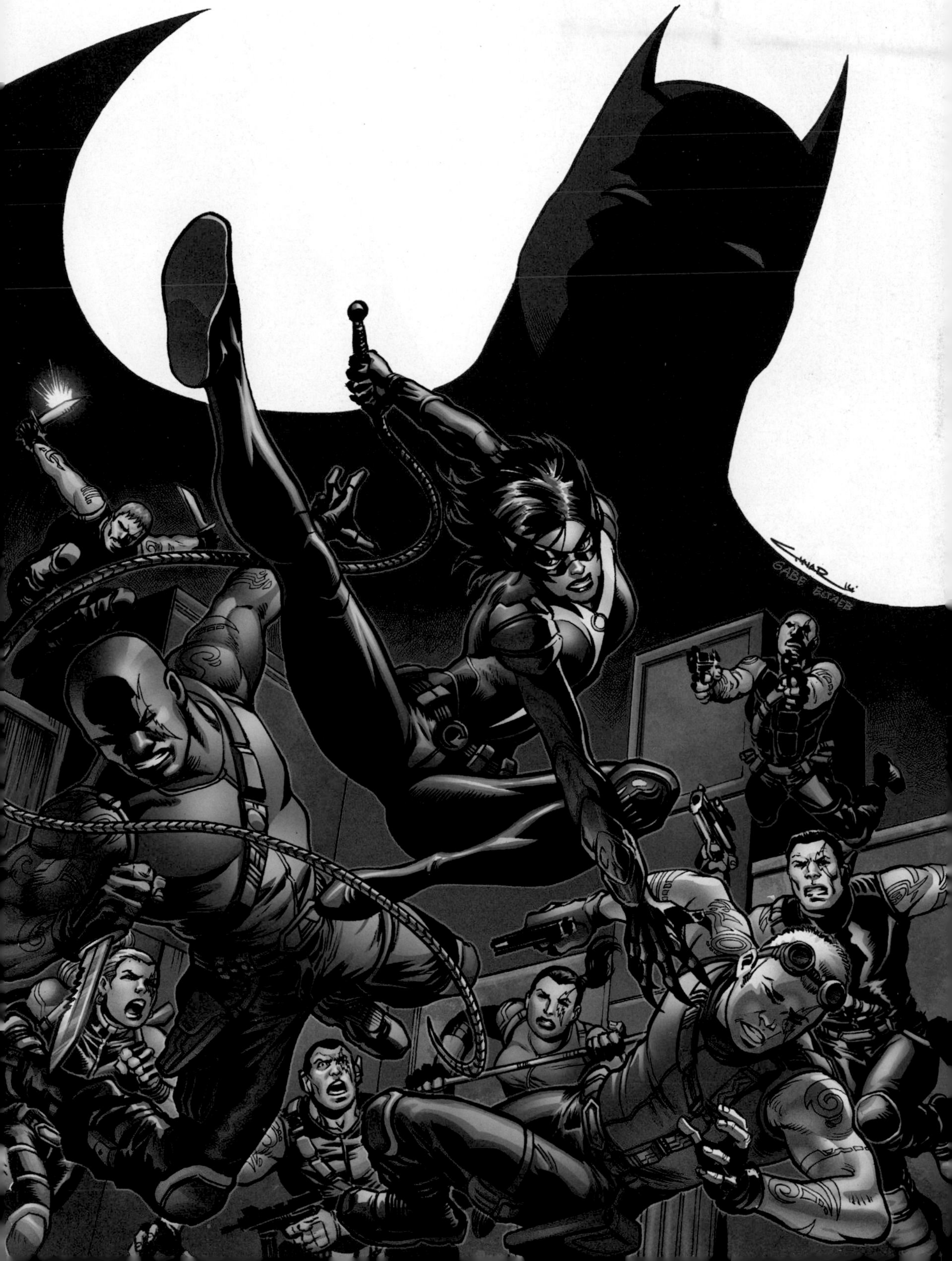

PART THREE: BINDINGS

PAUL LEVITZ writer **JED DOUGHERTY** artist **CHRIS SOTOMAYOR** colorist
TRAVIS LANHAM letterer cover art by **YILDIRAY CINAR & GABE ELTAEB**

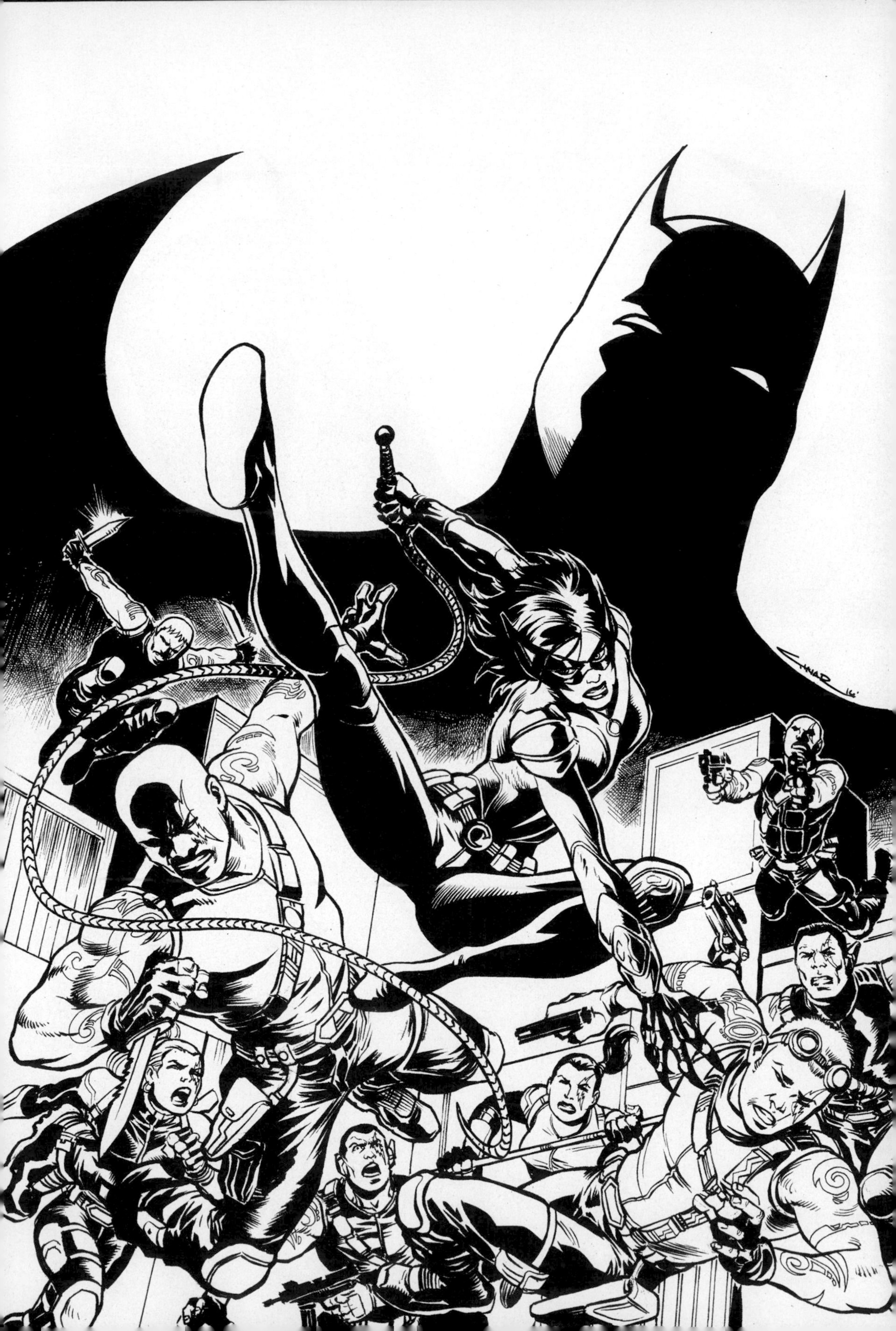

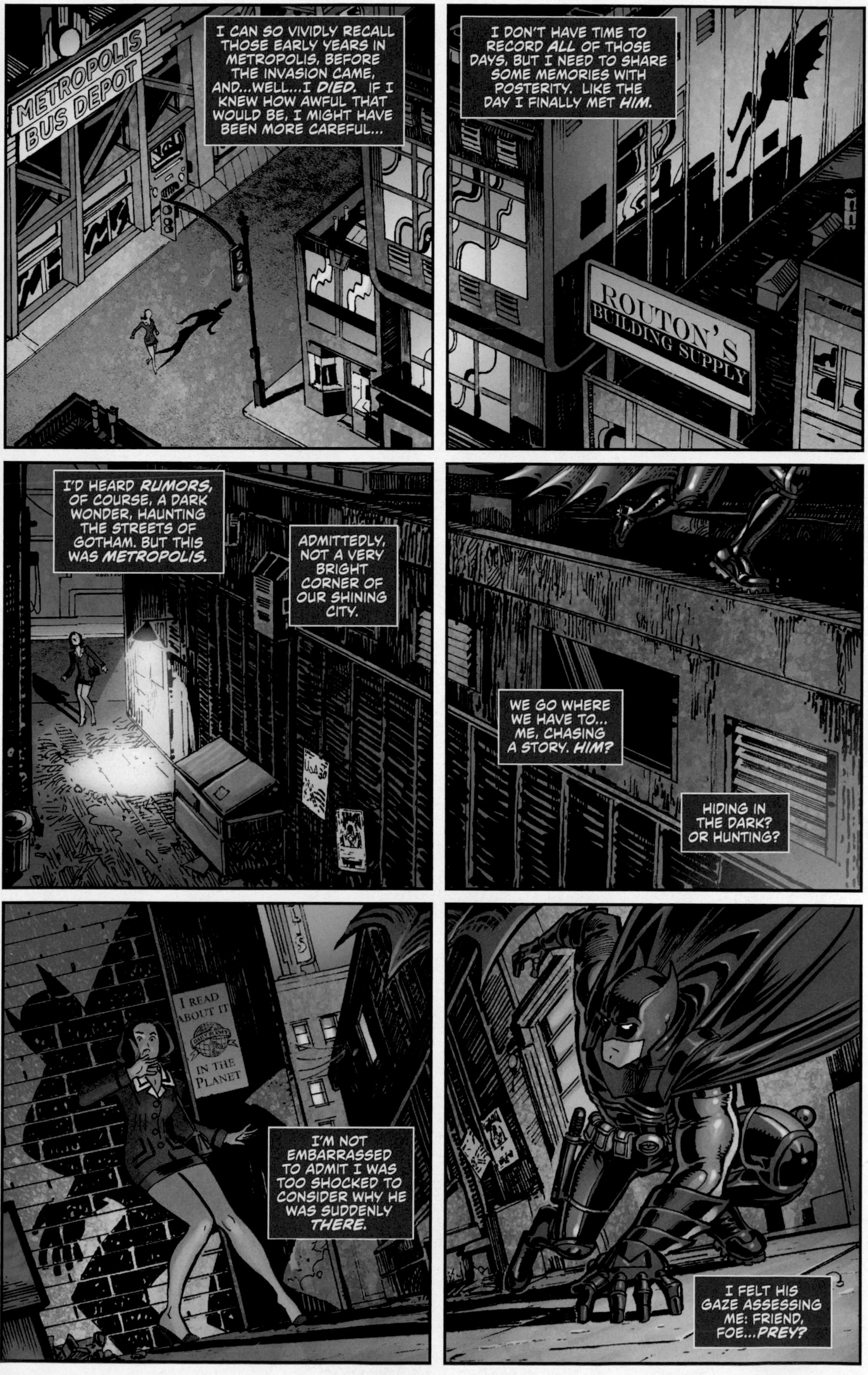
METROPOLIS BUS DEPOT
I CAN SO VIVIDLY RECALL THOSE EARLY YEARS IN METROPOLIS, BEFORE THE INVASION CAME, AND...WELL...I DIED. IF I KNEW HOW AWFUL THAT WOULD BE, I MIGHT HAVE BEEN MORE CAREFUL...
I DON'T HAVE TIME TO RECORD ALL OF THOSE DAYS, BUT I NEED TO SHARE SOME MEMORIES WITH POSTERITY. LIKE THE DAY I FINALLY MET HIM.
ROUTON'S BUILDING SUPPLY
I'D HEARD RUMORS, OF COURSE, A DARK WONDER, HAUNTING THE STREETS OF GOTHAM. BUT THIS WAS METROPOLIS.
ADMITTEDLY, NOT A VERY BRIGHT CORNER OF OUR SHINING CITY.
WE GO WHERE WE HAVE TO... ME, CHASING A STORY. HIM?
HIDING IN THE DARK? OR HUNTING?
I READ ABOUT IT IN THE PLANET
I'M NOT EMBARRASSED TO ADMIT I WAS TOO SHOCKED TO CONSIDER WHY HE WAS SUDDENLY THERE.
I FELT HIS GAZE ASSESSING ME: FRIEND, FOE...PREY?

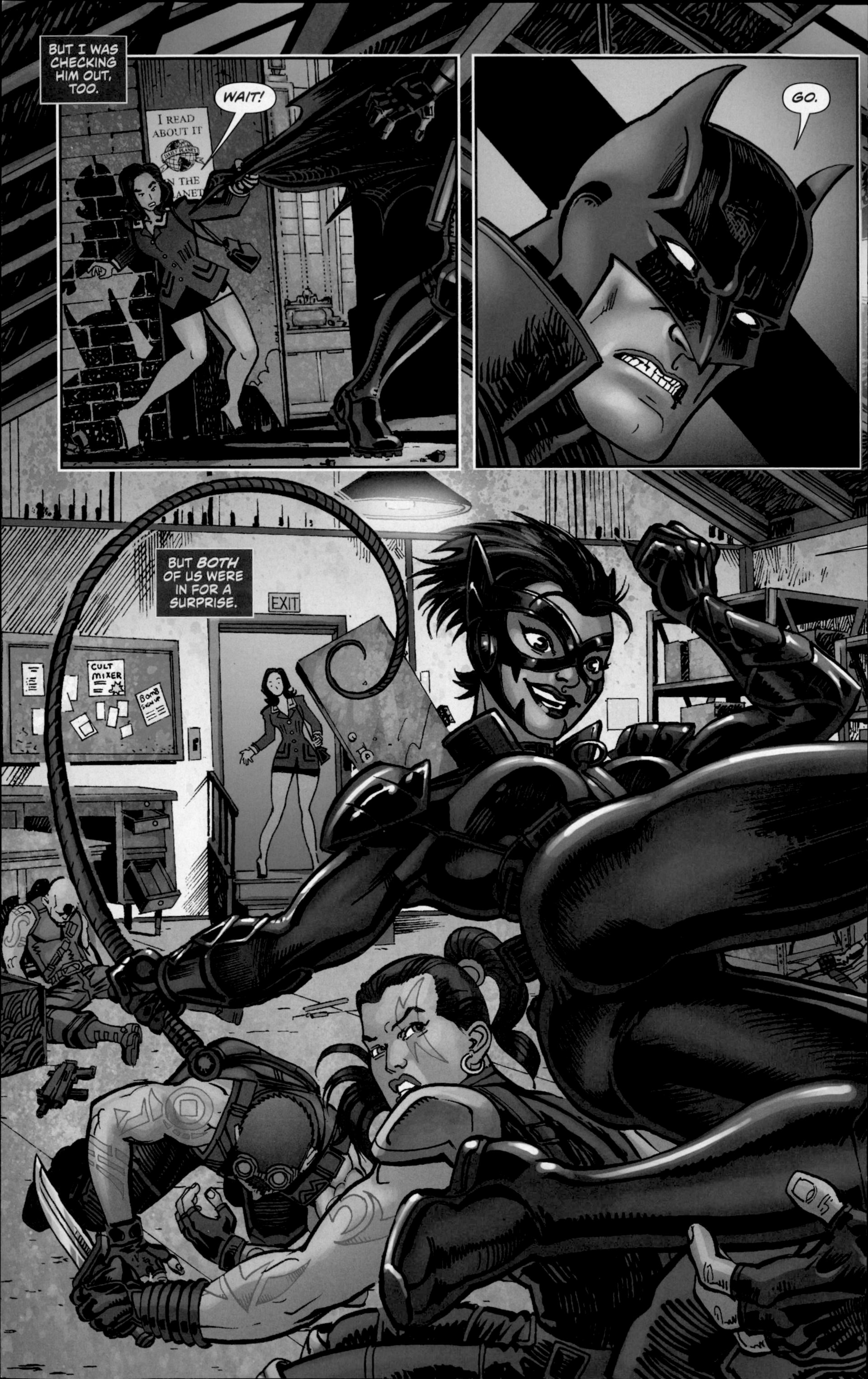

BUT I WAS CHECKING HIM OUT, TOO.
I READ ABOUT IT
DAILY PLANET
WAIT!
GO.
BUT BOTH OF US WERE IN FOR A SURPRISE.
EXIT
CULT MIXER
BOMB SIGN UP

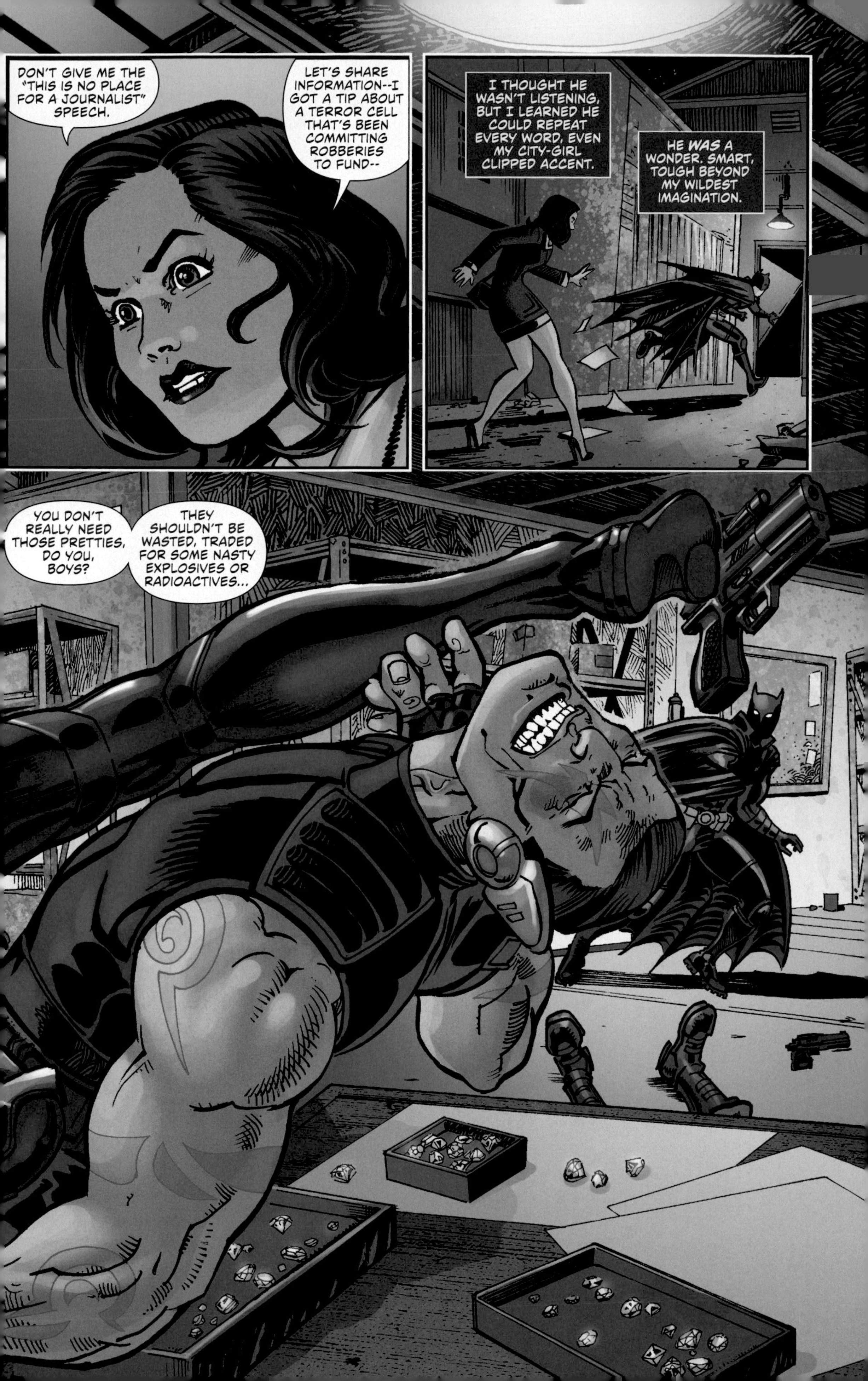
DON'T GIVE ME THE "THIS IS NO PLACE FOR A JOURNALIST" SPEECH.
LET'S SHARE INFORMATION--I GOT A TIP ABOUT A TERROR CELL THAT'S BEEN COMMITTING ROBBERIES TO FUND--
I THOUGHT HE WASN'T LISTENING, BUT I LEARNED HE COULD REPEAT EVERY WORD, EVEN MY CITY-GIRL CLIPPED ACCENT.
HE *WAS* A WONDER. SMART, TOUGH BEYOND MY WILDEST IMAGINATION.
YOU DON'T REALLY NEED THOSE PRETTIES, DO YOU, BOYS?
THEY SHOULDN'T BE WASTED, TRADED FOR SOME NASTY EXPLOSIVES OR RADIOACTIVES...

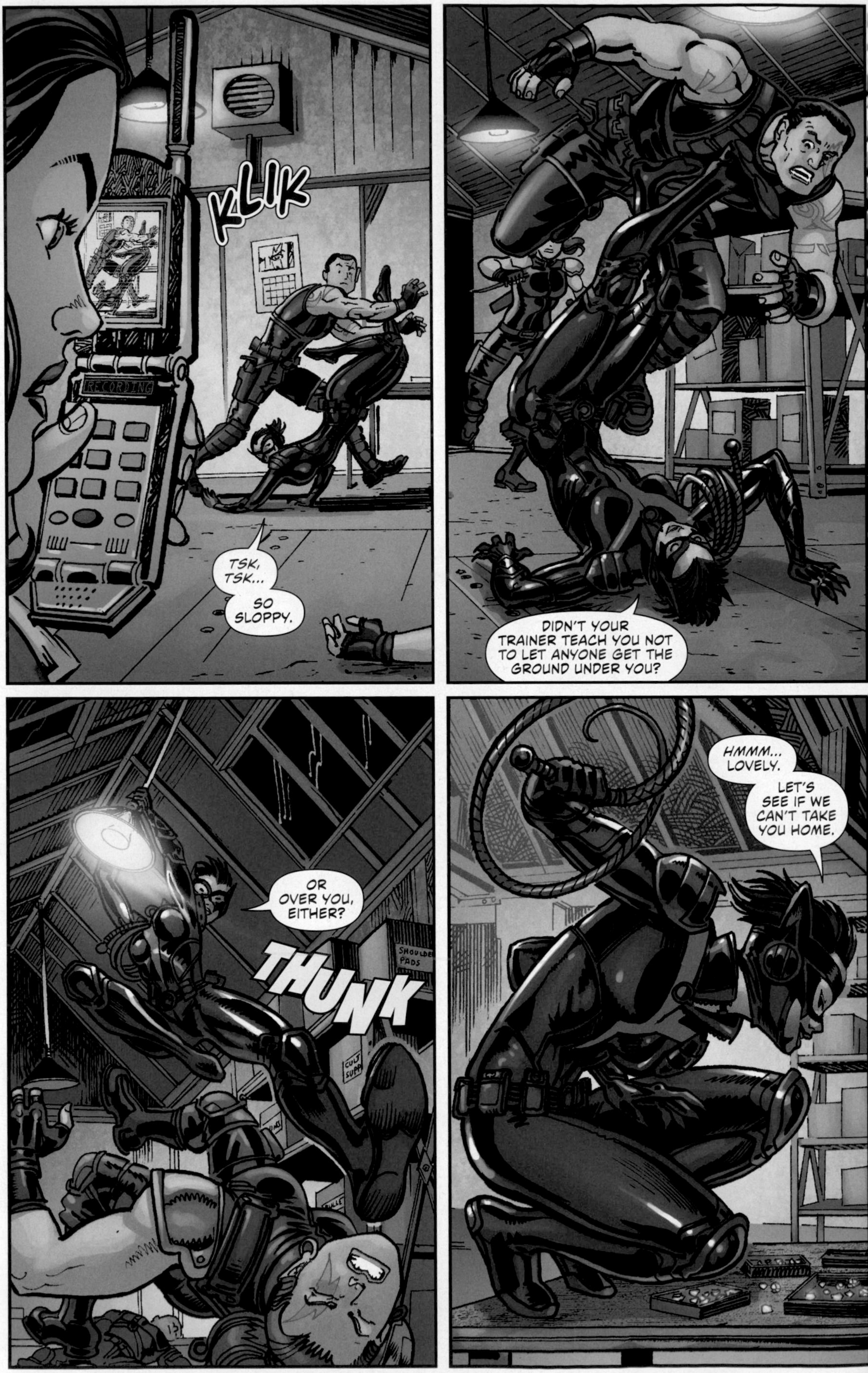
RECORDING
KLIK
TSK, TSK...
SO SLOPPY.
DIDN'T YOUR TRAINER TEACH YOU NOT TO LET ANYONE GET THE GROUND UNDER YOU?
OR OVER YOU, EITHER?
THUNK
HMMM... LOVELY.
LET'S SEE IF WE CAN'T TAKE YOU HOME.

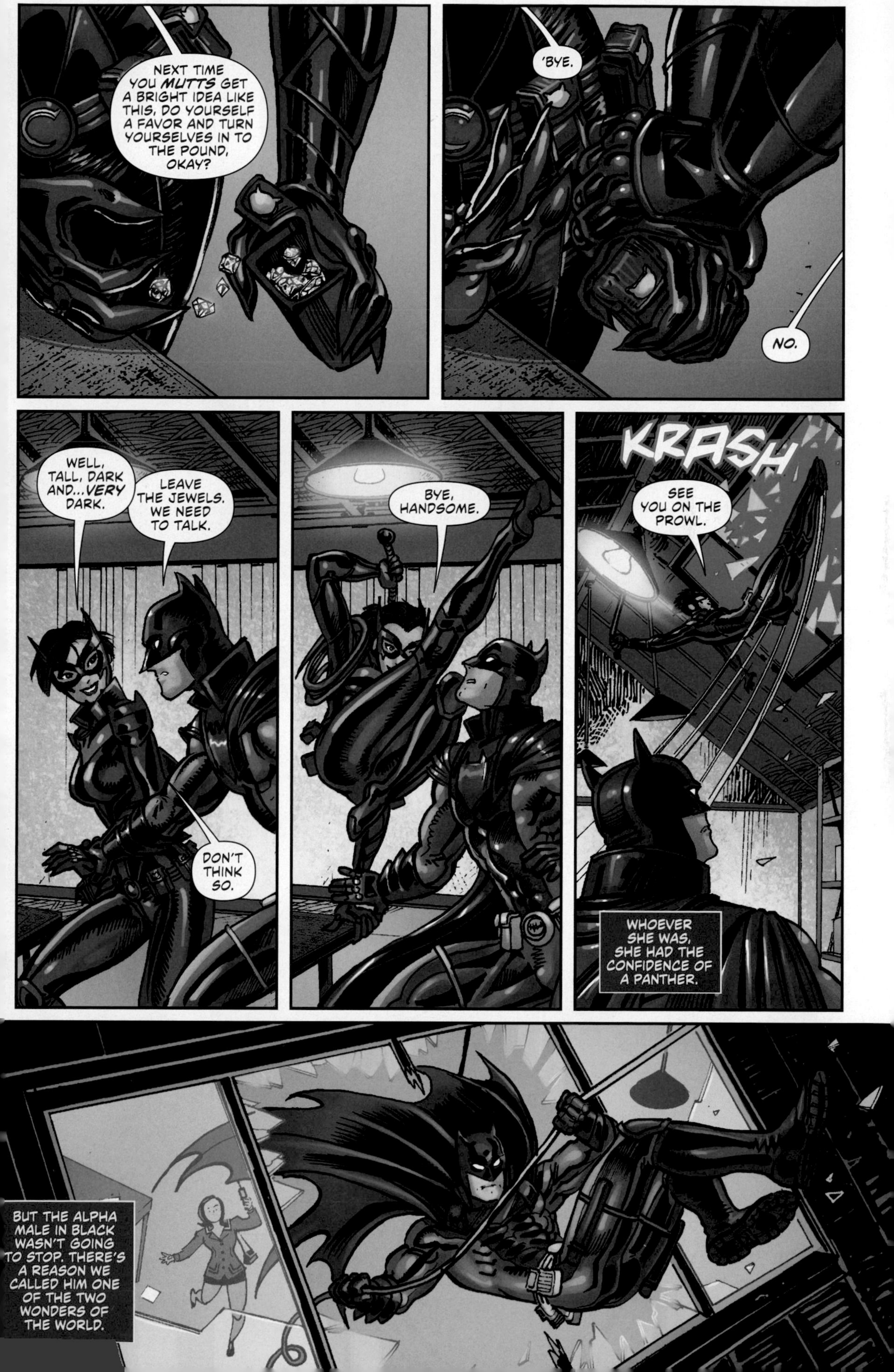
NEXT TIME YOU MUTTS GET A BRIGHT IDEA LIKE THIS, DO YOURSELF A FAVOR AND TURN YOURSELVES IN TO THE POUND, OKAY?
'BYE.
NO.
WELL, TALL, DARK AND...VERY DARK.
LEAVE THE JEWELS. WE NEED TO TALK.
DON'T THINK SO.
BYE, HANDSOME.
KRASH
SEE YOU ON THE PROWL.
WHOEVER SHE WAS, SHE HAD THE CONFIDENCE OF A PANTHER.
BUT THE ALPHA MALE IN BLACK WASN'T GOING TO STOP. THERE'S A REASON WE CALLED HIM ONE OF THE TWO WONDERS OF THE WORLD.

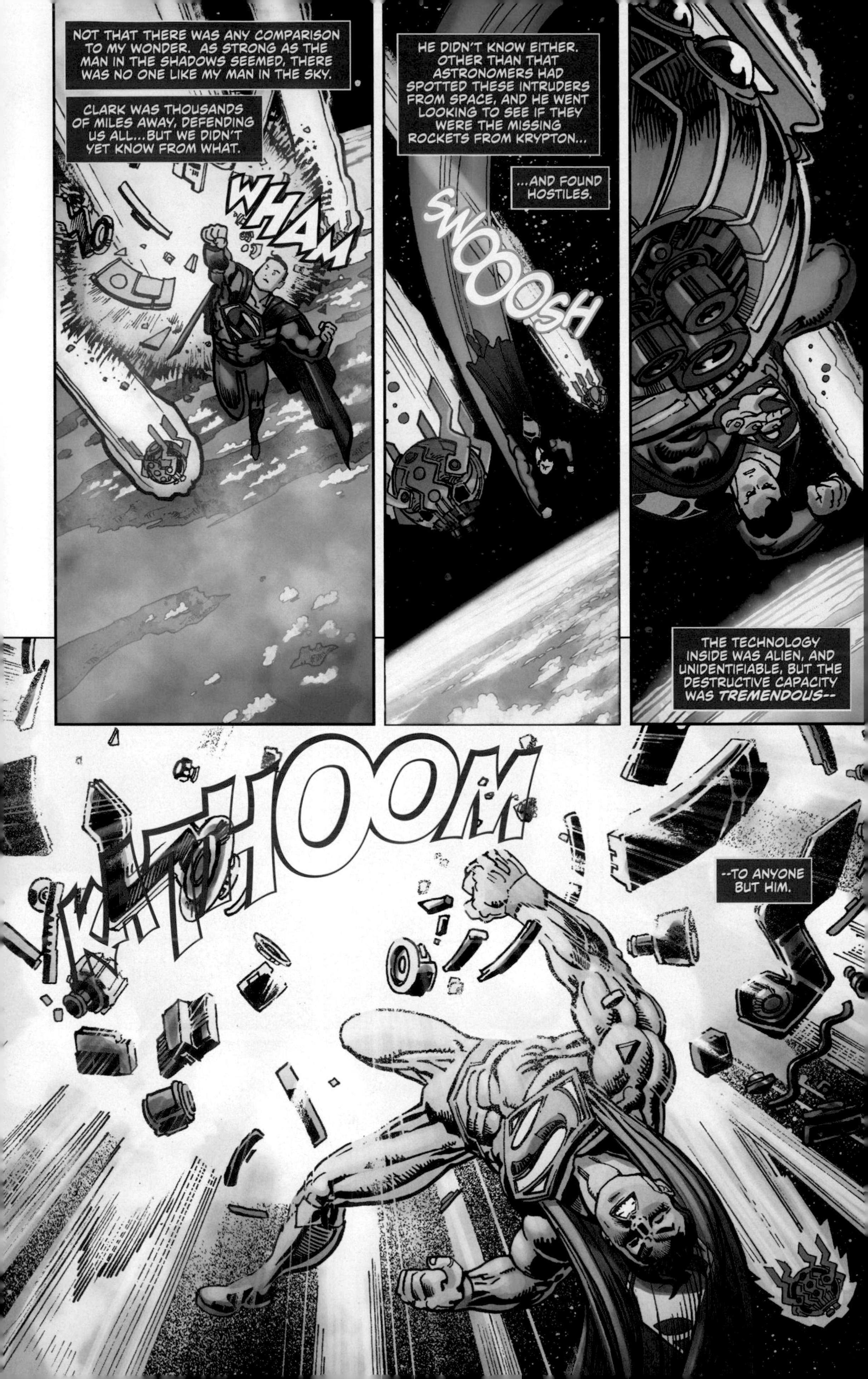
NOT THAT THERE WAS ANY COMPARISON TO MY WONDER. AS STRONG AS THE MAN IN THE SHADOWS SEEMED, THERE WAS NO ONE LIKE MY MAN IN THE SKY.
CLARK WAS THOUSANDS OF MILES AWAY, DEFENDING US ALL...BUT WE DIDN'T YET KNOW FROM WHAT.
WHAM
HE DIDN'T KNOW EITHER. OTHER THAN THAT ASTRONOMERS HAD SPOTTED THESE INTRUDERS FROM SPACE, AND HE WENT LOOKING TO SEE IF THEY WERE THE MISSING ROCKETS FROM KRYPTON...
...AND FOUND HOSTILES.
SWOOOSH
THE TECHNOLOGY INSIDE WAS ALIEN, AND UNIDENTIFIABLE, BUT THE DESTRUCTIVE CAPACITY WAS *TREMENDOUS*--
KTHOOM
--TO ANYONE BUT HIM.

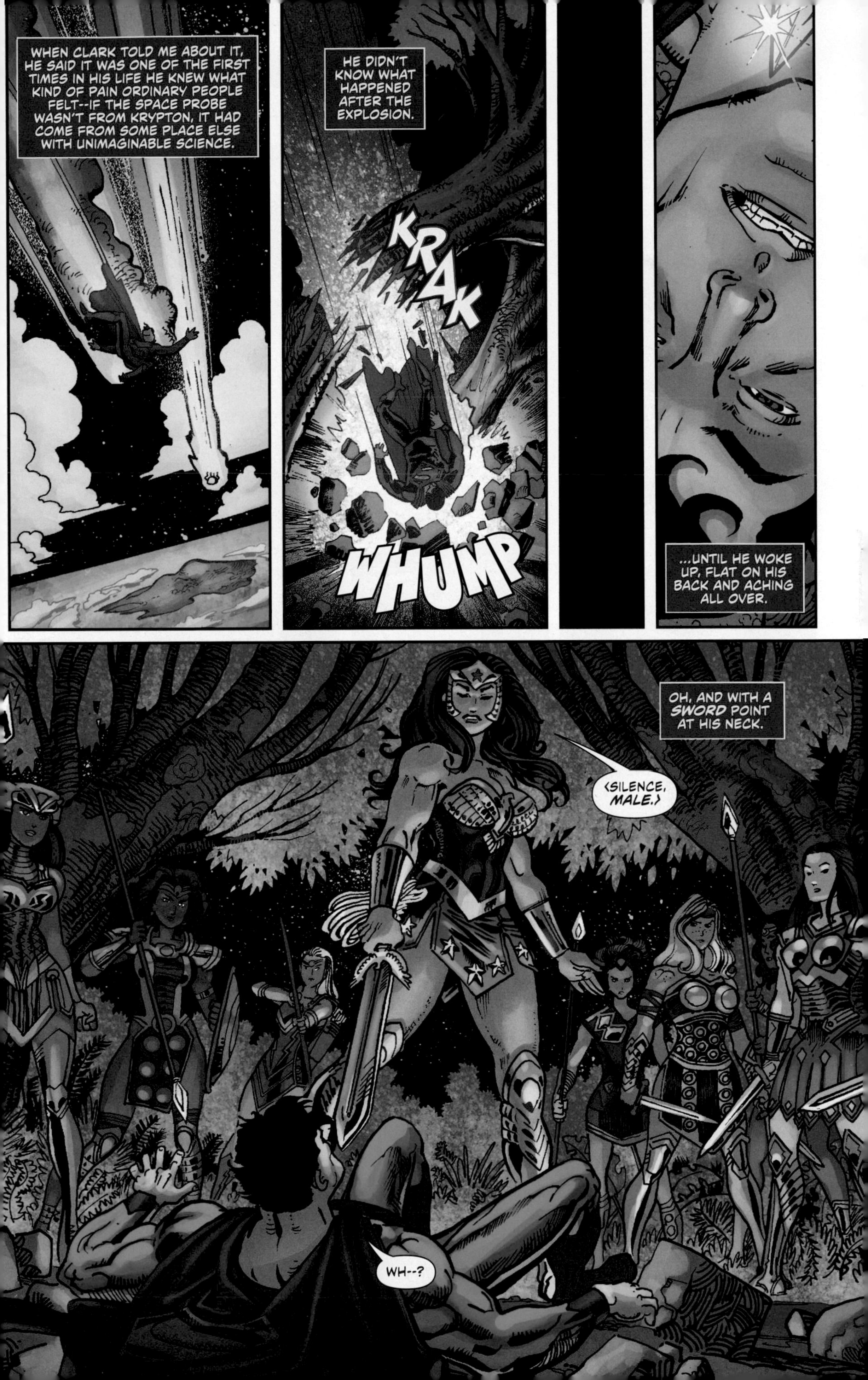
WHEN CLARK TOLD ME ABOUT IT, HE SAID IT WAS ONE OF THE FIRST TIMES IN HIS LIFE HE KNEW WHAT KIND OF PAIN ORDINARY PEOPLE FELT--IF THE SPACE PROBE WASN'T FROM KRYPTON, IT HAD COME FROM SOME PLACE ELSE WITH UNIMAGINABLE SCIENCE.
HE DIDN'T KNOW WHAT HAPPENED AFTER THE EXPLOSION.
KRAK
WHUMP
...UNTIL HE WOKE UP, FLAT ON HIS BACK AND ACHING ALL OVER.
OH, AND WITH A SWORD POINT AT HIS NECK.
‹SILENCE, MALE.›
WH--?

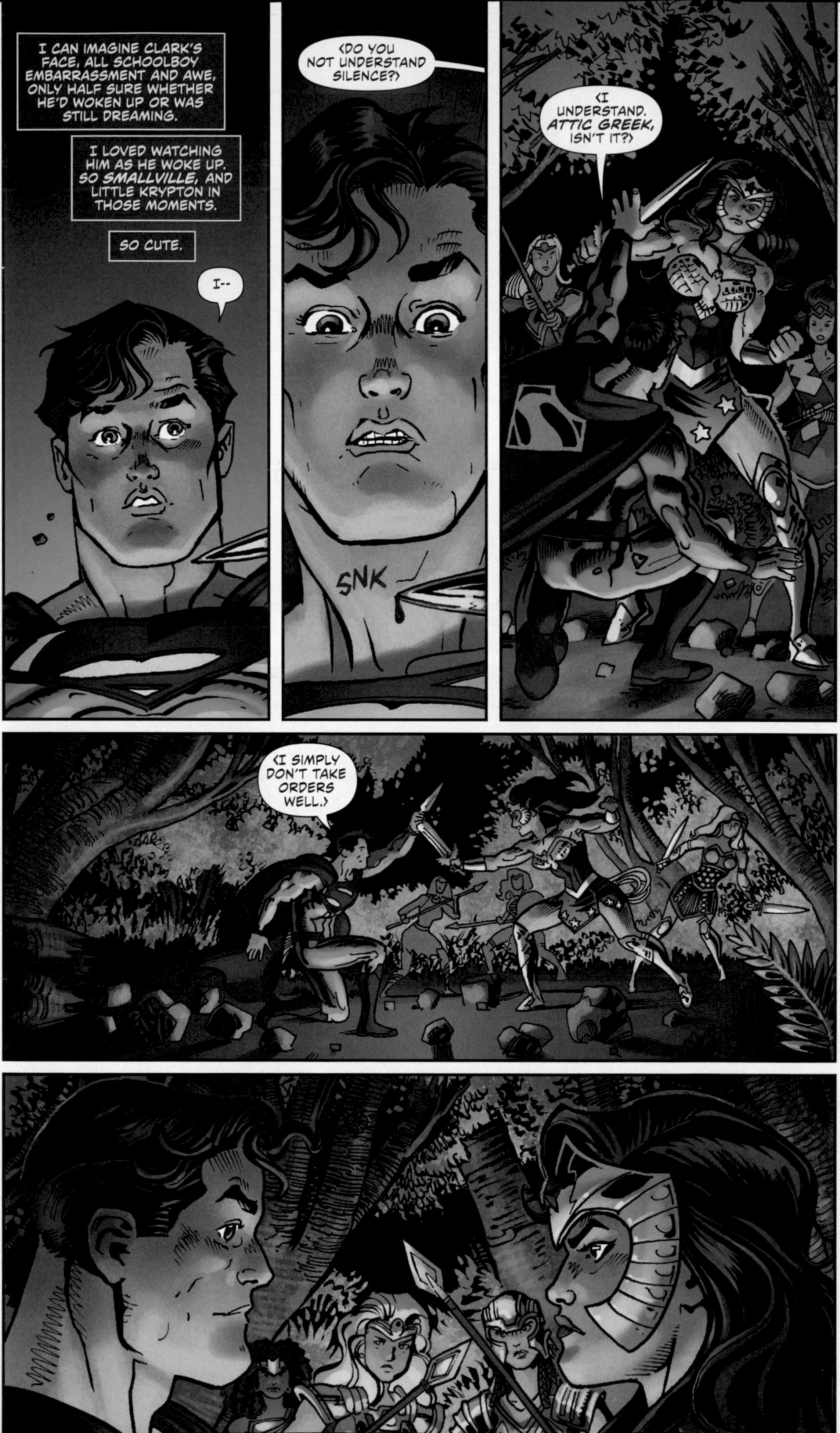
I CAN IMAGINE CLARK'S FACE, ALL SCHOOLBOY EMBARRASSMENT AND AWE, ONLY HALF SURE WHETHER HE'D WOKEN UP OR WAS STILL DREAMING.
I LOVED WATCHING HIM AS HE WOKE UP. SO *SMALLVILLE*, AND LITTLE KRYPTON IN THOSE MOMENTS.
SO CUTE.
I--
<DO YOU NOT UNDERSTAND SILENCE?>
SNK
<I UNDERSTAND. *ATTIC GREEK*, ISN'T IT?>
<I SIMPLY DON'T TAKE ORDERS WELL.>

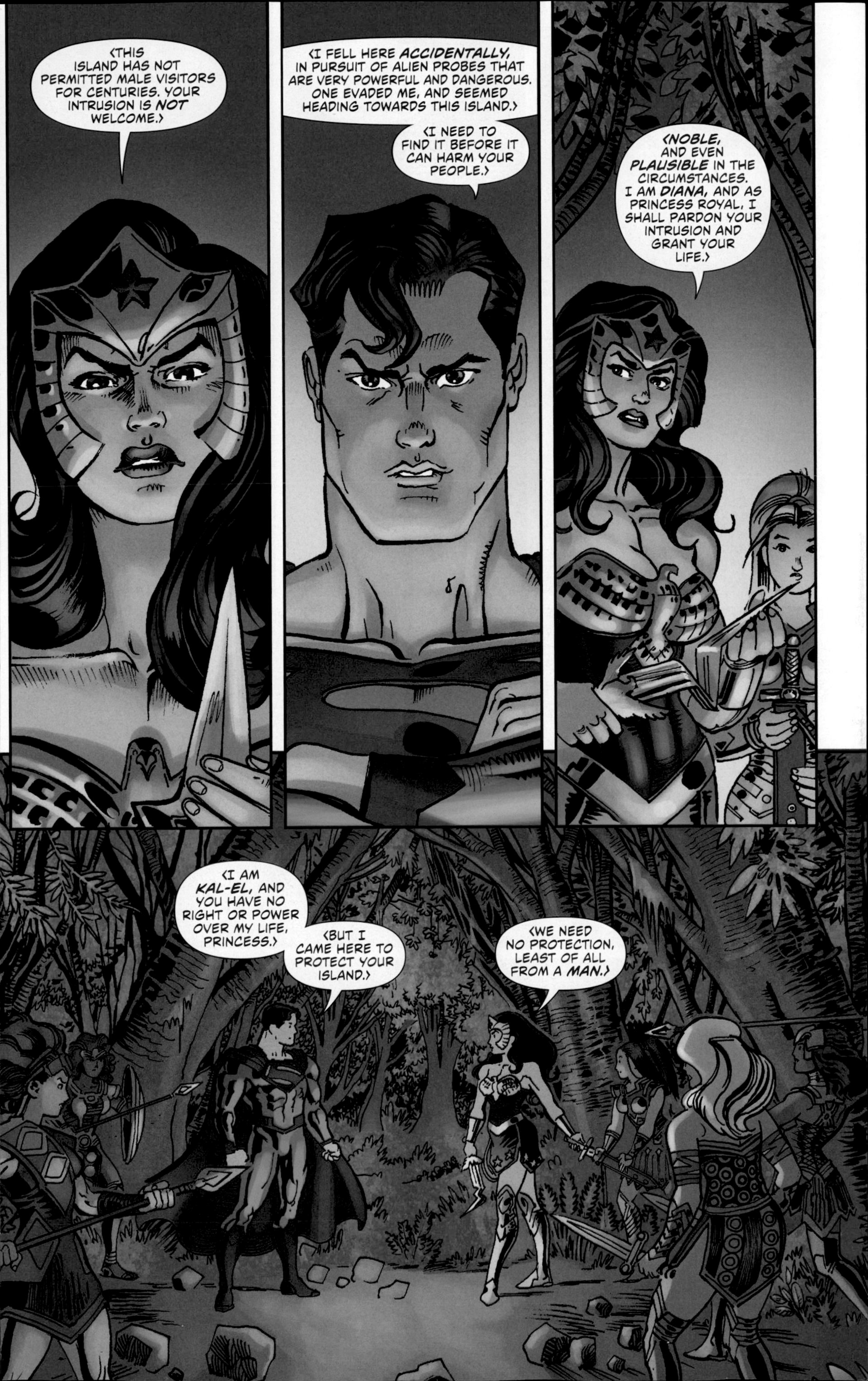

<THIS ISLAND HAS NOT PERMITTED MALE VISITORS FOR CENTURIES. YOUR INTRUSION IS NOT WELCOME.>
<I FELL HERE ACCIDENTALLY, IN PURSUIT OF ALIEN PROBES THAT ARE VERY POWERFUL AND DANGEROUS. ONE EVADED ME, AND SEEMED HEADING TOWARDS THIS ISLAND.>
<I NEED TO FIND IT BEFORE IT CAN HARM YOUR PEOPLE.>
<NOBLE, AND EVEN PLAUSIBLE IN THE CIRCUMSTANCES. I AM DIANA, AND AS PRINCESS ROYAL, I SHALL PARDON YOUR INTRUSION AND GRANT YOUR LIFE.>
<I AM KAL-EL, AND YOU HAVE NO RIGHT OR POWER OVER MY LIFE, PRINCESS.>
<BUT I CAME HERE TO PROTECT YOUR ISLAND.>
<WE NEED NO PROTECTION, LEAST OF ALL FROM A MAN.>

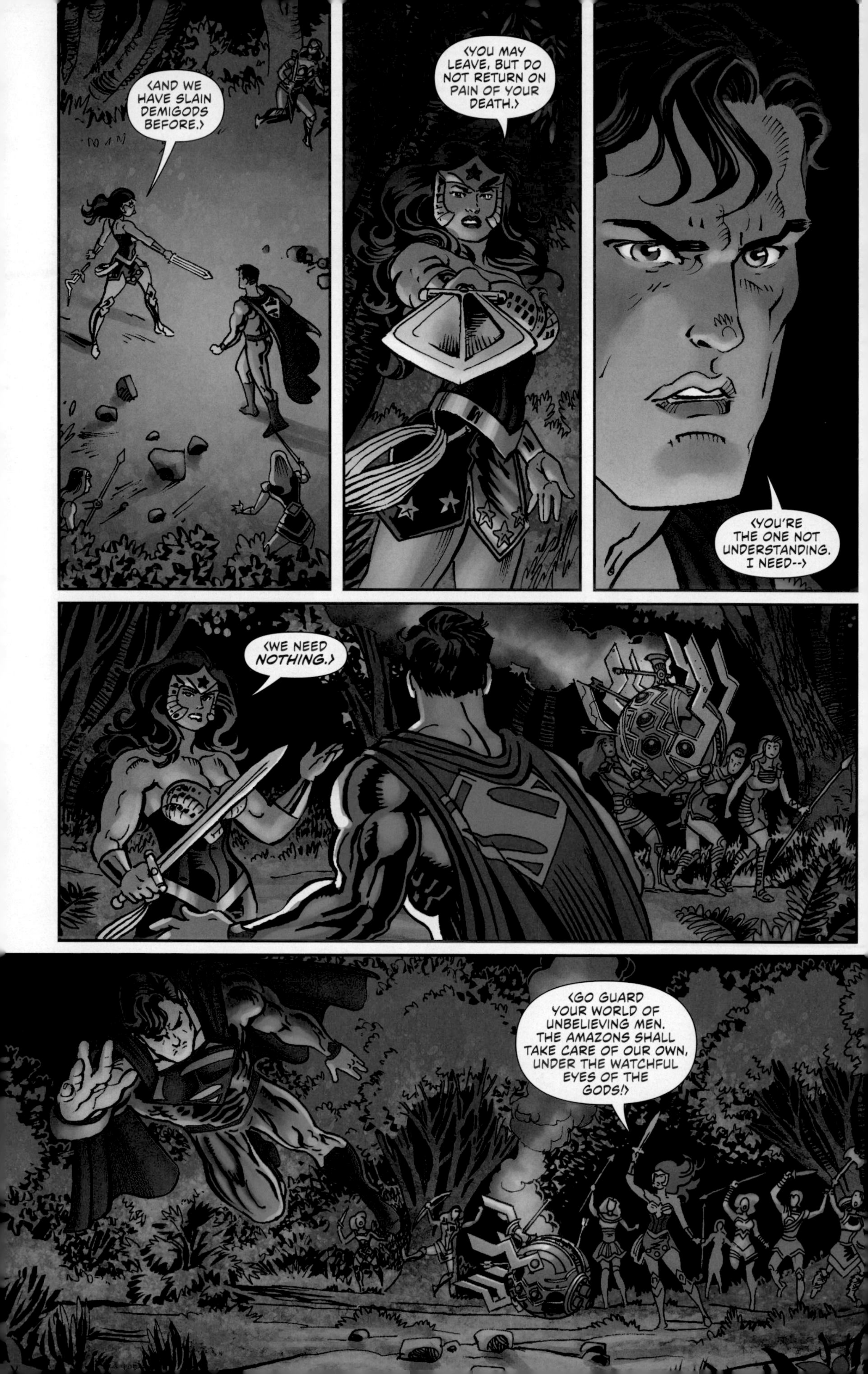

‹AND WE HAVE SLAIN DEMIGODS BEFORE.›
‹YOU MAY LEAVE, BUT DO NOT RETURN ON PAIN OF YOUR DEATH.›
‹YOU'RE THE ONE NOT UNDERSTANDING. I NEED--›
‹WE NEED *NOTHING.*›
‹GO GUARD YOUR WORLD OF UNBELIEVING MEN. THE AMAZONS SHALL TAKE CARE OF OUR OWN, UNDER THE WATCHFUL EYES OF THE GODS!›

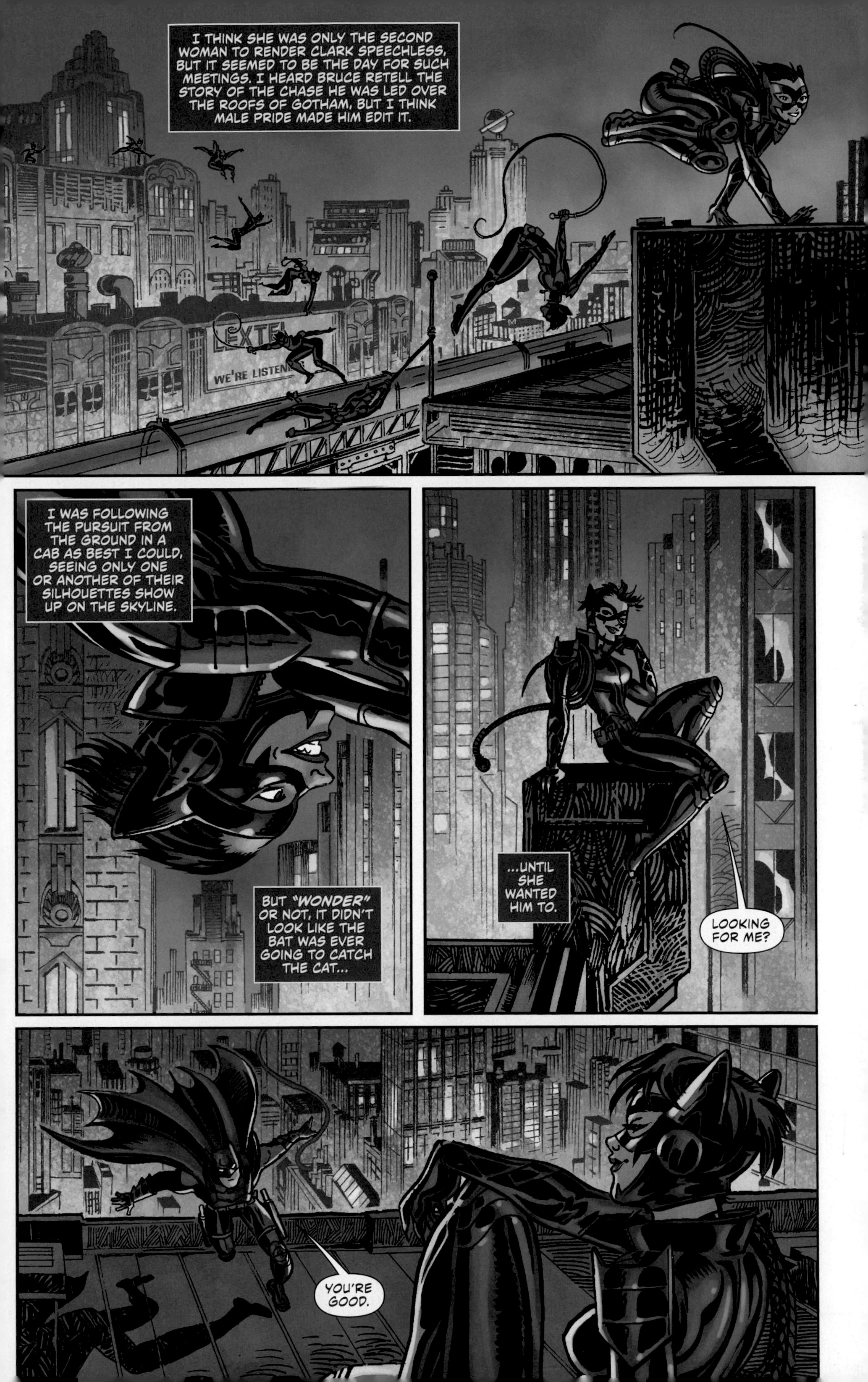
I THINK SHE WAS ONLY THE SECOND WOMAN TO RENDER CLARK SPEECHLESS, BUT IT SEEMED TO BE THE DAY FOR SUCH MEETINGS. I HEARD BRUCE RETELL THE STORY OF THE CHASE HE WAS LED OVER THE ROOFS OF GOTHAM, BUT I THINK MALE PRIDE MADE HIM EDIT IT.
WE'RE LISTEN
I WAS FOLLOWING THE PURSUIT FROM THE GROUND IN A CAB AS BEST I COULD, SEEING ONLY ONE OR ANOTHER OF THEIR SILHOUETTES SHOW UP ON THE SKYLINE.
BUT *"WONDER"* OR NOT, IT DIDN'T LOOK LIKE THE BAT WAS EVER GOING TO CATCH THE CAT...
...UNTIL SHE WANTED HIM TO.
LOOKING FOR ME?
YOU'RE GOOD.

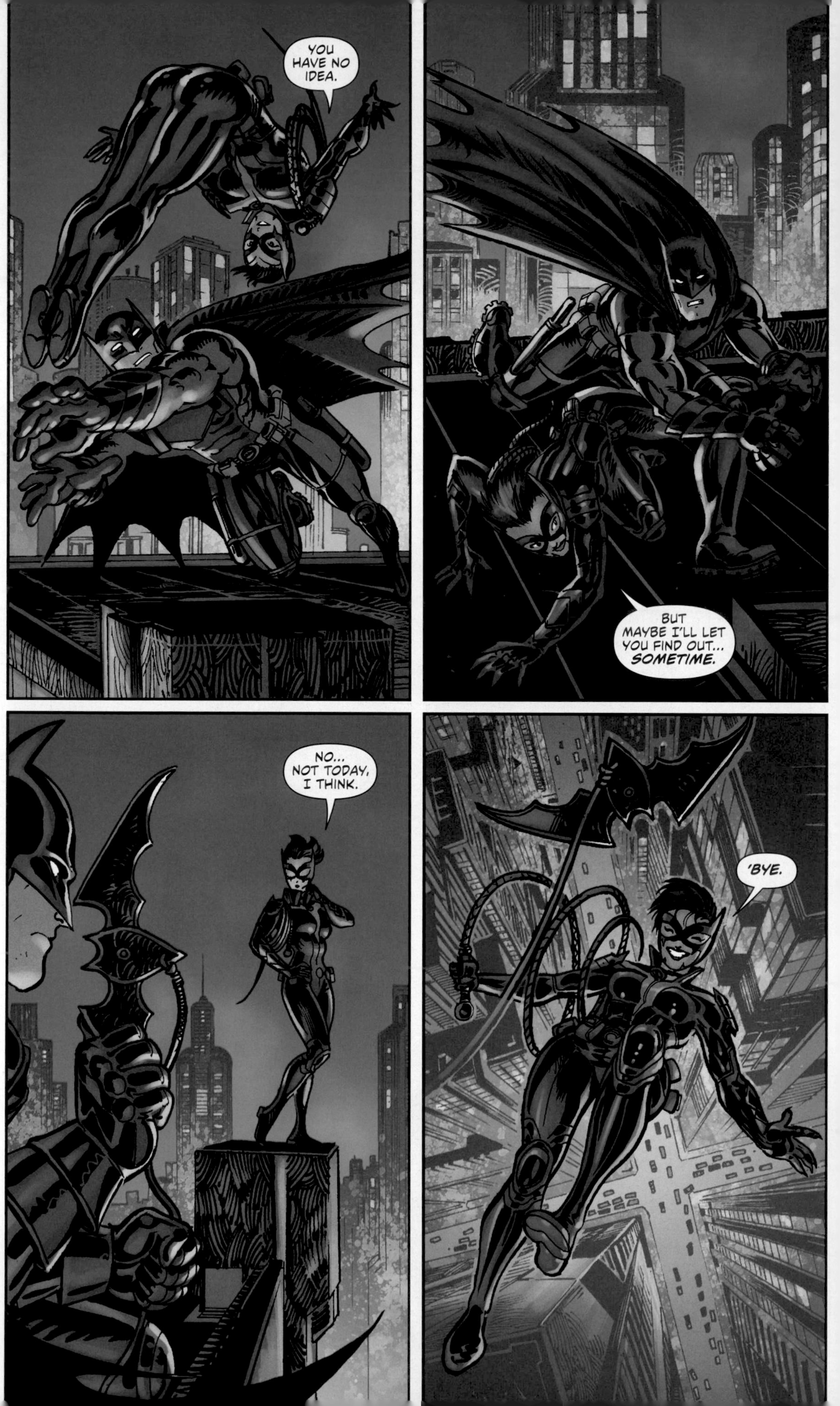
YOU HAVE NO IDEA.
BUT MAYBE I'LL LET YOU FIND OUT... SOMETIME.
NO... NOT TODAY, I THINK.
'BYE.

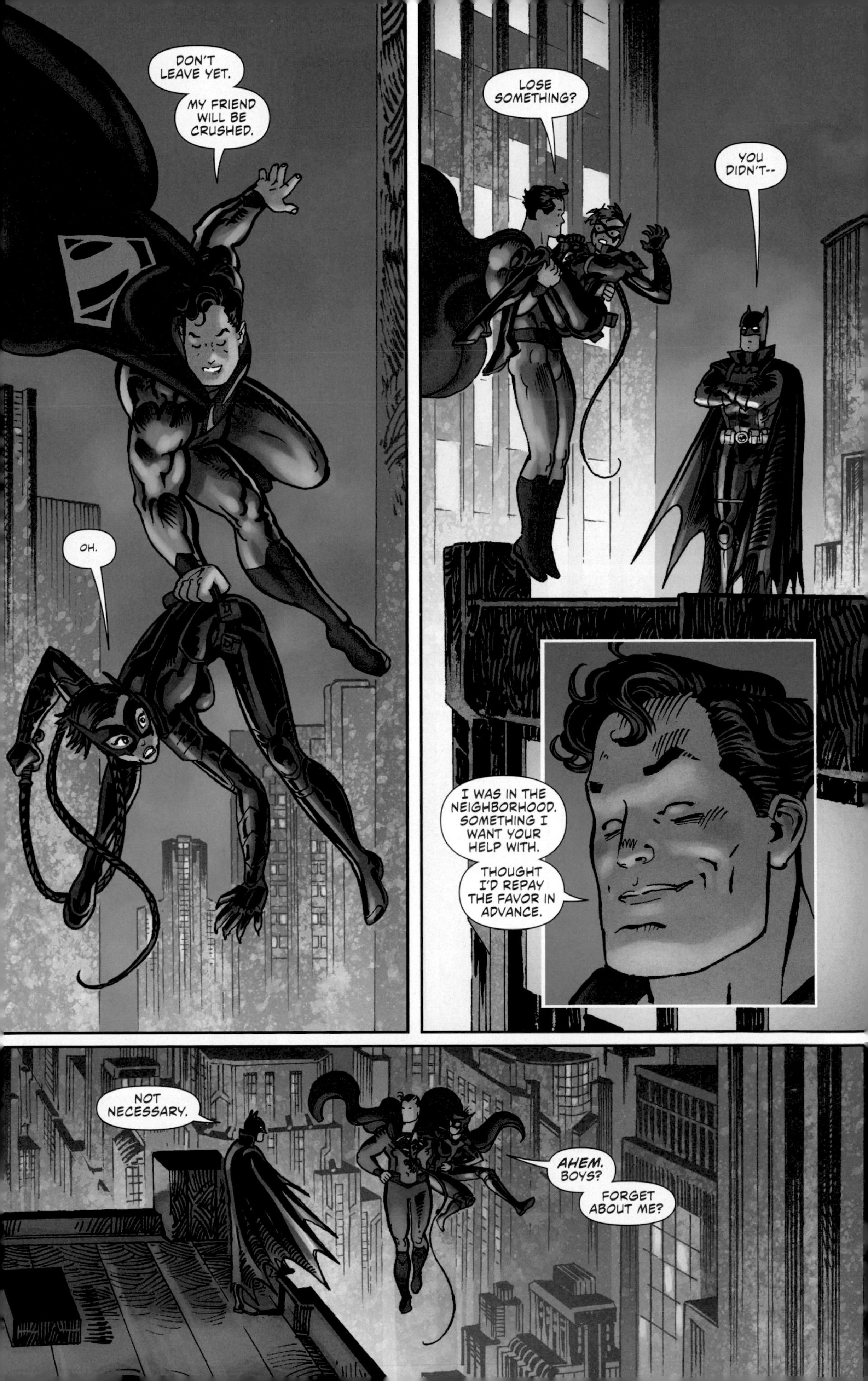
DON'T LEAVE YET.
MY FRIEND WILL BE CRUSHED.
OH.
LOSE SOMETHING?
YOU DIDN'T--
I WAS IN THE NEIGHBORHOOD. SOMETHING I WANT YOUR HELP WITH.
THOUGHT I'D REPAY THE FAVOR IN ADVANCE.
NOT NECESSARY.
AHEM. BOYS?
FORGET ABOUT ME?

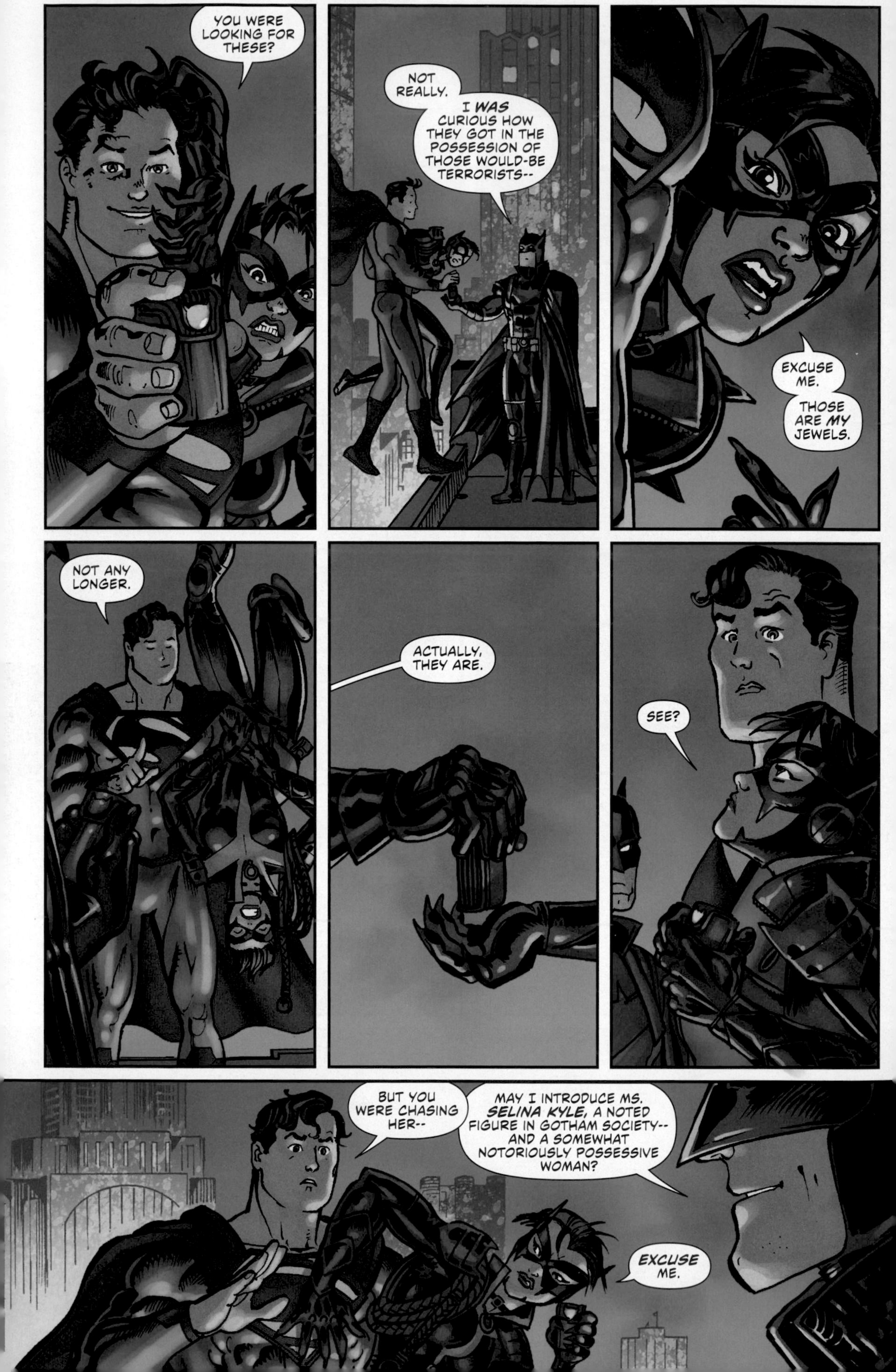
YOU WERE LOOKING FOR THESE?
NOT REALLY.
I WAS CURIOUS HOW THEY GOT IN THE POSSESSION OF THOSE WOULD-BE TERRORISTS--
EXCUSE ME.
THOSE ARE MY JEWELS.
NOT ANY LONGER.
ACTUALLY, THEY ARE.
SEE?
BUT YOU WERE CHASING HER--
MAY I INTRODUCE MS. SELINA KYLE, A NOTED FIGURE IN GOTHAM SOCIETY-- AND A SOMEWHAT NOTORIOUSLY POSSESSIVE WOMAN?
EXCUSE ME.

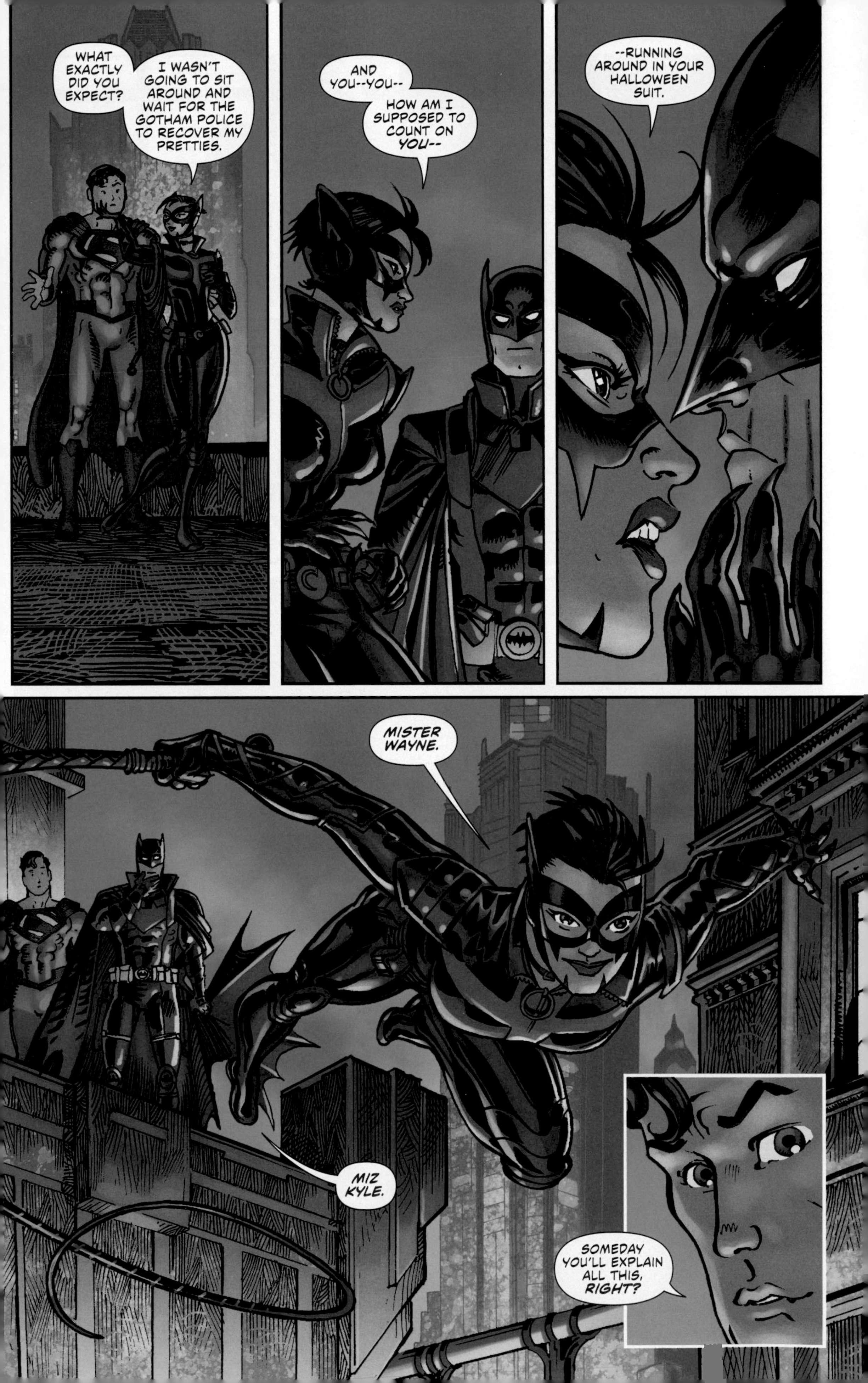
WHAT EXACTLY DID YOU EXPECT?
I WASN'T GOING TO SIT AROUND AND WAIT FOR THE GOTHAM POLICE TO RECOVER MY PRETTIES.
AND YOU--YOU--
HOW AM I SUPPOSED TO COUNT ON YOU--
--RUNNING AROUND IN YOUR HALLOWEEN SUIT.
MISTER WAYNE.
MIZ KYLE.
SOMEDAY YOU'LL EXPLAIN ALL THIS, RIGHT?

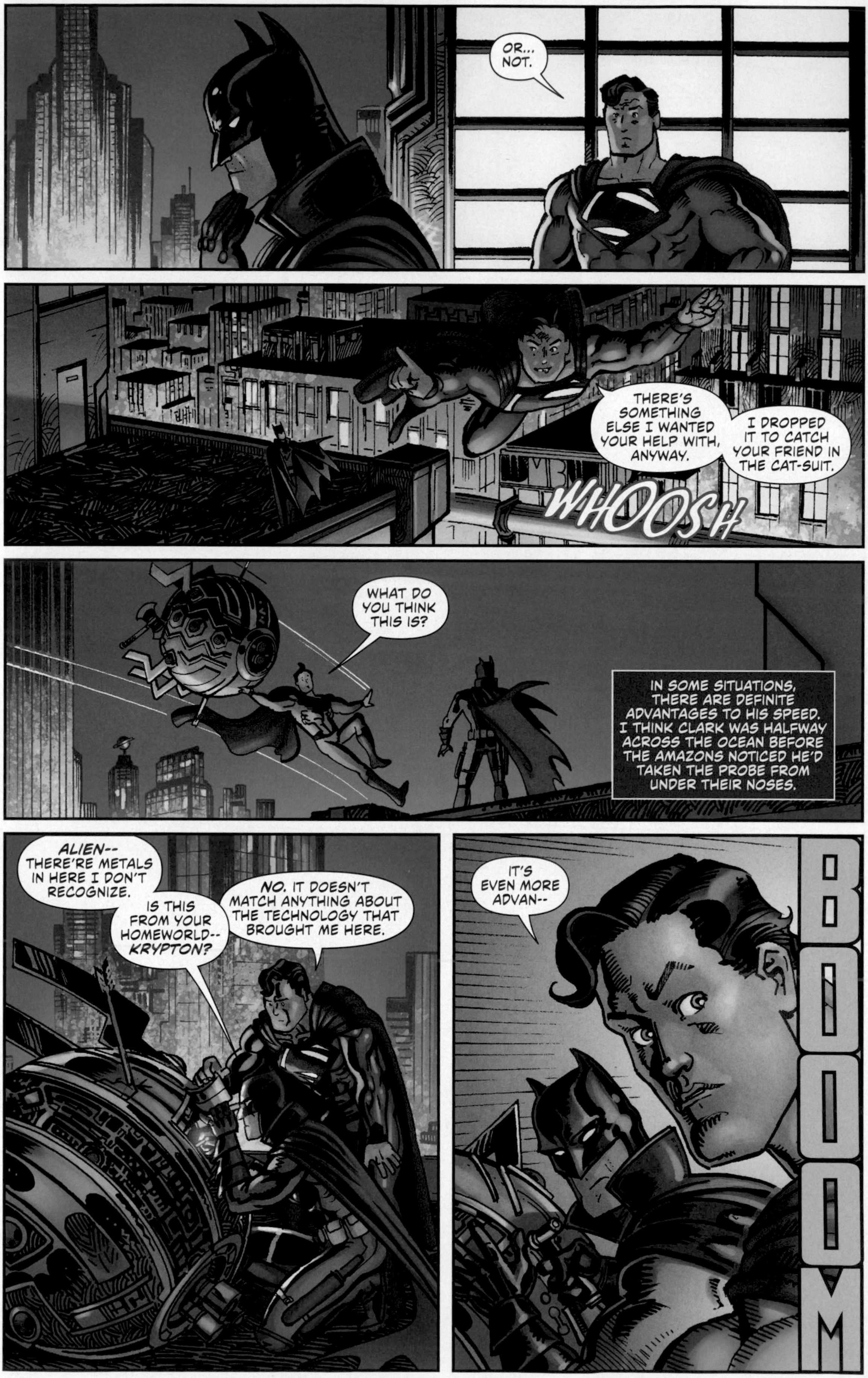
OR... NOT.
THERE'S SOMETHING ELSE I WANTED YOUR HELP WITH, ANYWAY.
I DROPPED IT TO CATCH YOUR FRIEND IN THE CAT-SUIT.
WHOOSH
WHAT DO YOU THINK THIS IS?
IN SOME SITUATIONS, THERE ARE DEFINITE ADVANTAGES TO HIS SPEED. I THINK CLARK WAS HALFWAY ACROSS THE OCEAN BEFORE THE AMAZONS NOTICED HE'D TAKEN THE PROBE FROM UNDER THEIR NOSES.
ALIEN-- THERE'RE METALS IN HERE I DON'T RECOGNIZE.
IS THIS FROM YOUR HOMEWORLD-- KRYPTON?
NO. IT DOESN'T MATCH ANYTHING ABOUT THE TECHNOLOGY THAT BROUGHT ME HERE.
IT'S EVEN MORE ADVAN--
BOOOOM

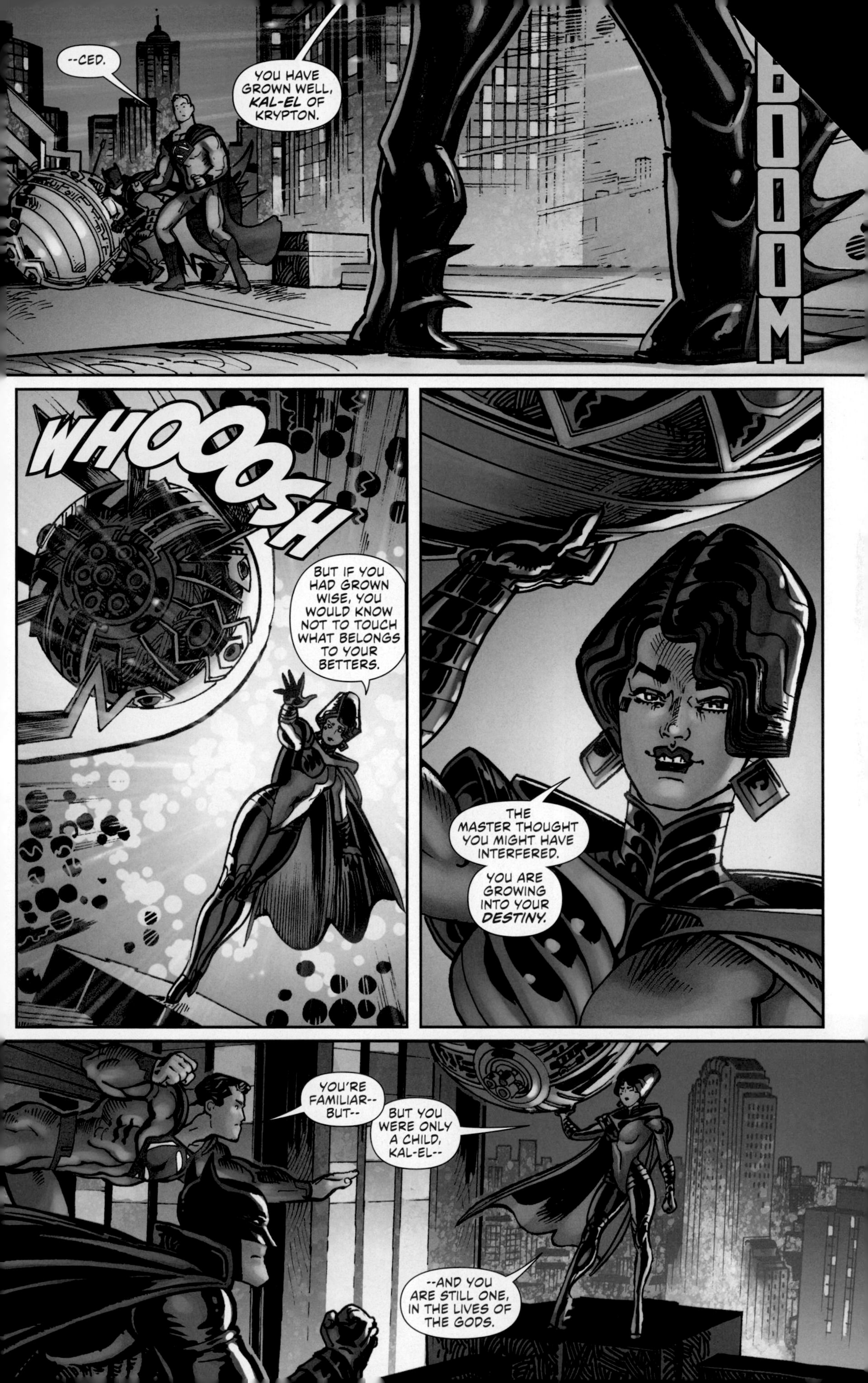
--CED.
YOU HAVE GROWN WELL, KAL-EL OF KRYPTON.
BOOOM
WHOOOSH
BUT IF YOU HAD GROWN WISE, YOU WOULD KNOW NOT TO TOUCH WHAT BELONGS TO YOUR BETTERS.
THE MASTER THOUGHT YOU MIGHT HAVE INTERFERED.
YOU ARE GROWING INTO YOUR DESTINY.
YOU'RE FAMILIAR-- BUT--
BUT YOU WERE ONLY A CHILD, KAL-EL--
--AND YOU ARE STILL ONE, IN THE LIVES OF THE GODS.

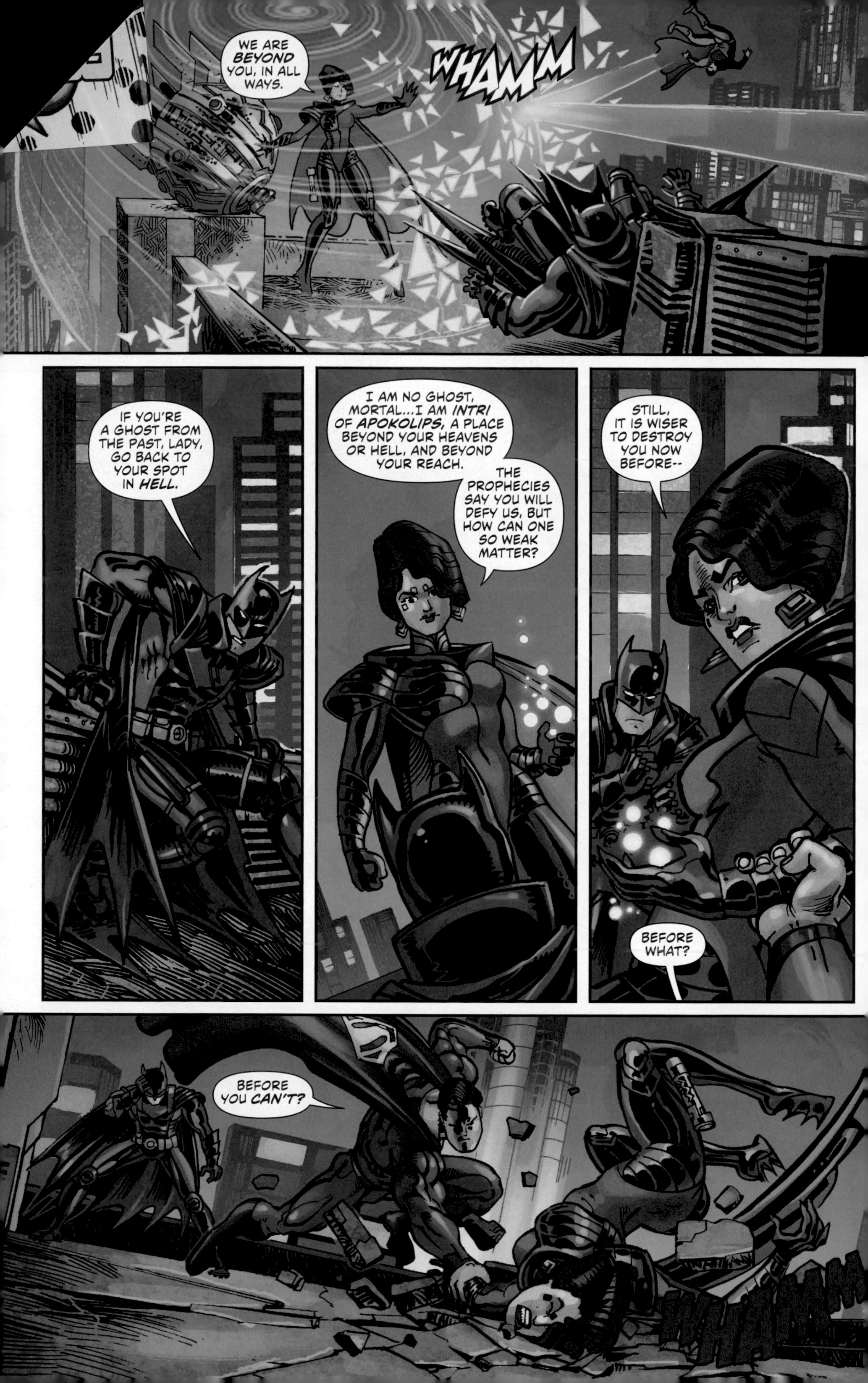
WE ARE BEYOND YOU, IN ALL WAYS.
WHAMM
IF YOU'RE A GHOST FROM THE PAST, LADY, GO BACK TO YOUR SPOT IN HELL.
I AM NO GHOST, MORTAL...I AM INTRI OF APOKOLIPS, A PLACE BEYOND YOUR HEAVENS OR HELL, AND BEYOND YOUR REACH.
THE PROPHECIES SAY YOU WILL DEFY US, BUT HOW CAN ONE SO WEAK MATTER?
STILL, IT IS WISER TO DESTROY YOU NOW BEFORE--
BEFORE WHAT?
BEFORE YOU CAN'T?

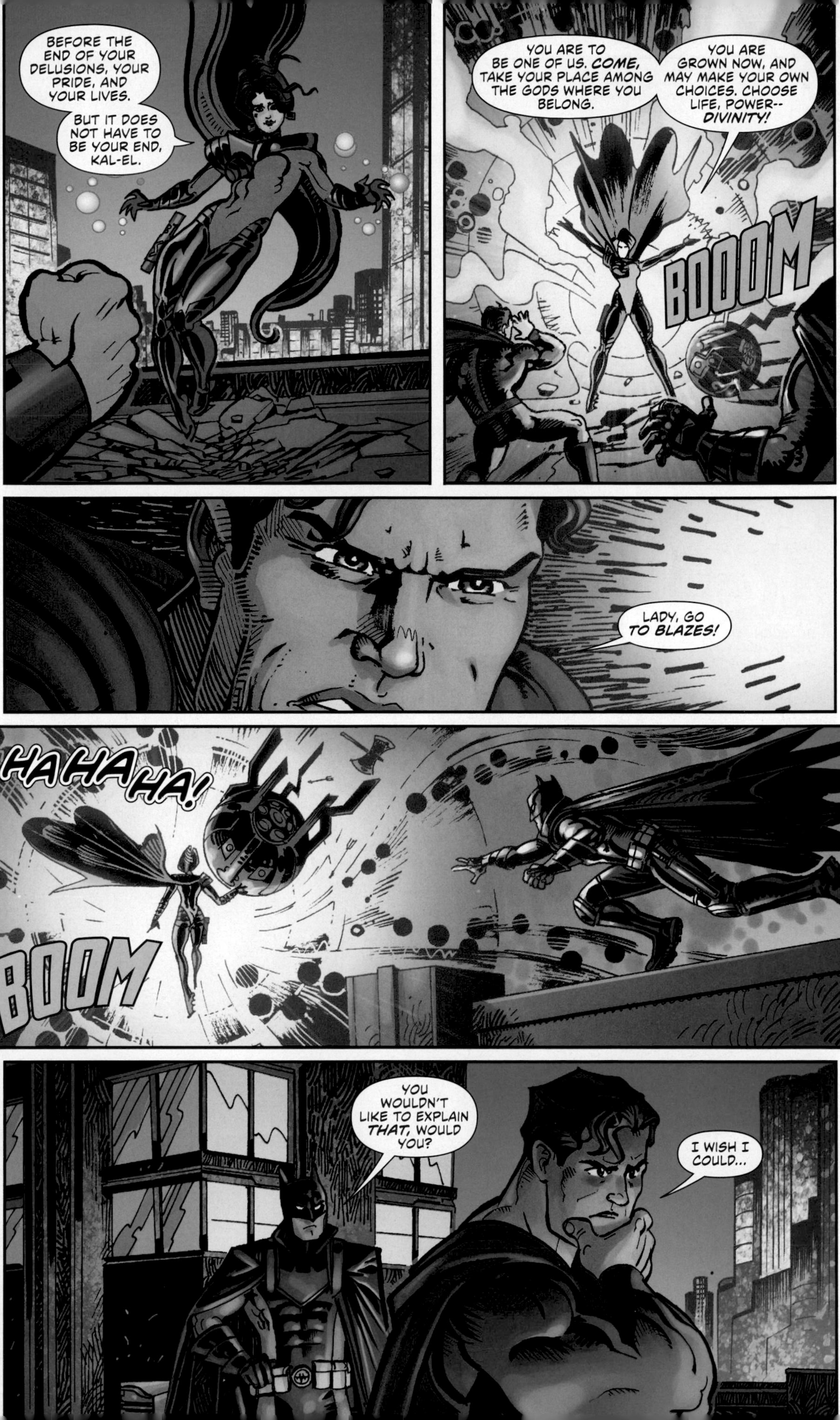
BEFORE THE END OF YOUR DELUSIONS, YOUR PRIDE, AND YOUR LIVES.
BUT IT DOES NOT HAVE TO BE YOUR END, KAL-EL.
YOU ARE TO BE ONE OF US. COME, TAKE YOUR PLACE AMONG THE GODS WHERE YOU BELONG.
YOU ARE GROWN NOW, AND MAY MAKE YOUR OWN CHOICES. CHOOSE LIFE, POWER-- DIVINITY!
BOOOM
LADY, GO TO BLAZES!
HAHAHAHA!
BOOM
YOU WOULDN'T LIKE TO EXPLAIN THAT, WOULD YOU?
I WISH I COULD...

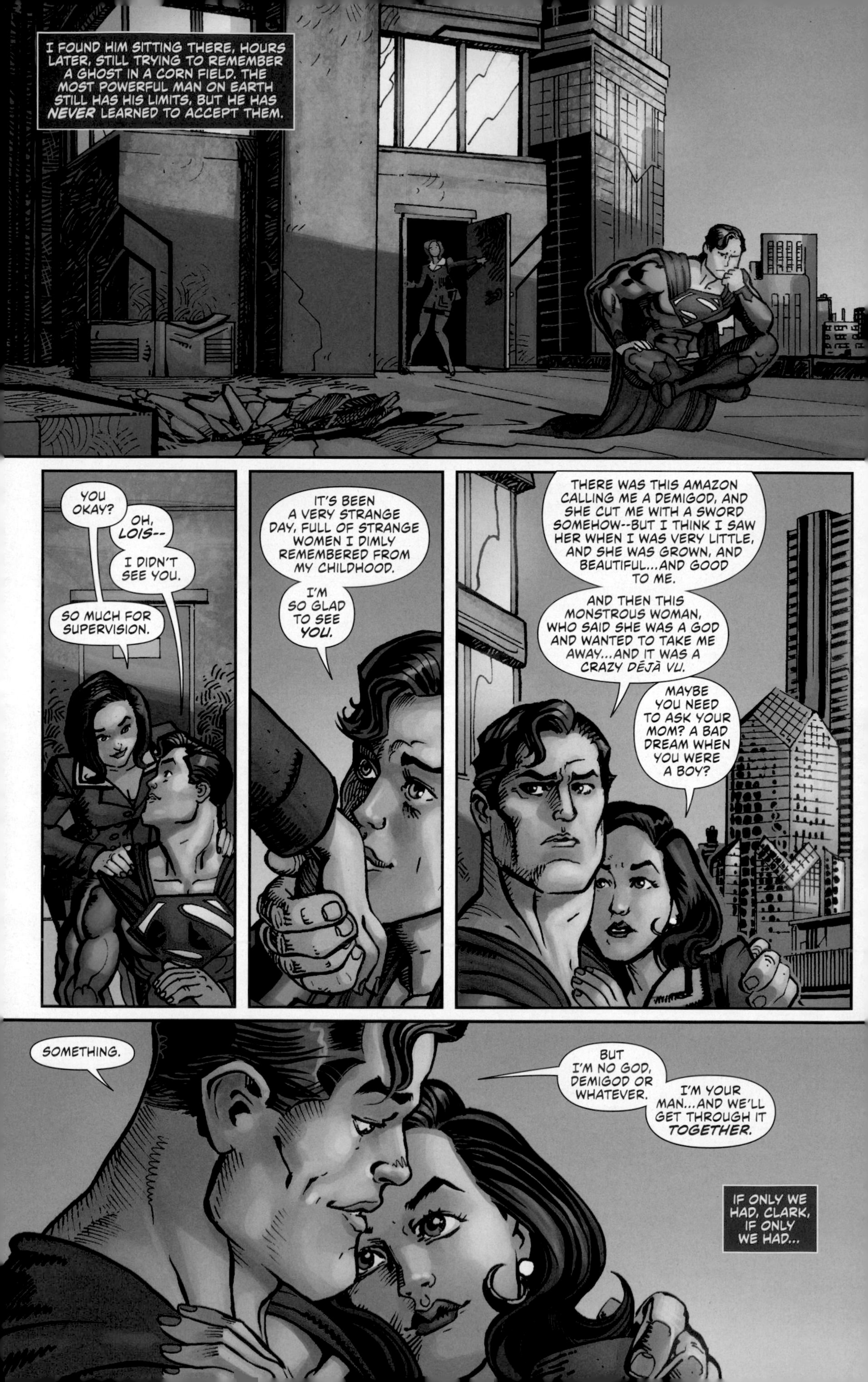
I FOUND HIM SITTING THERE, HOURS LATER, STILL TRYING TO REMEMBER A GHOST IN A CORN FIELD. THE MOST POWERFUL MAN ON EARTH STILL HAS HIS LIMITS, BUT HE HAS NEVER LEARNED TO ACCEPT THEM.
YOU OKAY?
OH, LOIS--
I DIDN'T SEE YOU.
SO MUCH FOR SUPERVISION.
IT'S BEEN A VERY STRANGE DAY, FULL OF STRANGE WOMEN I DIMLY REMEMBERED FROM MY CHILDHOOD.
I'M SO GLAD TO SEE YOU.
THERE WAS THIS AMAZON CALLING ME A DEMIGOD, AND SHE CUT ME WITH A SWORD SOMEHOW--BUT I THINK I SAW HER WHEN I WAS VERY LITTLE, AND SHE WAS GROWN, AND BEAUTIFUL...AND GOOD TO ME.
AND THEN THIS MONSTROUS WOMAN, WHO SAID SHE WAS A GOD AND WANTED TO TAKE ME AWAY...AND IT WAS A CRAZY DÉJÀ VU.
MAYBE YOU NEED TO ASK YOUR MOM? A BAD DREAM WHEN YOU WERE A BOY?
SOMETHING.
BUT I'M NO GOD, DEMIGOD OR WHATEVER.
I'M YOUR MAN...AND WE'LL GET THROUGH IT TOGETHER.
IF ONLY WE HAD, CLARK, IF ONLY WE HAD...

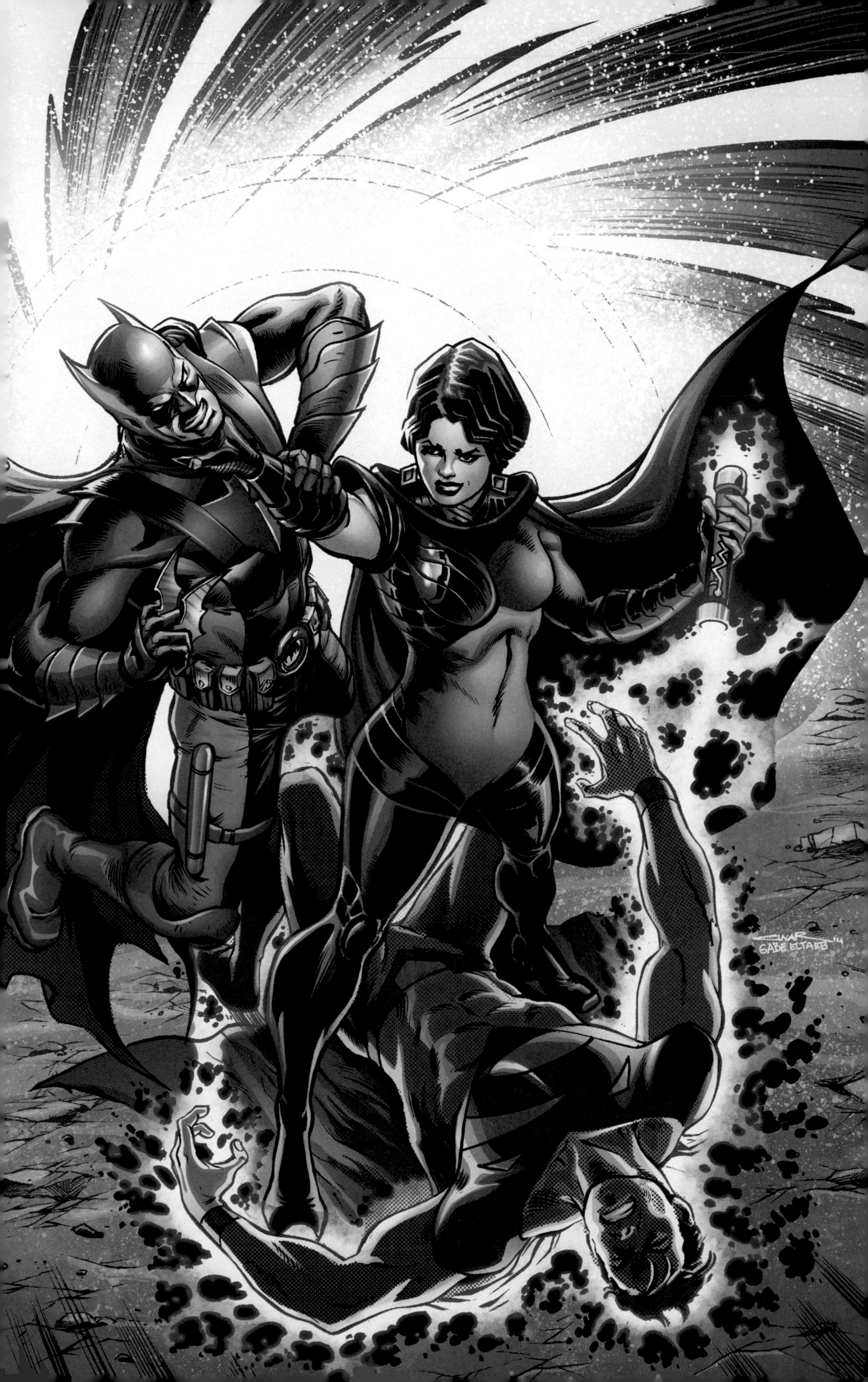
GABE ELTAEB

PART FOUR: GENERATIONS

PAUL LEVITZ writer **JED DOUGHERTY** artist **CHRIS SOTOMAYOR** colorist **TRAVIS LANHAM** letterer cover art by **YILDIRAY CINAR** & **GABE ELTAEB**

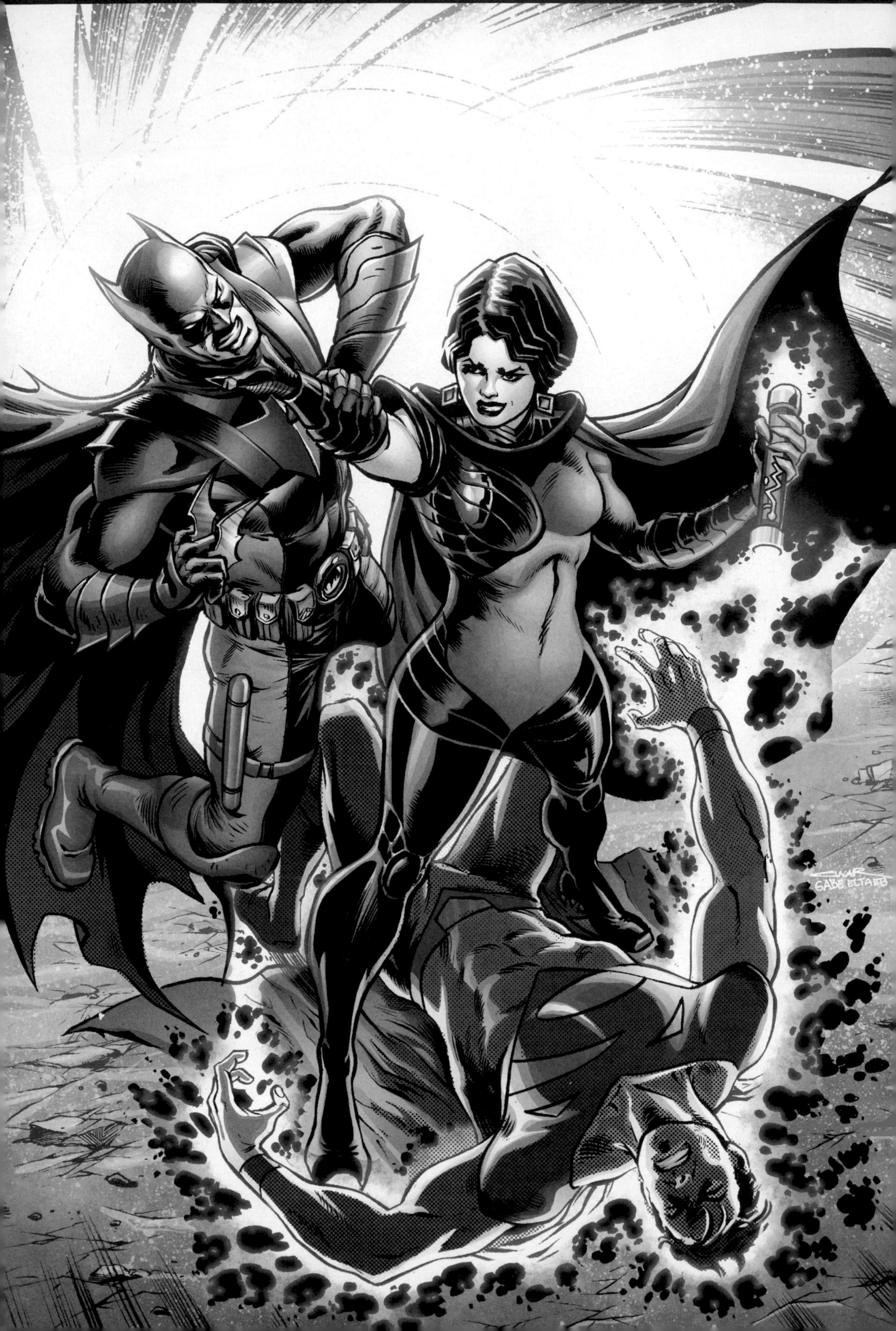

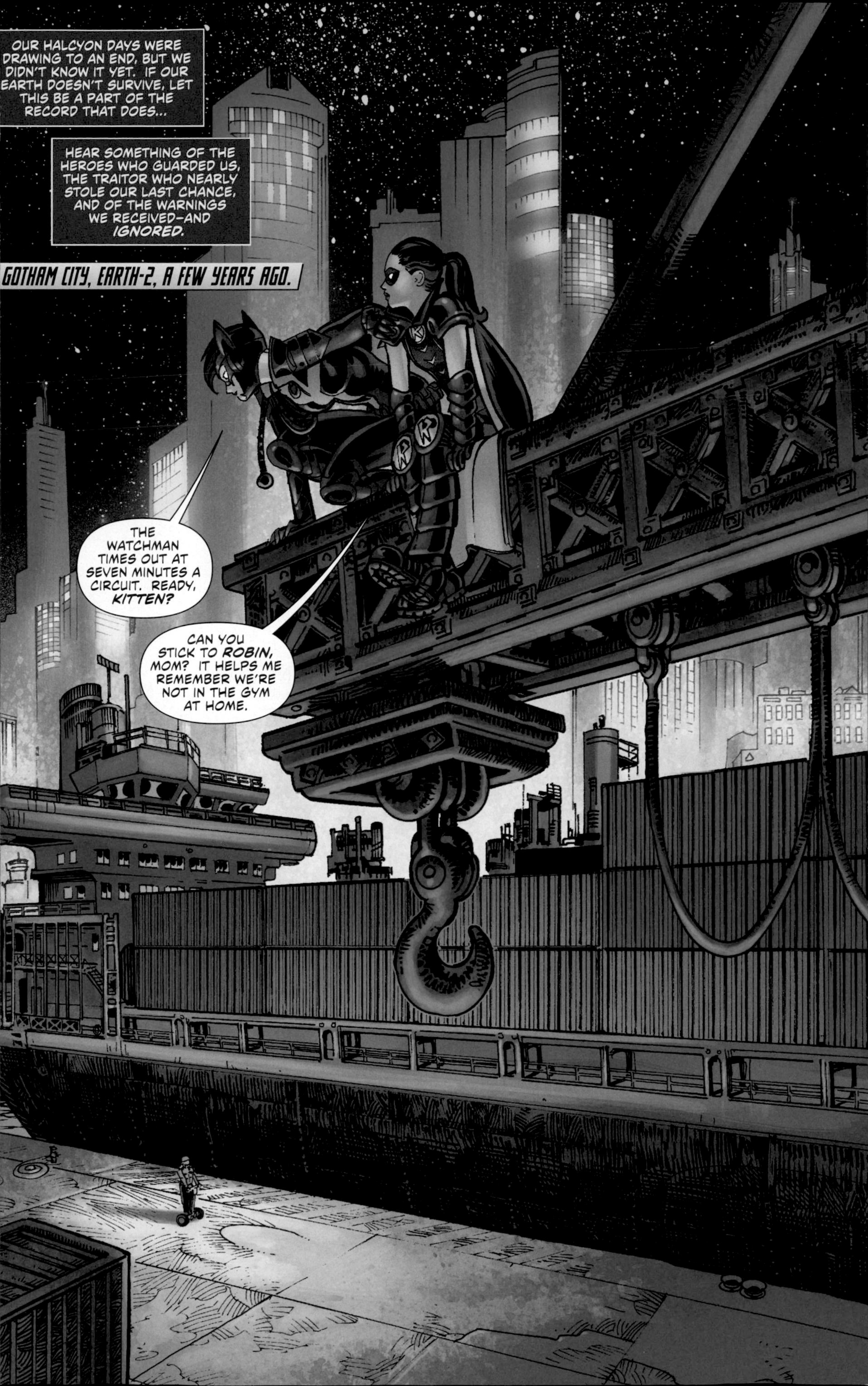
OUR HALCYON DAYS WERE DRAWING TO AN END, BUT WE DIDN'T KNOW IT YET. IF OUR EARTH DOESN'T SURVIVE, LET THIS BE A PART OF THE RECORD THAT DOES...
HEAR SOMETHING OF THE HEROES WHO GUARDED US, THE TRAITOR WHO NEARLY STOLE OUR LAST CHANCE, AND OF THE WARNINGS WE RECEIVED—AND *IGNORED*.
GOTHAM CITY, EARTH-2, A FEW YEARS AGO.
THE WATCHMAN TIMES OUT AT SEVEN MINUTES A CIRCUIT. READY, *KITTEN?*
CAN YOU STICK TO *ROBIN,* MOM? IT HELPS ME REMEMBER WE'RE NOT IN THE GYM AT HOME.

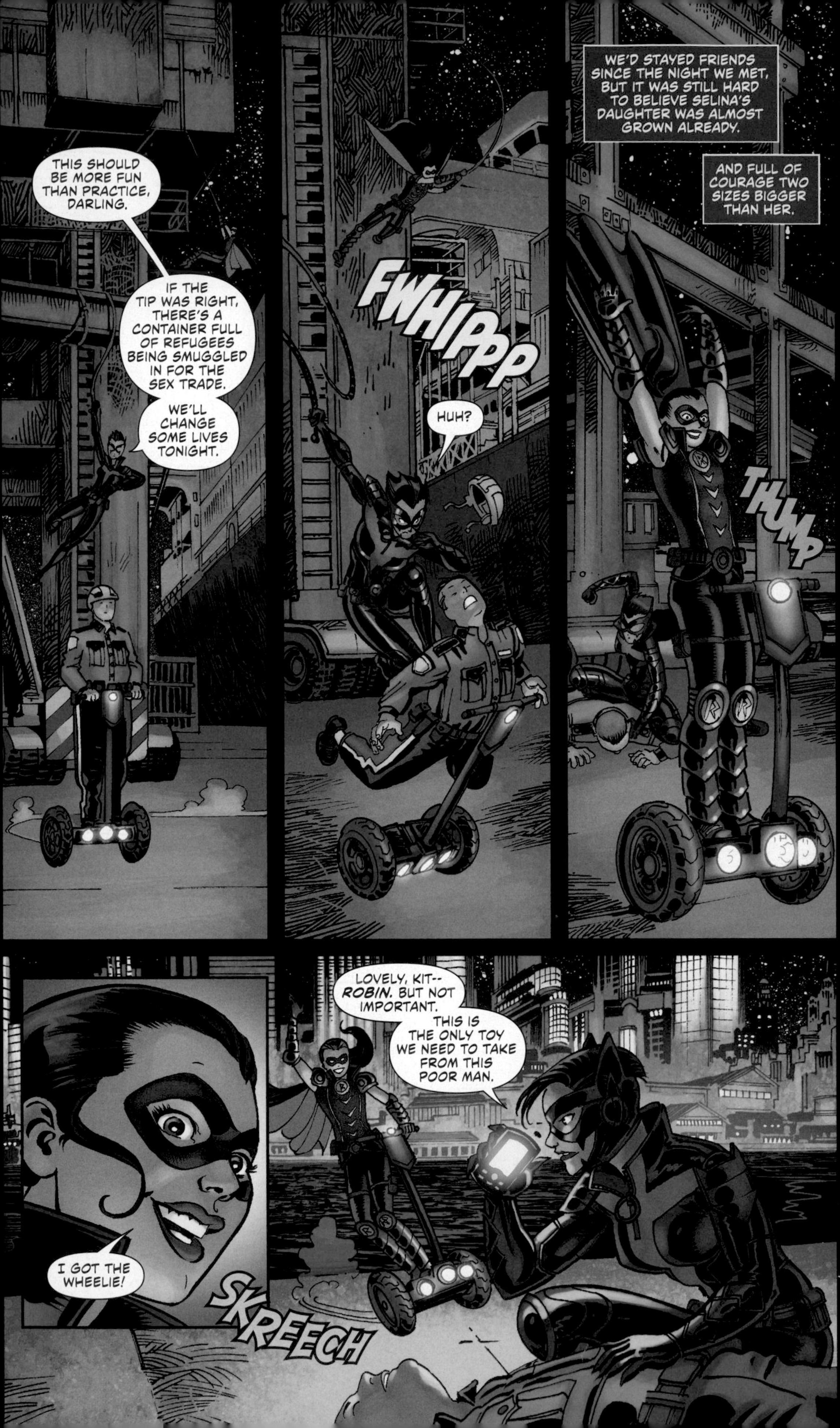
THIS SHOULD BE MORE FUN THAN PRACTICE, DARLING.
IF THE TIP WAS RIGHT, THERE'S A CONTAINER FULL OF REFUGEES BEING SMUGGLED IN FOR THE SEX TRADE.
WE'LL CHANGE SOME LIVES TONIGHT.
FWHIPPP
HUH?
WE'D STAYED FRIENDS SINCE THE NIGHT WE MET, BUT IT WAS STILL HARD TO BELIEVE SELINA'S DAUGHTER WAS ALMOST GROWN ALREADY.
AND FULL OF COURAGE TWO SIZES BIGGER THAN HER.
THUMP
I GOT THE WHEELIE!
SKREECH
LOVELY, KIT-- ROBIN. BUT NOT IMPORTANT.
THIS IS THE ONLY TOY WE NEED TO TAKE FROM THIS POOR MAN.

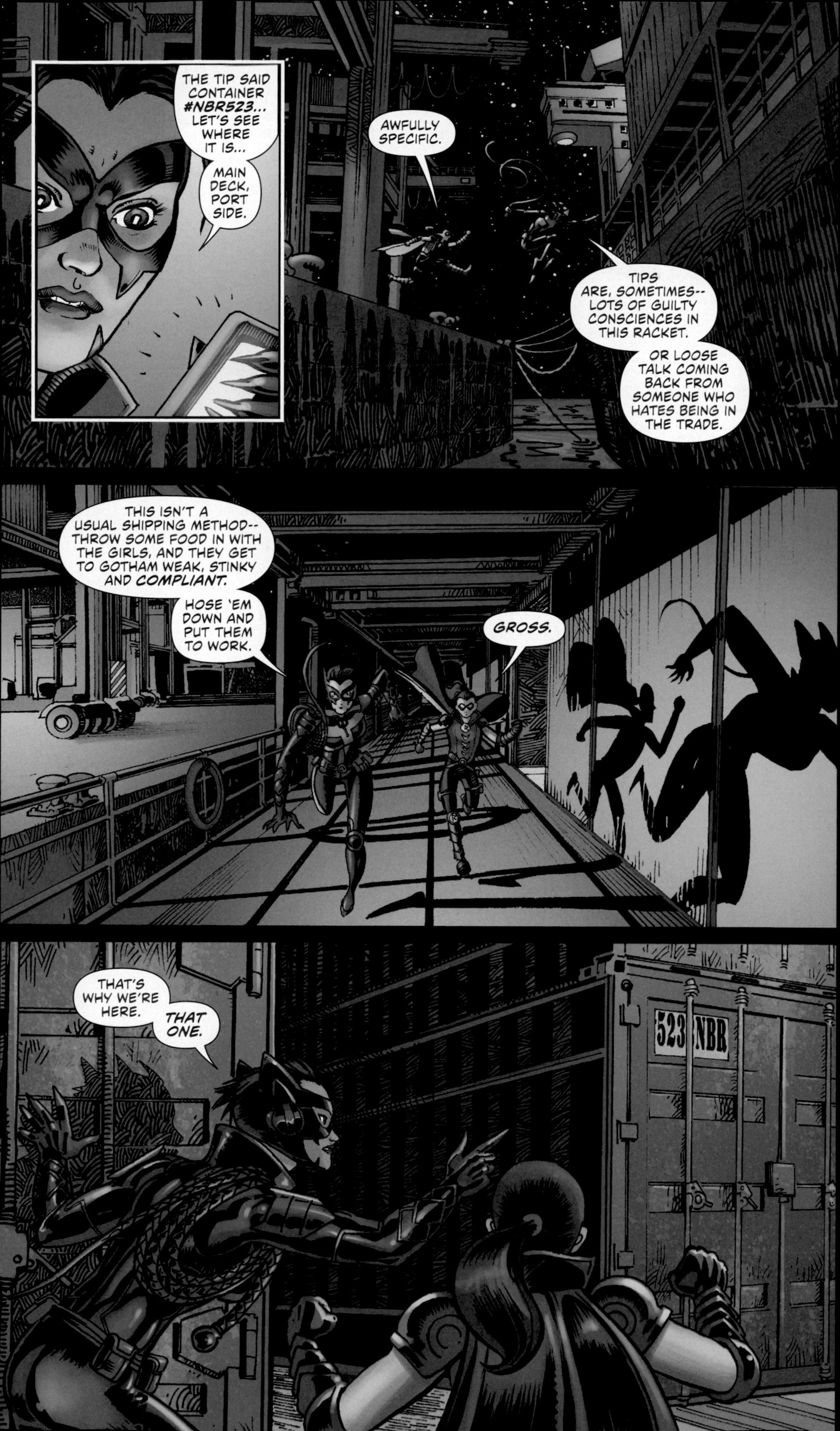
THE TIP SAID CONTAINER #NBR523... LET'S SEE WHERE IT IS...
MAIN DECK, PORT SIDE.
AWFULLY SPECIFIC.
TIPS ARE, SOMETIMES-- LOTS OF GUILTY CONSCIENCES IN THIS RACKET.
OR LOOSE TALK COMING BACK FROM SOMEONE WHO HATES BEING IN THE TRADE.
THIS ISN'T A USUAL SHIPPING METHOD-- THROW SOME FOOD IN WITH THE GIRLS, AND THEY GET TO GOTHAM WEAK, STINKY AND COMPLIANT.
HOSE 'EM DOWN AND PUT THEM TO WORK.
GROSS.
THAT'S WHY WE'RE HERE.
THAT ONE.
523 NBR

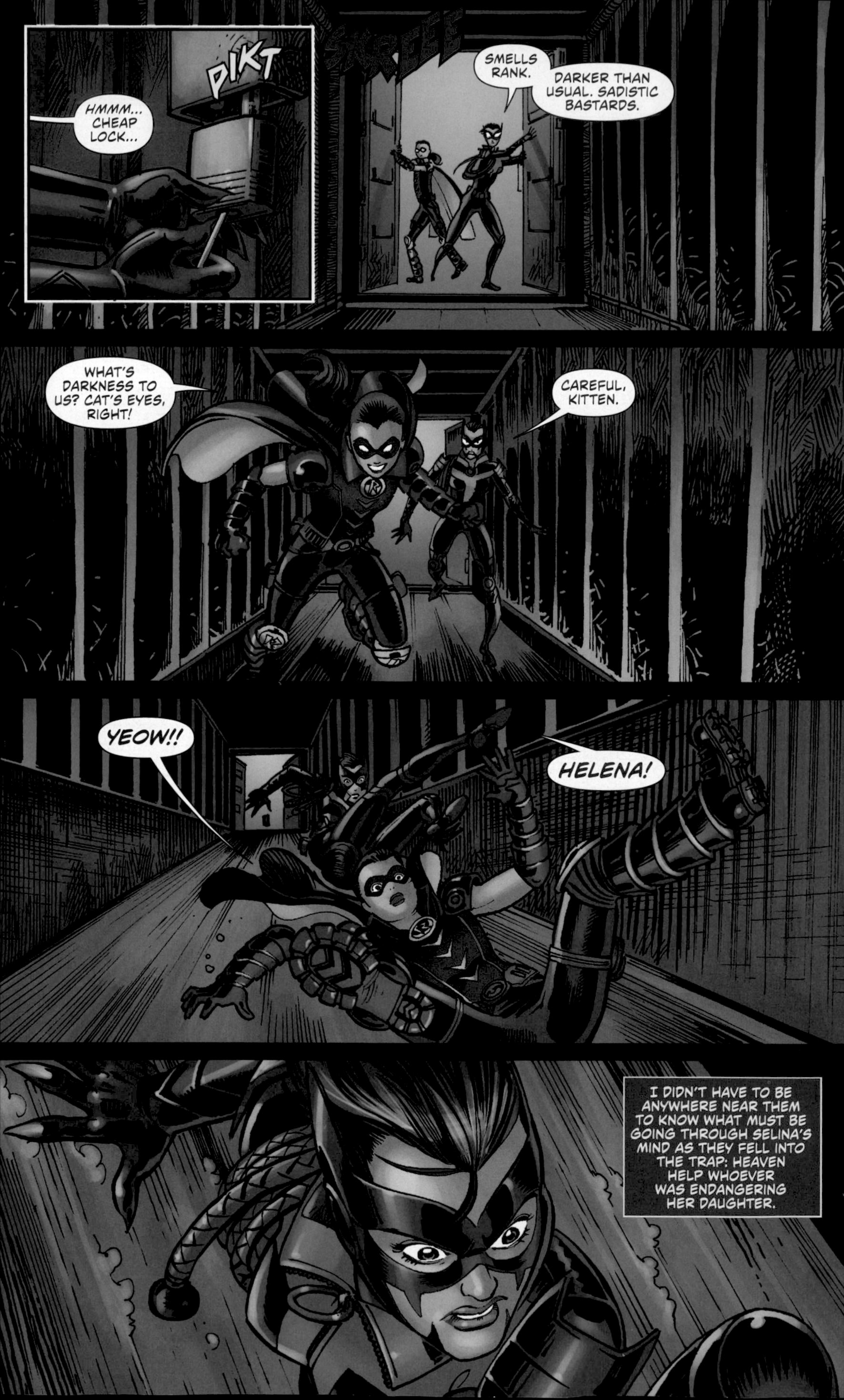
PIKT
HMMM... CHEAP LOCK...
SMELLS RANK.
DARKER THAN USUAL. SADISTIC BASTARDS.
WHAT'S DARKNESS TO US? CAT'S EYES, RIGHT!
CAREFUL, KITTEN.
YEOW!!
HELENA!
I DIDN'T HAVE TO BE ANYWHERE NEAR THEM TO KNOW WHAT MUST BE GOING THROUGH SELINA'S MIND AS THEY FELL INTO THE TRAP: HEAVEN HELP WHOEVER WAS ENDANGERING HER DAUGHTER.

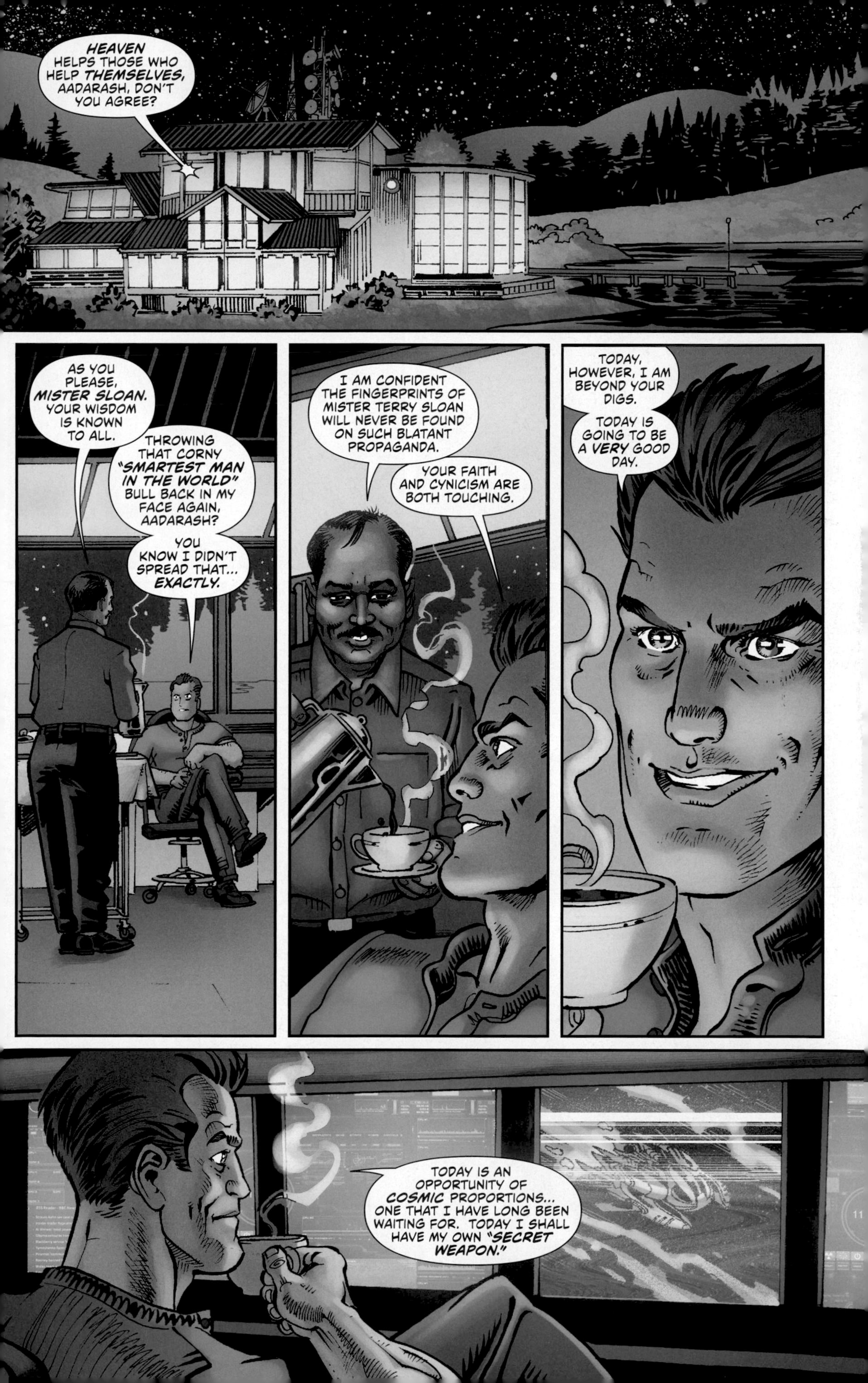
HEAVEN HELPS THOSE WHO HELP THEMSELVES, AADARASH, DON'T YOU AGREE?
AS YOU PLEASE, MISTER SLOAN. YOUR WISDOM IS KNOWN TO ALL.
THROWING THAT CORNY "SMARTEST MAN IN THE WORLD" BULL BACK IN MY FACE AGAIN, AADARASH?
YOU KNOW I DIDN'T SPREAD THAT... EXACTLY.
I AM CONFIDENT THE FINGERPRINTS OF MISTER TERRY SLOAN WILL NEVER BE FOUND ON SUCH BLATANT PROPAGANDA.
YOUR FAITH AND CYNICISM ARE BOTH TOUCHING.
TODAY, HOWEVER, I AM BEYOND YOUR DIGS.
TODAY IS GOING TO BE A VERY GOOD DAY.
TODAY IS AN OPPORTUNITY OF COSMIC PROPORTIONS... ONE THAT I HAVE LONG BEEN WAITING FOR. TODAY I SHALL HAVE MY OWN "SECRET WEAPON."

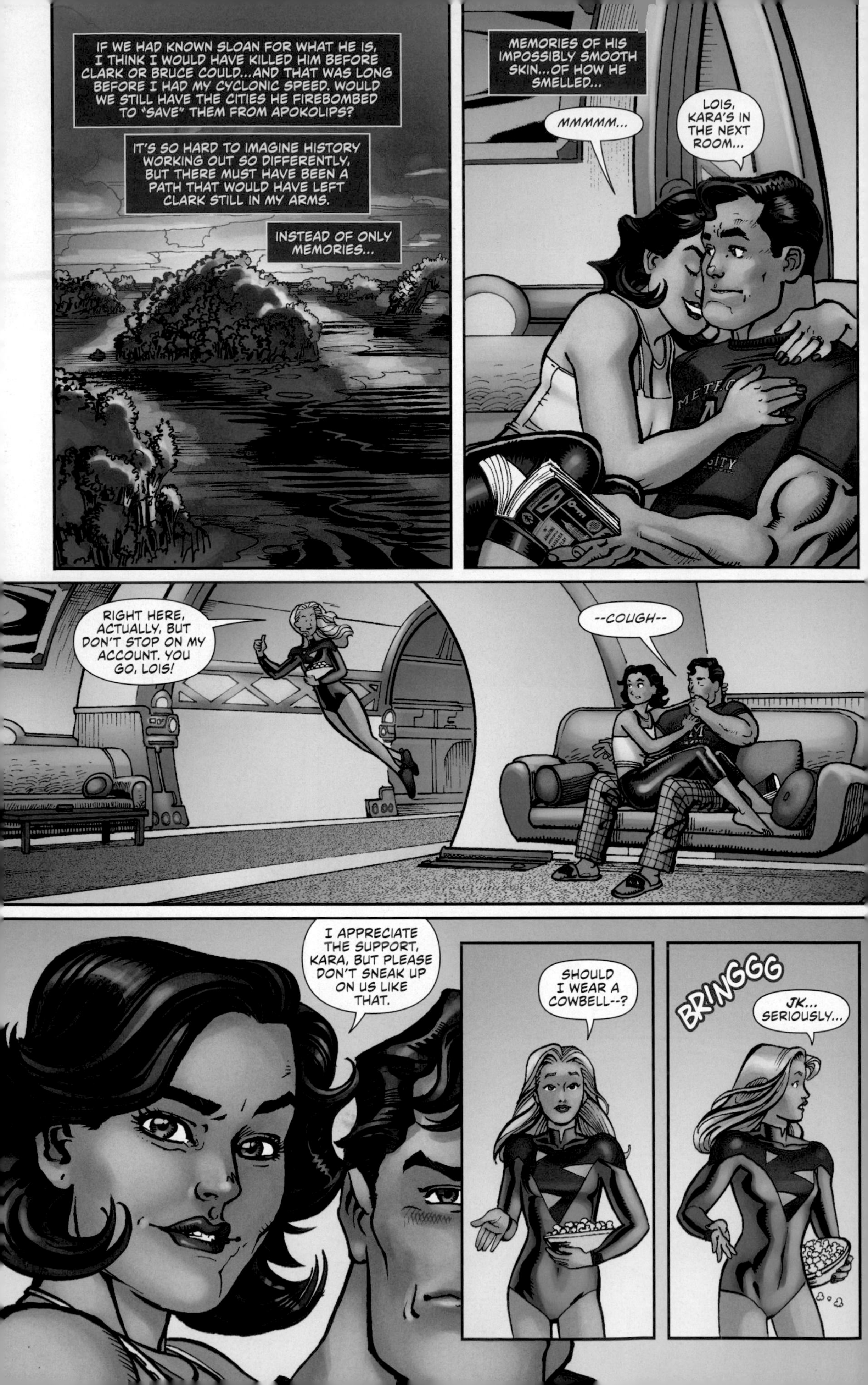
IF WE HAD KNOWN SLOAN FOR WHAT HE IS, I THINK I WOULD HAVE KILLED HIM BEFORE CLARK OR BRUCE COULD...AND THAT WAS LONG BEFORE I HAD MY CYCLONIC SPEED. WOULD WE STILL HAVE THE CITIES HE FIREBOMBED TO "SAVE" THEM FROM APOKOLIPS?
IT'S SO HARD TO IMAGINE HISTORY WORKING OUT SO DIFFERENTLY, BUT THERE MUST HAVE BEEN A PATH THAT WOULD HAVE LEFT CLARK STILL IN MY ARMS.
INSTEAD OF ONLY MEMORIES...
MEMORIES OF HIS IMPOSSIBLY SMOOTH SKIN...OF HOW HE SMELLED...
MMMMM...
LOIS, KARA'S IN THE NEXT ROOM...
RIGHT HERE, ACTUALLY, BUT DON'T STOP ON MY ACCOUNT. YOU GO, LOIS!
--COUGH--
I APPRECIATE THE SUPPORT, KARA, BUT PLEASE DON'T SNEAK UP ON US LIKE THAT.
SHOULD I WEAR A COWBELL--?
BRINGGG
JK... SERIOUSLY...

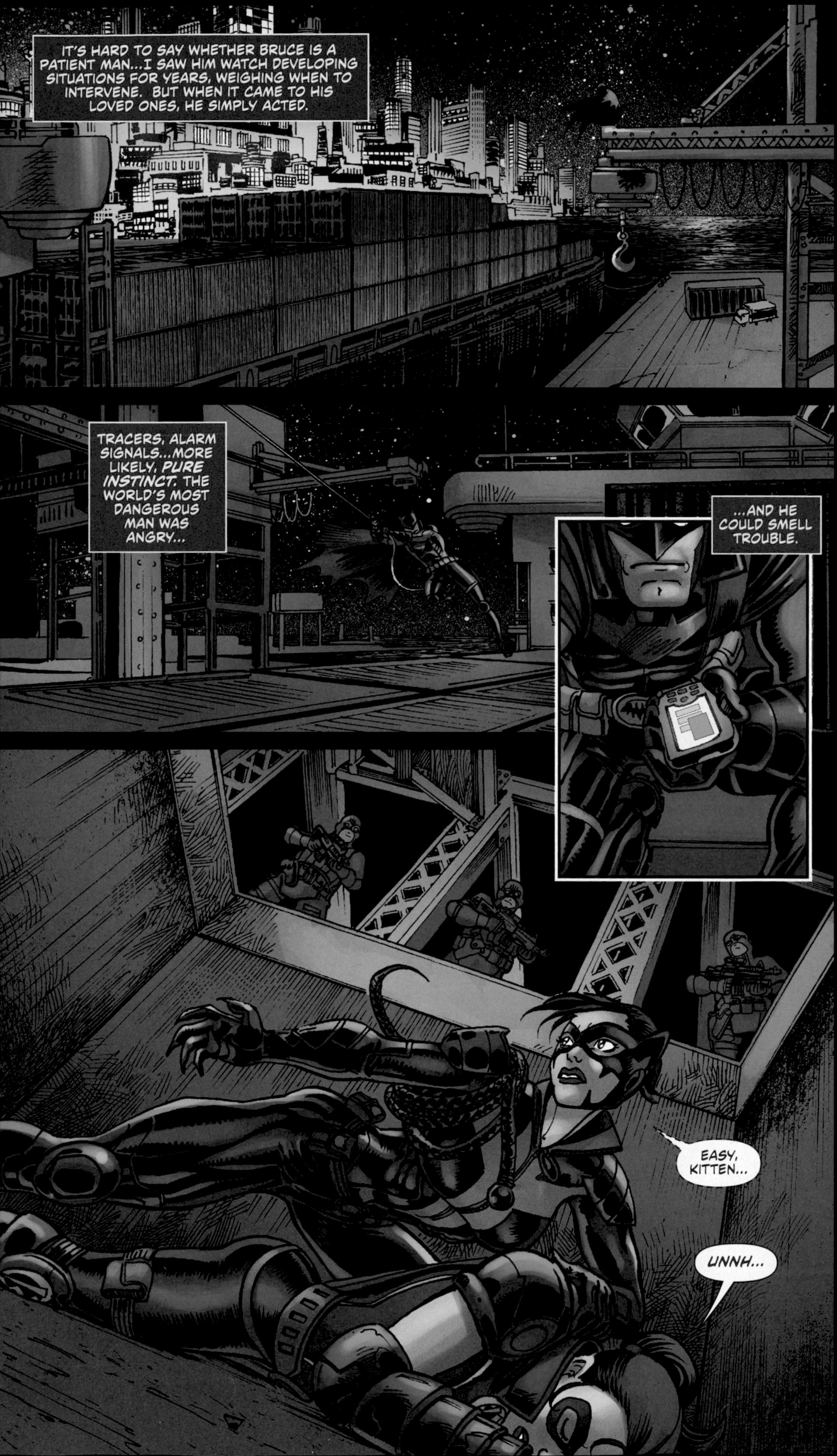

IT'S HARD TO SAY WHETHER BRUCE IS A PATIENT MAN...I SAW HIM WATCH DEVELOPING SITUATIONS FOR YEARS, WEIGHING WHEN TO INTERVENE. BUT WHEN IT CAME TO HIS LOVED ONES, HE SIMPLY ACTED.
TRACERS, ALARM SIGNALS...MORE LIKELY, *PURE INSTINCT.* THE WORLD'S MOST DANGEROUS MAN WAS ANGRY...
...AND HE COULD SMELL TROUBLE.
EASY, KITTEN...
UNNH...

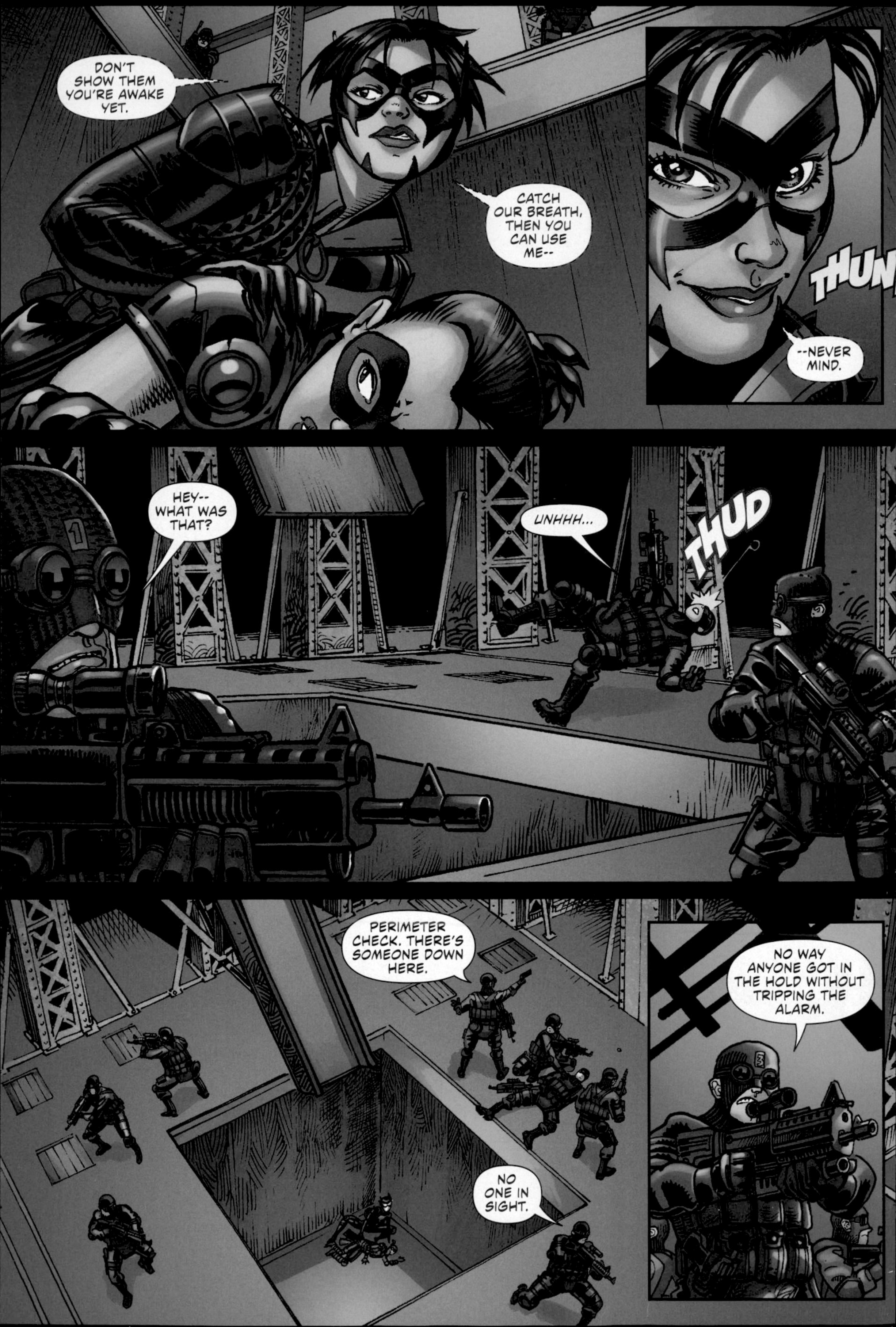
DON'T SHOW THEM YOU'RE AWAKE YET.
CATCH OUR BREATH, THEN YOU CAN USE ME--
THUN
--NEVER MIND.
HEY-- WHAT WAS THAT?
UNHHH...
THUD
PERIMETER CHECK. THERE'S SOMEONE DOWN HERE.
NO ONE IN SIGHT.
NO WAY ANYONE GOT IN THE HOLD WITHOUT TRIPPING THE ALARM.

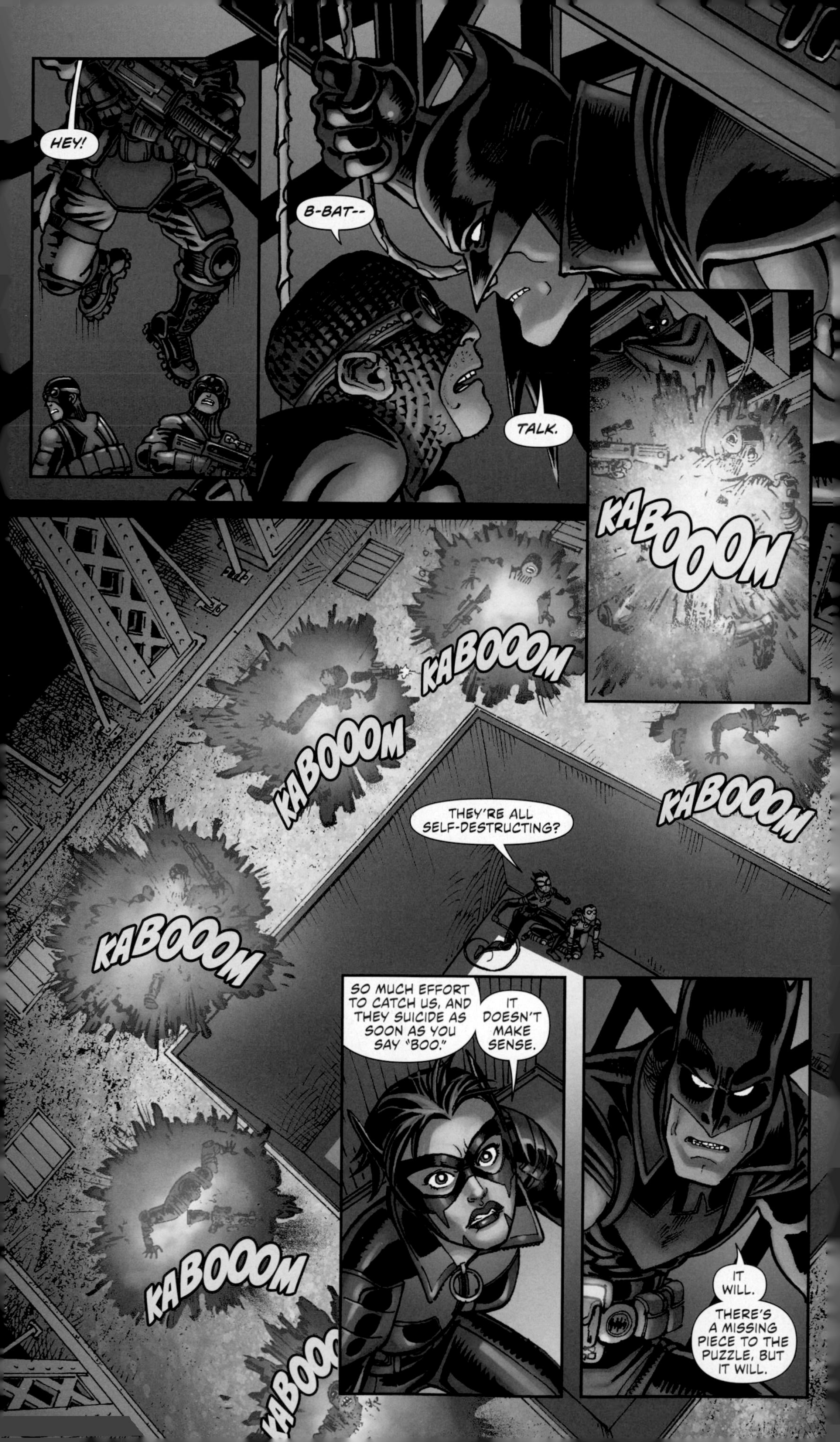
HEY!
B-BAT--
TALK.
KABOOOM
KABOOOM
KABOOOM
KABOOOM
THEY'RE ALL SELF-DESTRUCTING?
KABOOOM
KABOOOM
SO MUCH EFFORT TO CATCH US, AND THEY SUICIDE AS SOON AS YOU SAY "BOO."
IT DOESN'T MAKE SENSE.
IT WILL.
THERE'S A MISSING PIECE TO THE PUZZLE, BUT IT WILL.

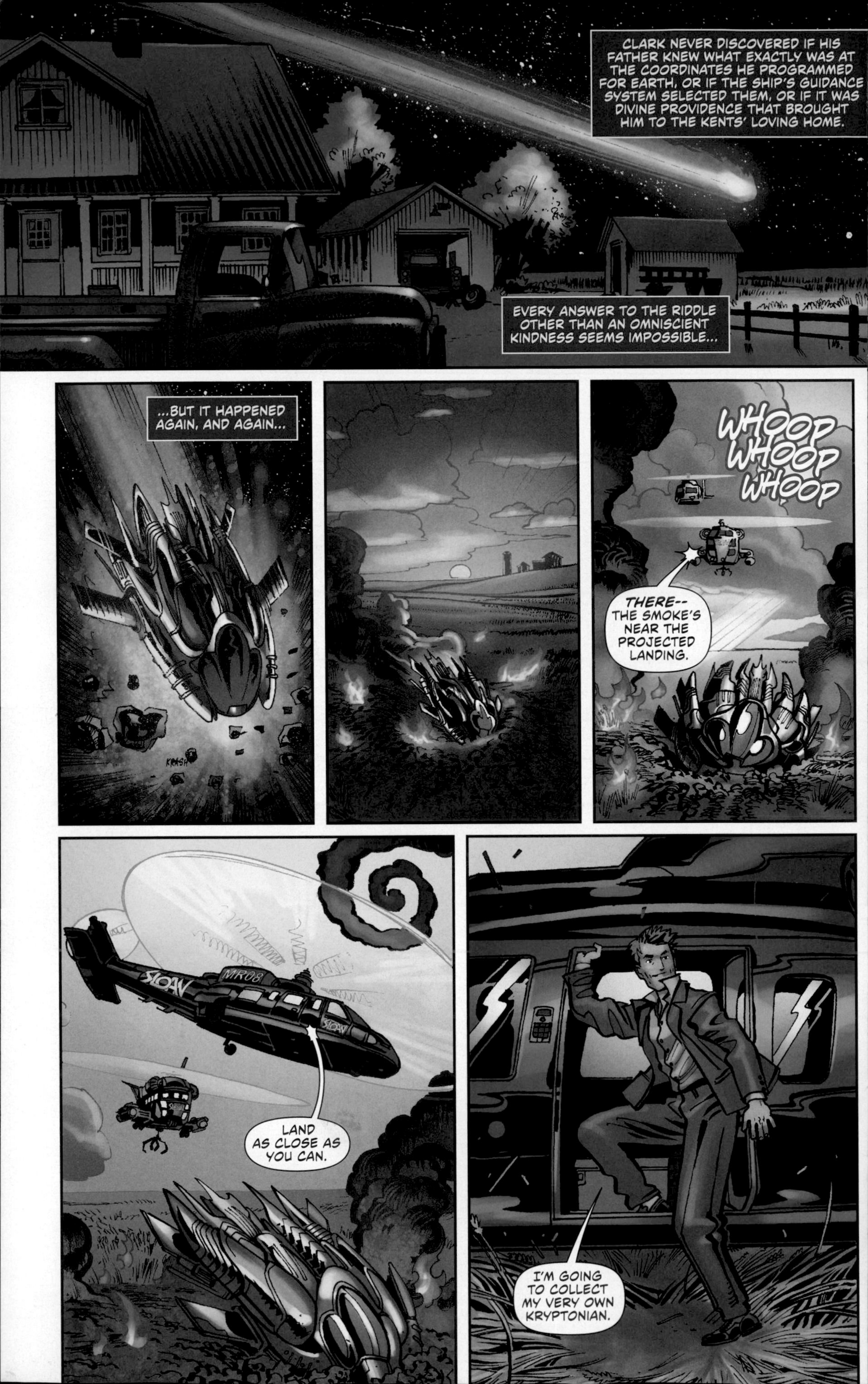
CLARK NEVER DISCOVERED IF HIS FATHER KNEW WHAT EXACTLY WAS AT THE COORDINATES HE PROGRAMMED FOR EARTH, OR IF THE SHIP'S GUIDANCE SYSTEM SELECTED THEM, OR IF IT WAS DIVINE PROVIDENCE THAT BROUGHT HIM TO THE KENTS' LOVING HOME.
EVERY ANSWER TO THE RIDDLE OTHER THAN AN OMNISCIENT KINDNESS SEEMS IMPOSSIBLE...
...BUT IT HAPPENED AGAIN, AND AGAIN...
KRASH
WHOOP WHOOP WHOOP
THERE-- THE SMOKE'S NEAR THE PROJECTED LANDING.
SLOAN
MR08
LAND AS CLOSE AS YOU CAN.
I'M GOING TO COLLECT MY VERY OWN KRYPTONIAN.

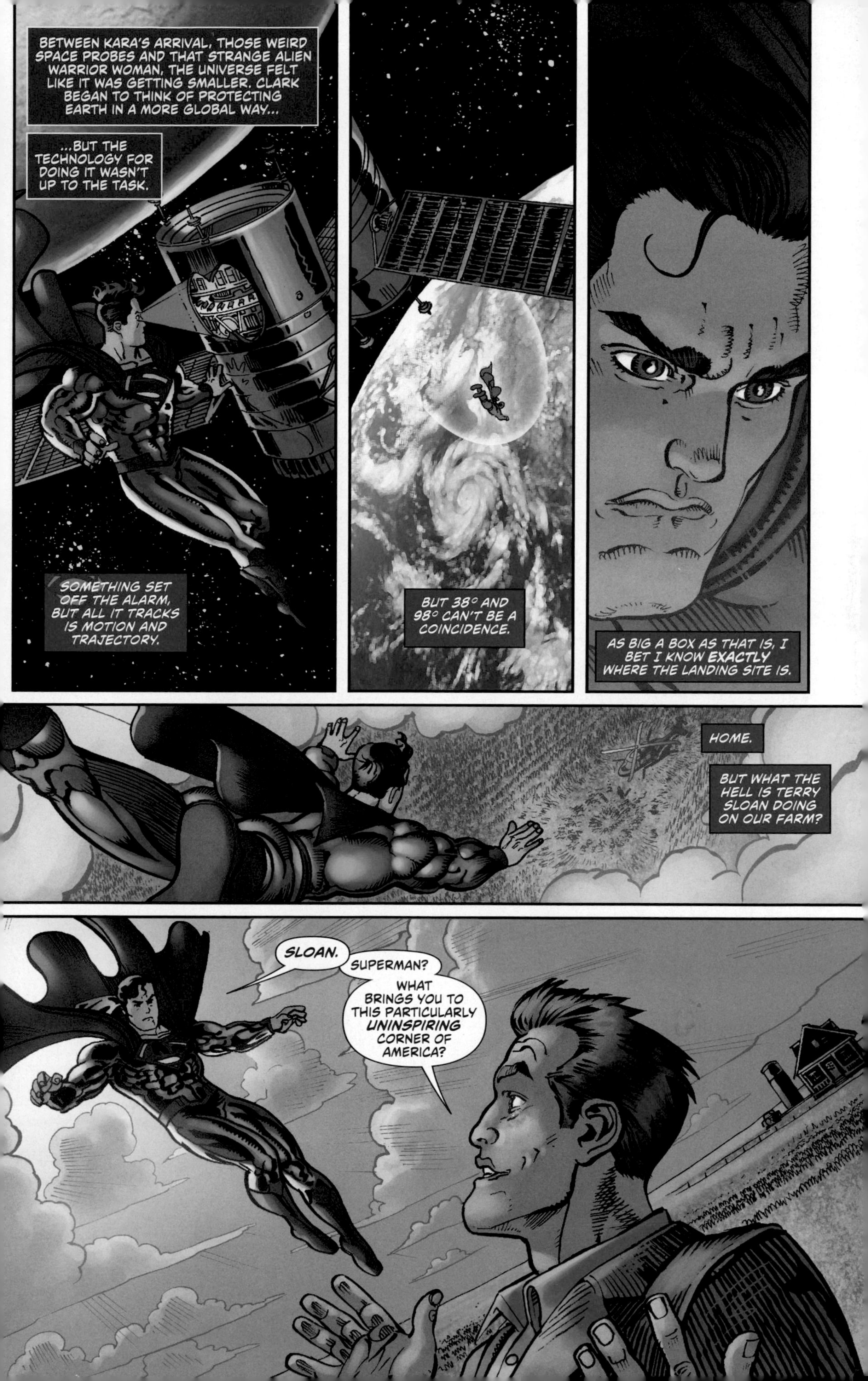
BETWEEN KARA'S ARRIVAL, THOSE WEIRD SPACE PROBES AND THAT STRANGE ALIEN WARRIOR WOMAN, THE UNIVERSE FELT LIKE IT WAS GETTING SMALLER. CLARK BEGAN TO THINK OF PROTECTING EARTH IN A MORE GLOBAL WAY...
...BUT THE TECHNOLOGY FOR DOING IT WASN'T UP TO THE TASK.
SOMETHING SET OFF THE ALARM, BUT ALL IT TRACKS IS MOTION AND TRAJECTORY.
BUT 38° AND 98° CAN'T BE A COINCIDENCE.
AS BIG A BOX AS THAT IS, I BET I KNOW EXACTLY WHERE THE LANDING SITE IS.
HOME.
BUT WHAT THE HELL IS TERRY SLOAN DOING ON OUR FARM?
SLOAN.
SUPERMAN?
WHAT BRINGS YOU TO THIS PARTICULARLY UNINSPIRING CORNER OF AMERICA?

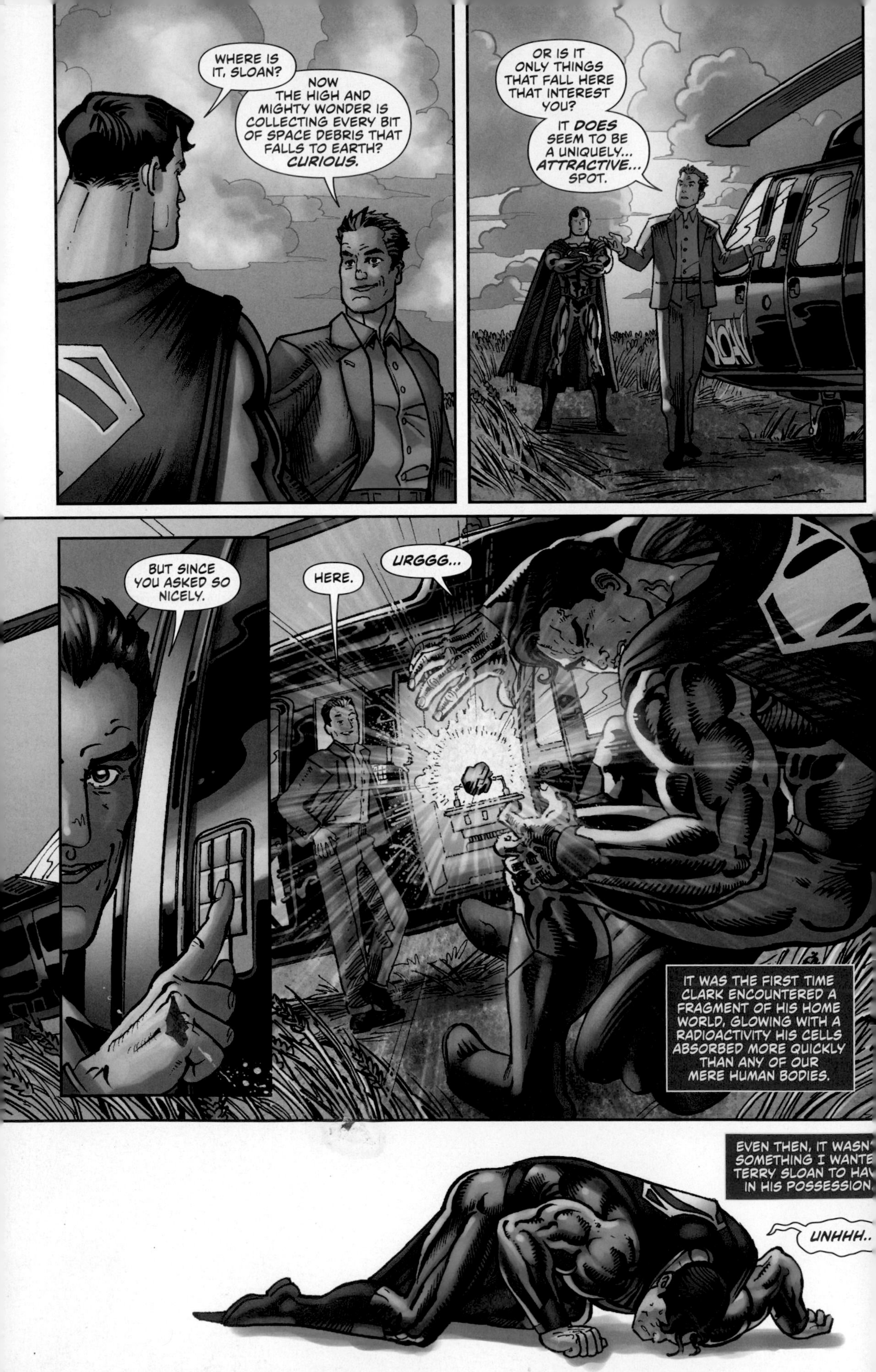
WHERE IS IT, SLOAN?
NOW THE HIGH AND MIGHTY WONDER IS COLLECTING EVERY BIT OF SPACE DEBRIS THAT FALLS TO EARTH? CURIOUS.
OR IS IT ONLY THINGS THAT FALL HERE THAT INTEREST YOU?
IT DOES SEEM TO BE A UNIQUELY... ATTRACTIVE... SPOT.
BUT SINCE YOU ASKED SO NICELY.
HERE.
URGGG...
IT WAS THE FIRST TIME CLARK ENCOUNTERED A FRAGMENT OF HIS HOME WORLD, GLOWING WITH A RADIOACTIVITY HIS CELLS ABSORBED MORE QUICKLY THAN ANY OF OUR MERE HUMAN BODIES.
EVEN THEN, IT WASN' SOMETHING I WANTE TERRY SLOAN TO HAV IN HIS POSSESSION.
UNHHH..

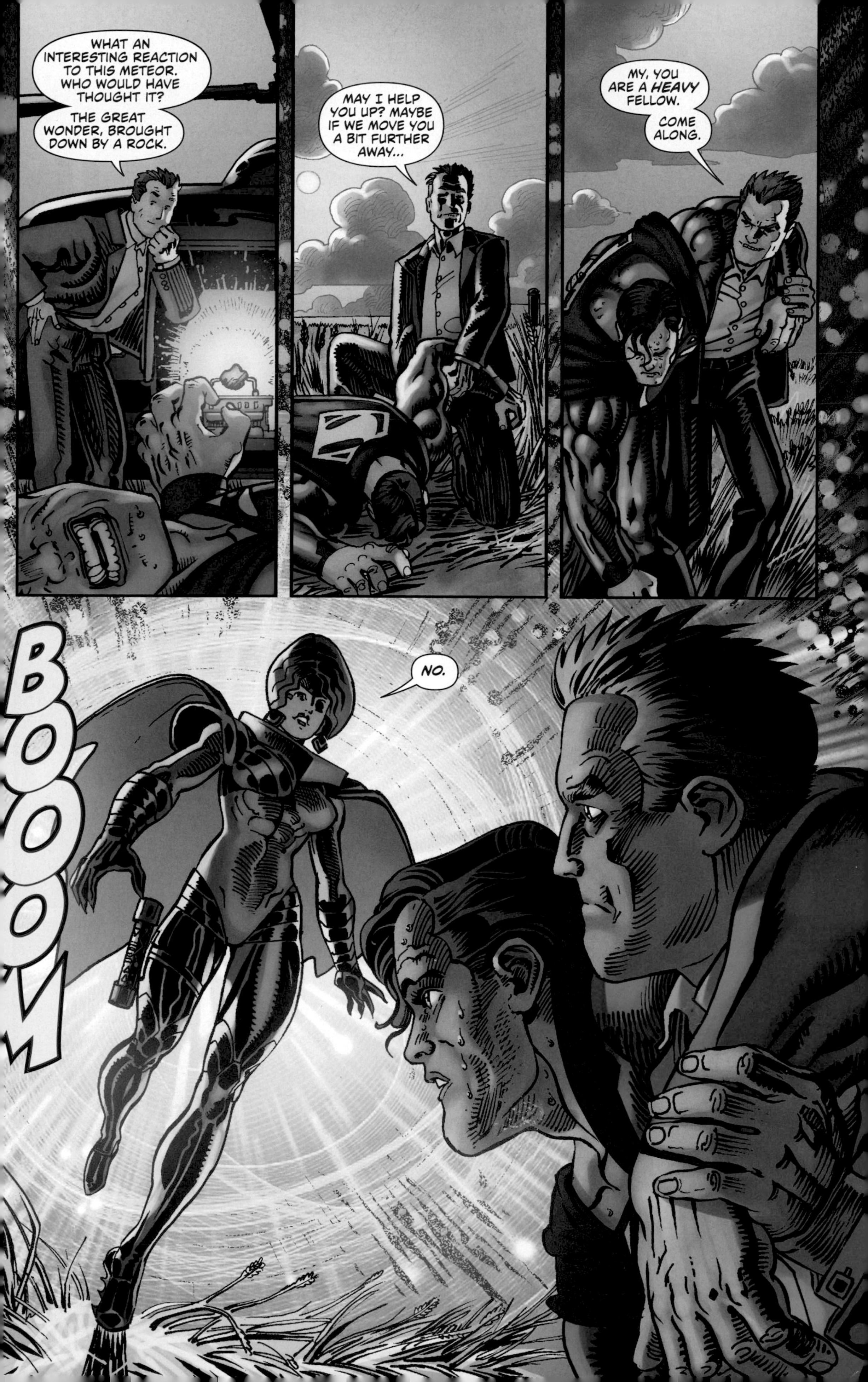
WHAT AN INTERESTING REACTION TO THIS METEOR. WHO WOULD HAVE THOUGHT IT?
THE GREAT WONDER, BROUGHT DOWN BY A ROCK.
MAY I HELP YOU UP? MAYBE IF WE MOVE YOU A BIT FURTHER AWAY...
MY, YOU ARE A HEAVY FELLOW.
COME ALONG.
BOOOOM
NO.

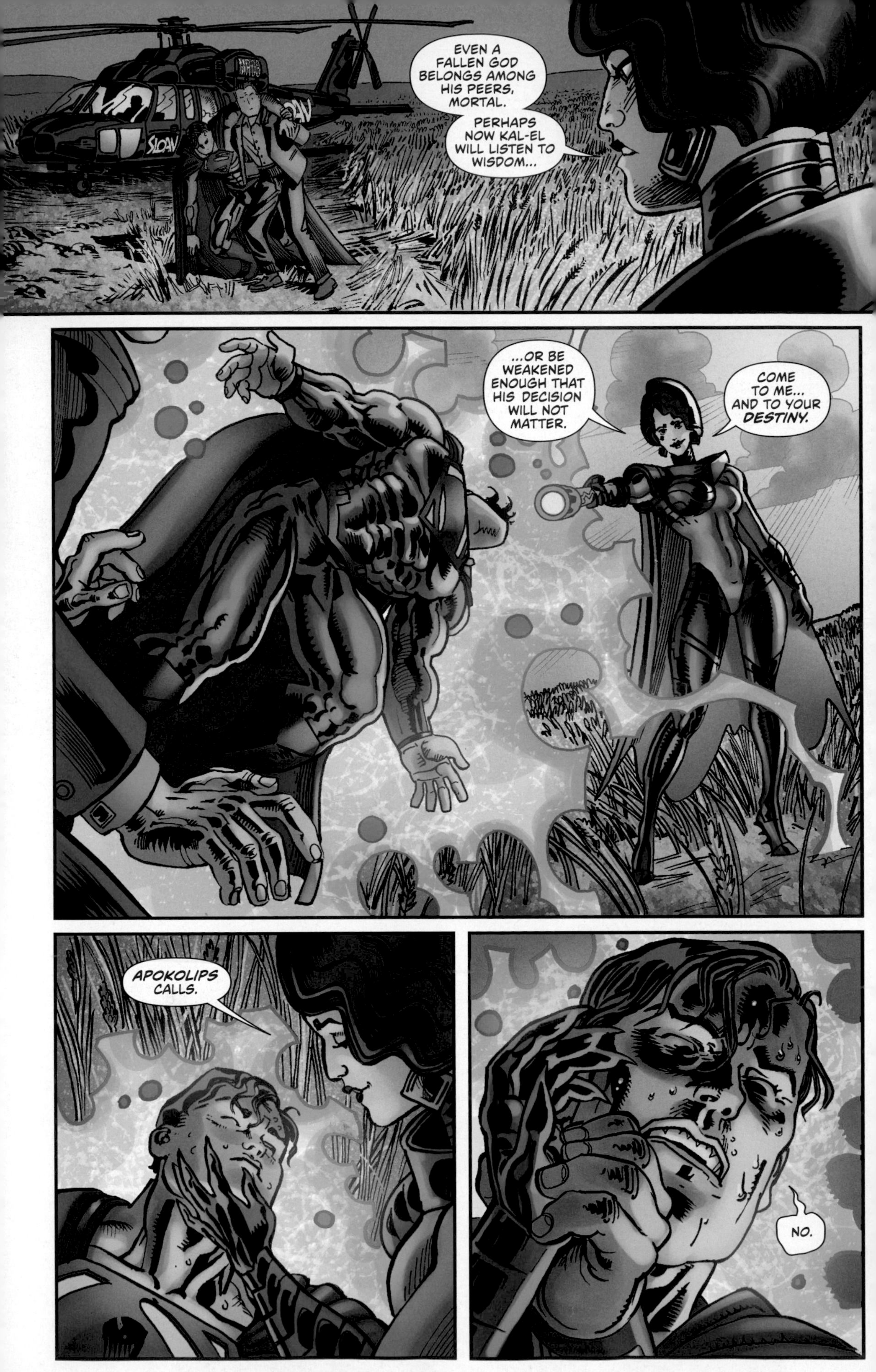

EVEN A FALLEN GOD BELONGS AMONG HIS PEERS, MORTAL.
PERHAPS NOW KAL-EL WILL LISTEN TO WISDOM...
...OR BE WEAKENED ENOUGH THAT HIS DECISION WILL NOT MATTER.
COME TO ME... AND TO YOUR DESTINY.
APOKOLIPS CALLS.
NO.

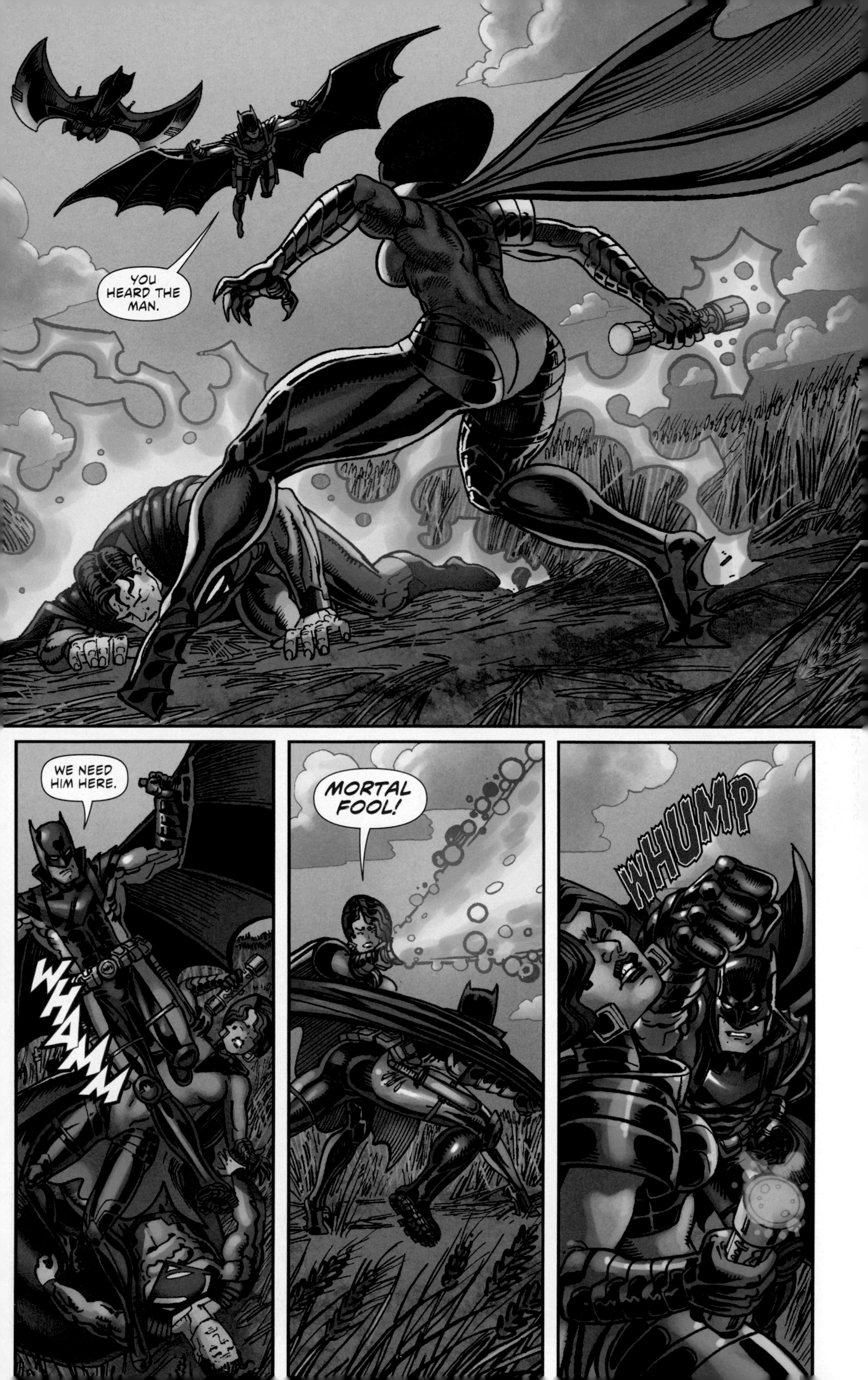
YOU HEARD THE MAN.
WE NEED HIM HERE.
WHAMM
MORTAL FOOL!
WHUMP

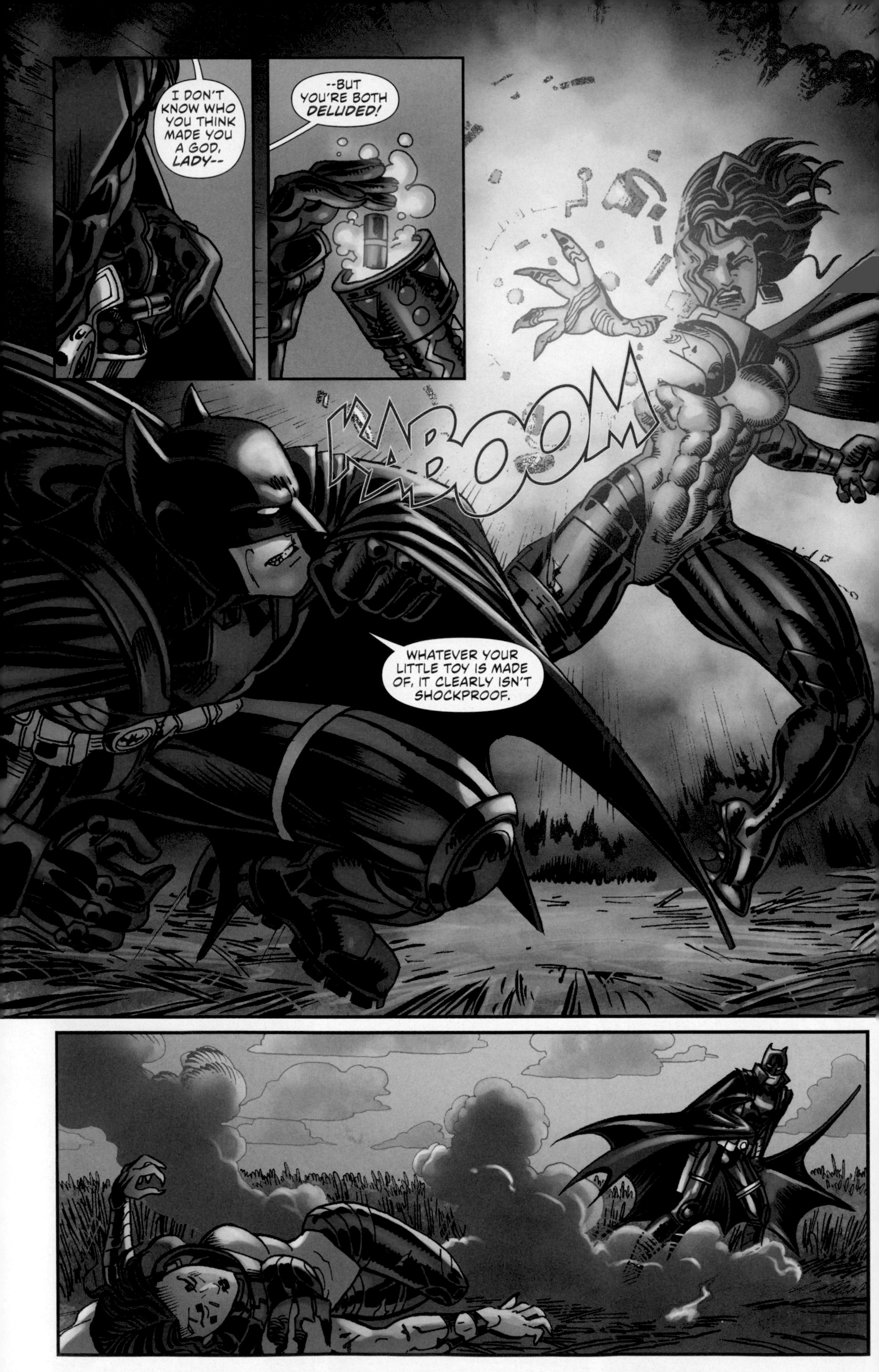
I DON'T KNOW WHO YOU THINK MADE YOU A GOD, LADY--
--BUT YOU'RE BOTH DELUDED!
KABOOM
WHATEVER YOUR LITTLE TOY IS MADE OF, IT CLEARLY ISN'T SHOCKPROOF.

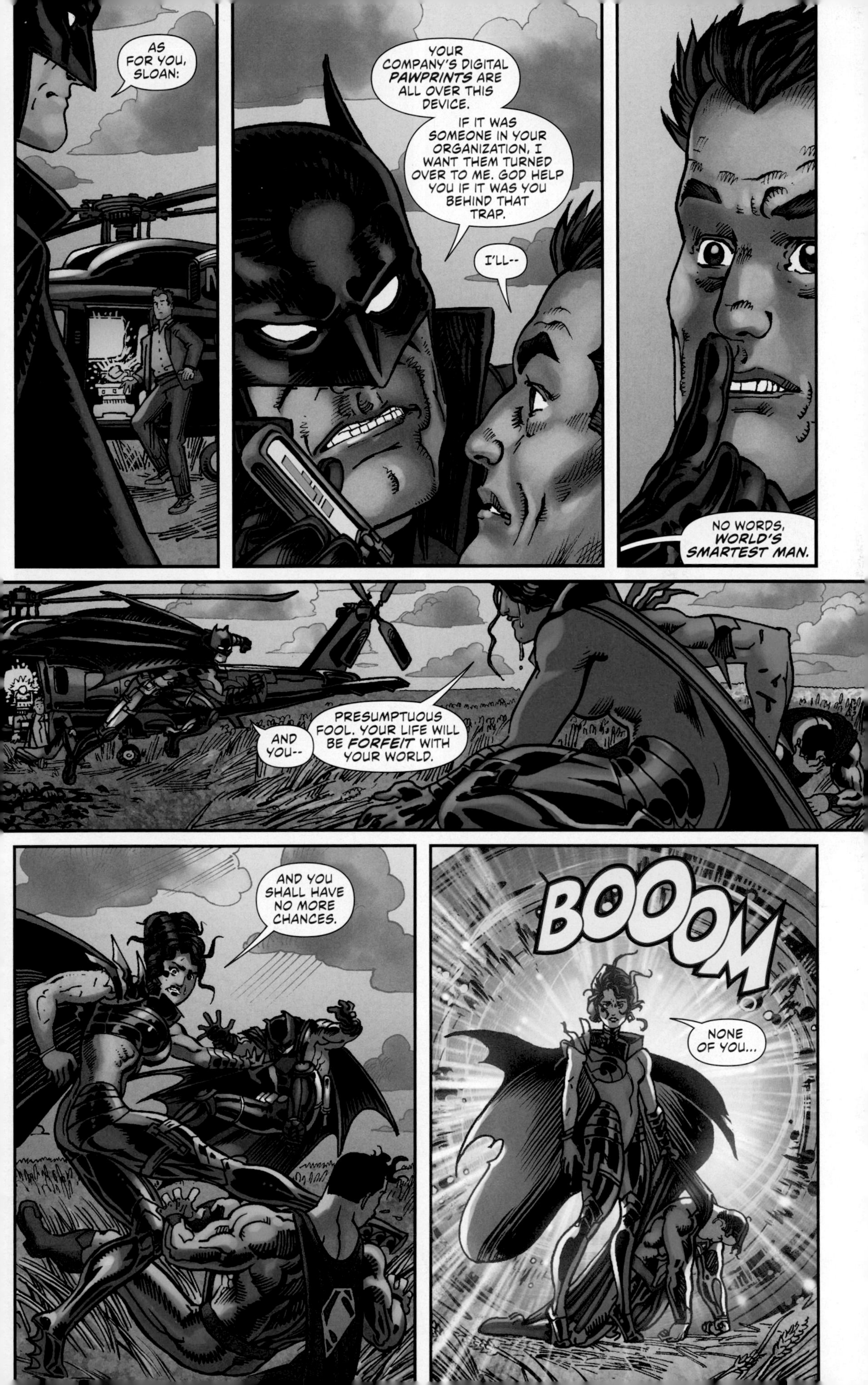
AS FOR YOU, SLOAN:
YOUR COMPANY'S DIGITAL PAWPRINTS ARE ALL OVER THIS DEVICE.
IF IT WAS SOMEONE IN YOUR ORGANIZATION, I WANT THEM TURNED OVER TO ME. GOD HELP YOU IF IT WAS YOU BEHIND THAT TRAP.
I'LL--
NO WORDS, WORLD'S SMARTEST MAN.
AND YOU--
PRESUMPTUOUS FOOL. YOUR LIFE WILL BE FORFEIT WITH YOUR WORLD.
AND YOU SHALL HAVE NO MORE CHANCES.
BOOOOM
NONE OF YOU...

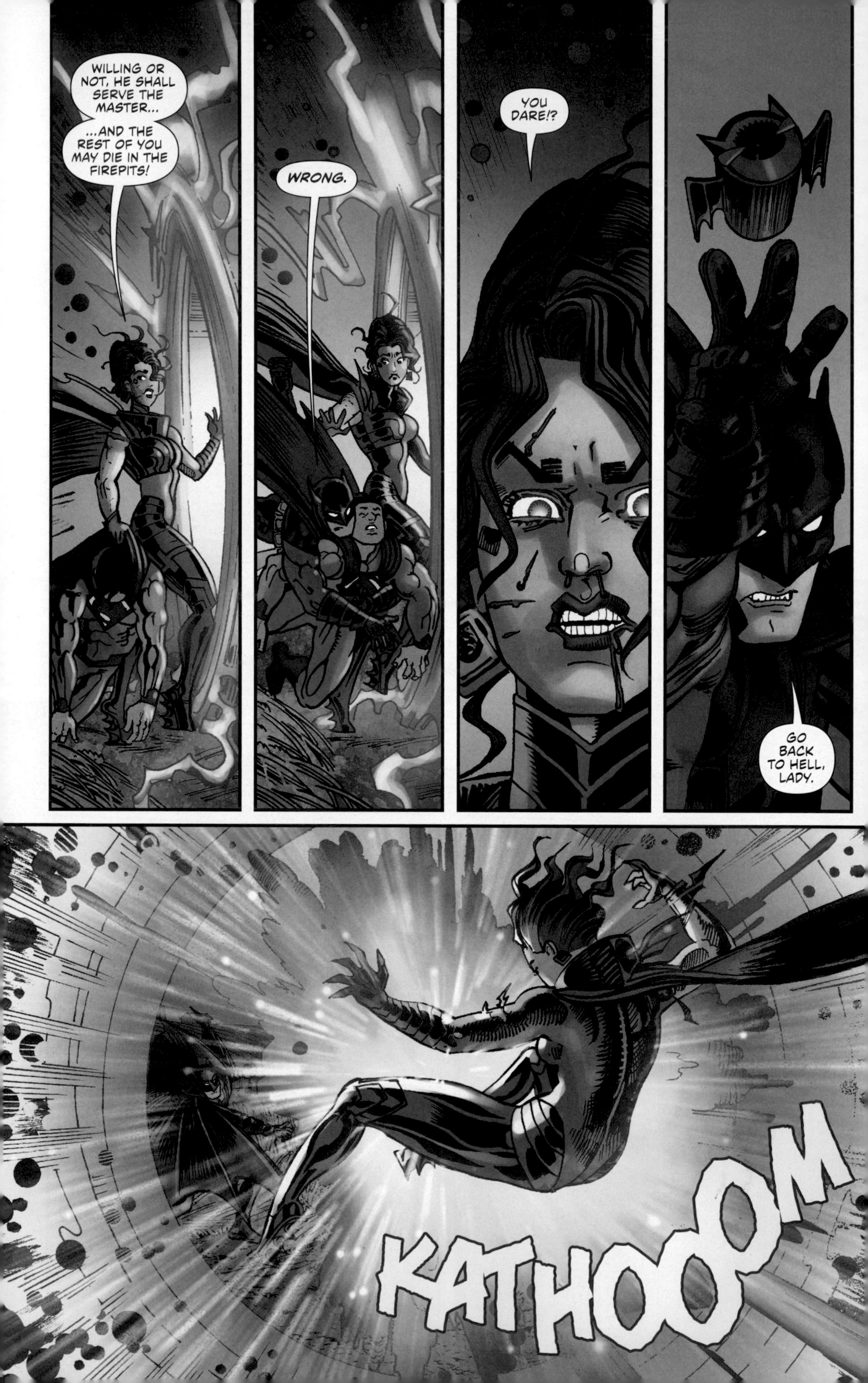
WILLING OR NOT, HE SHALL SERVE THE MASTER...
...AND THE REST OF YOU MAY DIE IN THE FIREPITS!
WRONG.
YOU DARE!?
GO BACK TO HELL, LADY.
KATHOOOOM

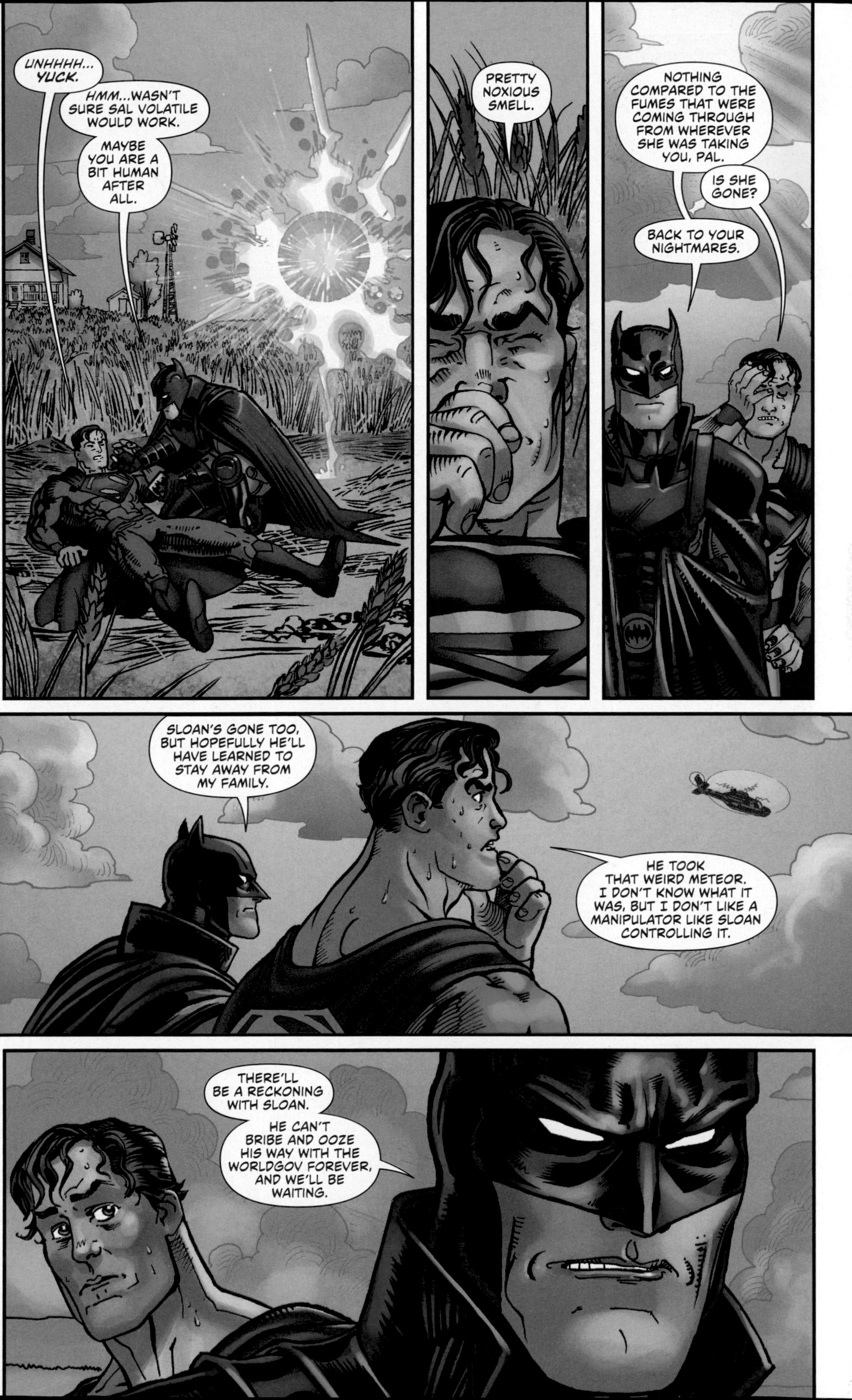
UNHHHH... YUCK.
HMM...WASN'T SURE SAL VOLATILE WOULD WORK.
MAYBE YOU ARE A BIT HUMAN AFTER ALL.
PRETTY NOXIOUS SMELL.
NOTHING COMPARED TO THE FUMES THAT WERE COMING THROUGH FROM WHEREVER SHE WAS TAKING YOU, PAL.
IS SHE GONE?
BACK TO YOUR NIGHTMARES.
SLOAN'S GONE TOO, BUT HOPEFULLY HE'LL HAVE LEARNED TO STAY AWAY FROM MY FAMILY.
HE TOOK THAT WEIRD METEOR. I DON'T KNOW WHAT IT WAS, BUT I DON'T LIKE A MANIPULATOR LIKE SLOAN CONTROLLING IT.
THERE'LL BE A RECKONING WITH SLOAN.
HE CAN'T BRIBE AND OOZE HIS WAY WITH THE WORLDGOV FOREVER, AND WE'LL BE WAITING.

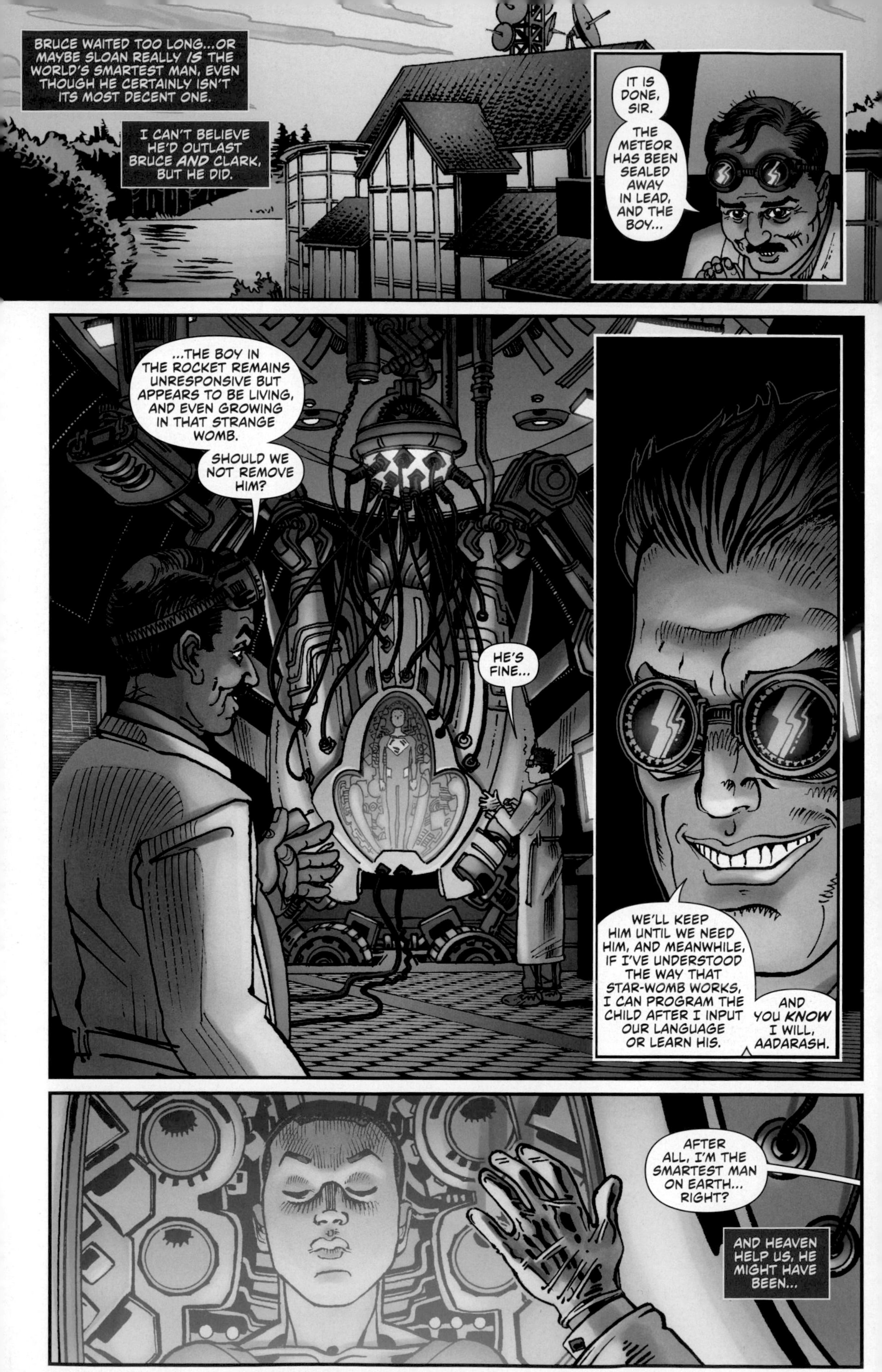

BRUCE WAITED TOO LONG...OR MAYBE SLOAN REALLY IS THE WORLD'S SMARTEST MAN, EVEN THOUGH HE CERTAINLY ISN'T ITS MOST DECENT ONE.
I CAN'T BELIEVE HE'D OUTLAST BRUCE AND CLARK, BUT HE DID.
IT IS DONE, SIR.
THE METEOR HAS BEEN SEALED AWAY IN LEAD, AND THE BOY...
...THE BOY IN THE ROCKET REMAINS UNRESPONSIVE BUT APPEARS TO BE LIVING, AND EVEN GROWING IN THAT STRANGE WOMB.
SHOULD WE NOT REMOVE HIM?
HE'S FINE...
WE'LL KEEP HIM UNTIL WE NEED HIM, AND MEANWHILE, IF I'VE UNDERSTOOD THE WAY THAT STAR-WOMB WORKS, I CAN PROGRAM THE CHILD AFTER I INPUT OUR LANGUAGE OR LEARN HIS.
AND YOU KNOW I WILL, AADARASH.
AFTER ALL, I'M THE SMARTEST MAN ON EARTH... RIGHT?
AND HEAVEN HELP US, HE MIGHT HAVE BEEN...

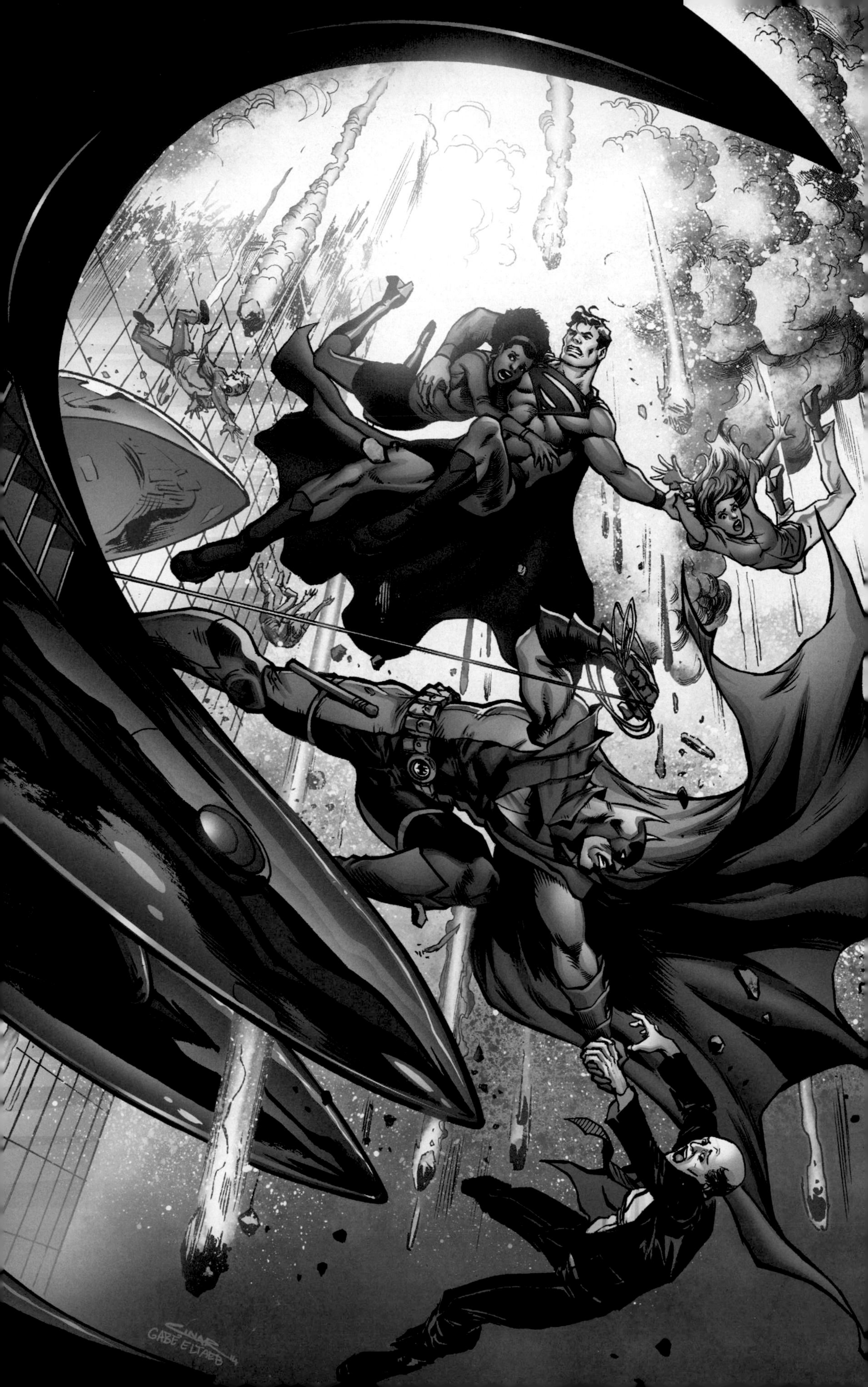
GABE ELTAEB

PART FIVE: SIGNS

PAUL LEVITZ writer **JED DOUGHERTY** artist **CHRIS SOTOMAYOR** colorist
TRAVIS LANHAM letterer cover art by **YILDIRAY CINAR & GABE ELTAEB**

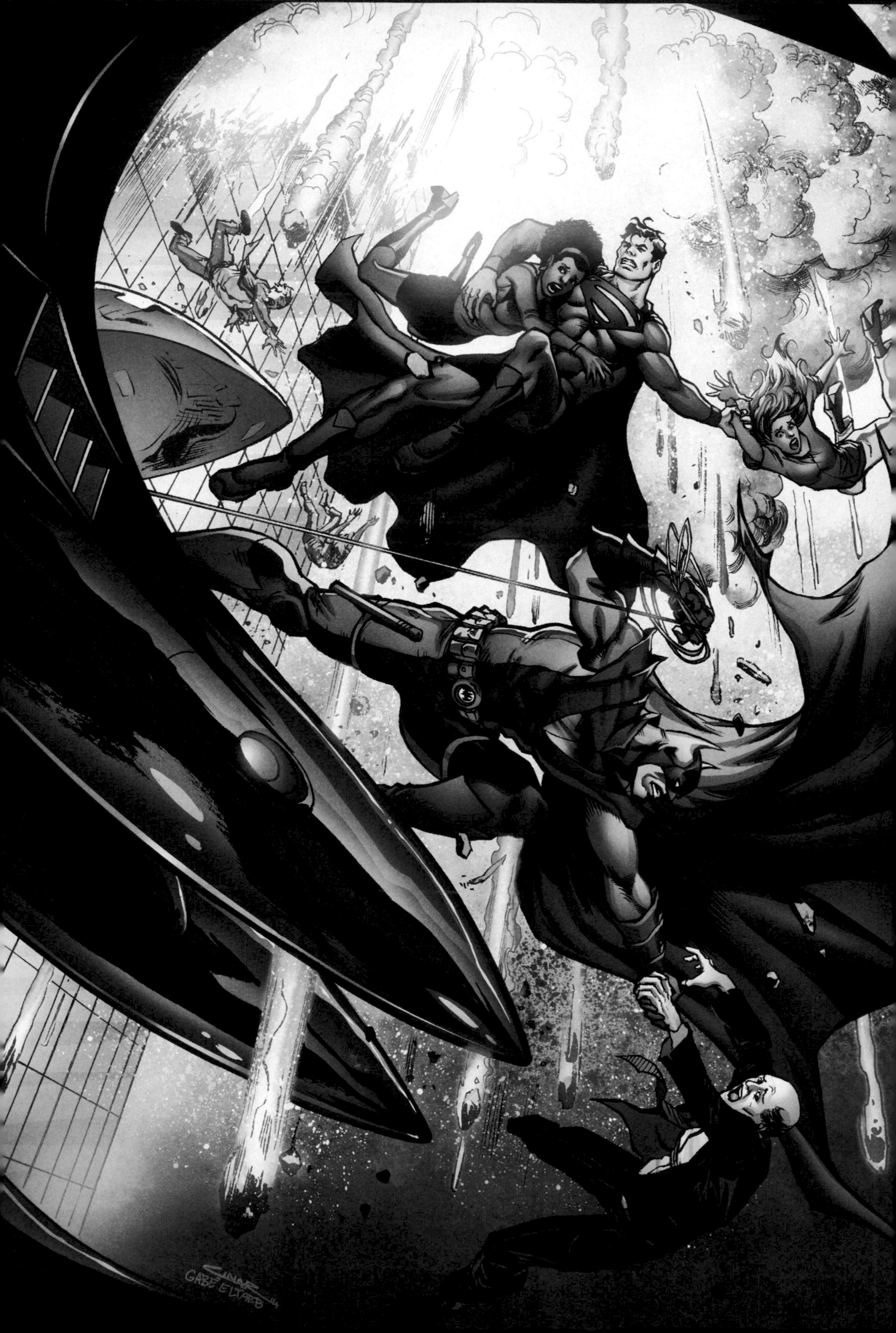
CINAR
GABE ELTAEB

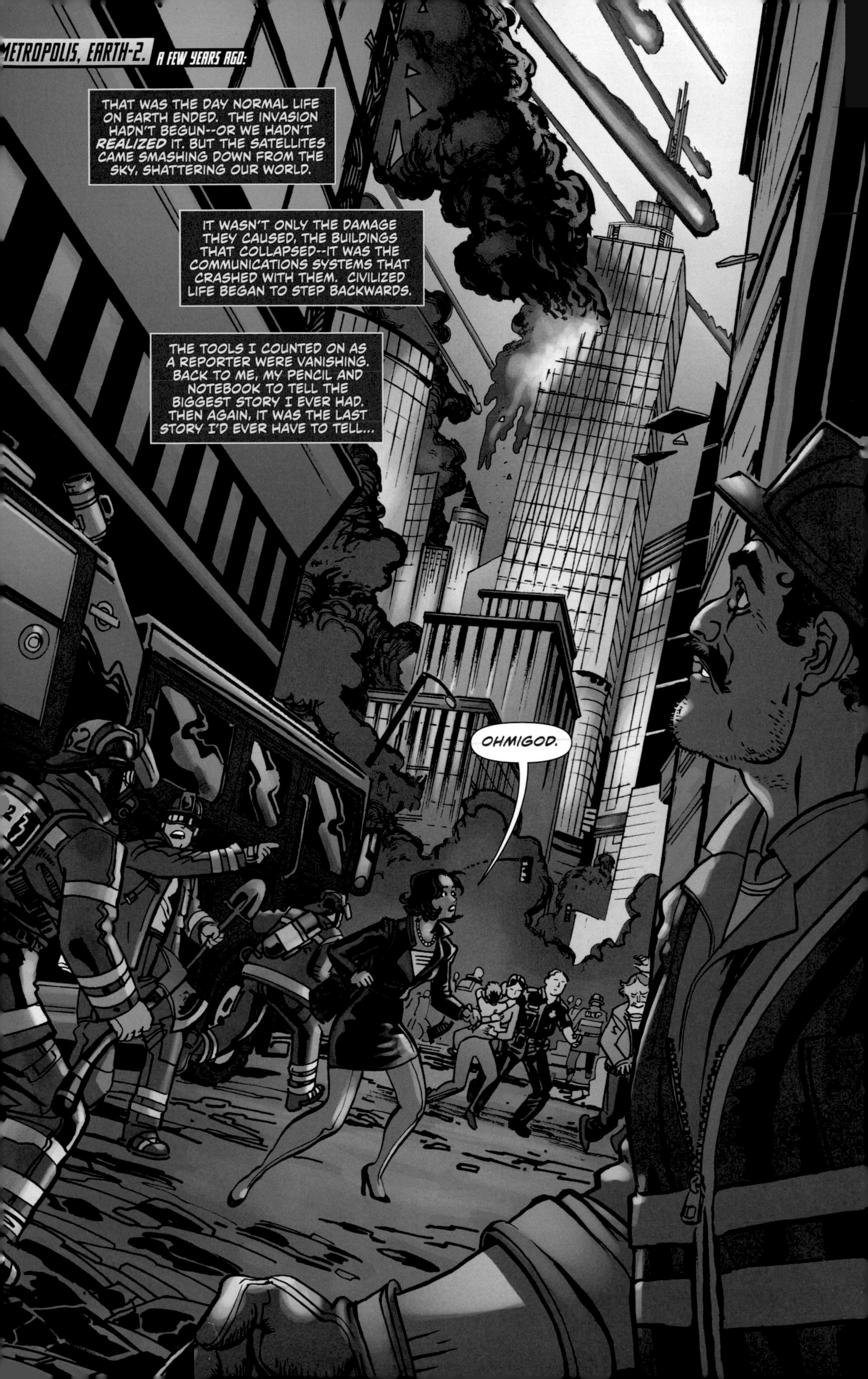
METROPOLIS, EARTH-2.
A FEW YEARS AGO:
THAT WAS THE DAY NORMAL LIFE ON EARTH ENDED. THE INVASION HADN'T BEGUN--OR WE HADN'T REALIZED IT. BUT THE SATELLITES CAME SMASHING DOWN FROM THE SKY, SHATTERING OUR WORLD.
IT WASN'T ONLY THE DAMAGE THEY CAUSED, THE BUILDINGS THAT COLLAPSED--IT WAS THE COMMUNICATIONS SYSTEMS THAT CRASHED WITH THEM. CIVILIZED LIFE BEGAN TO STEP BACKWARDS.
THE TOOLS I COUNTED ON AS A REPORTER WERE VANISHING. BACK TO ME, MY PENCIL AND NOTEBOOK TO TELL THE BIGGEST STORY I EVER HAD. THEN AGAIN, IT WAS THE LAST STORY I'D EVER HAVE TO TELL...
OHMIGOD.

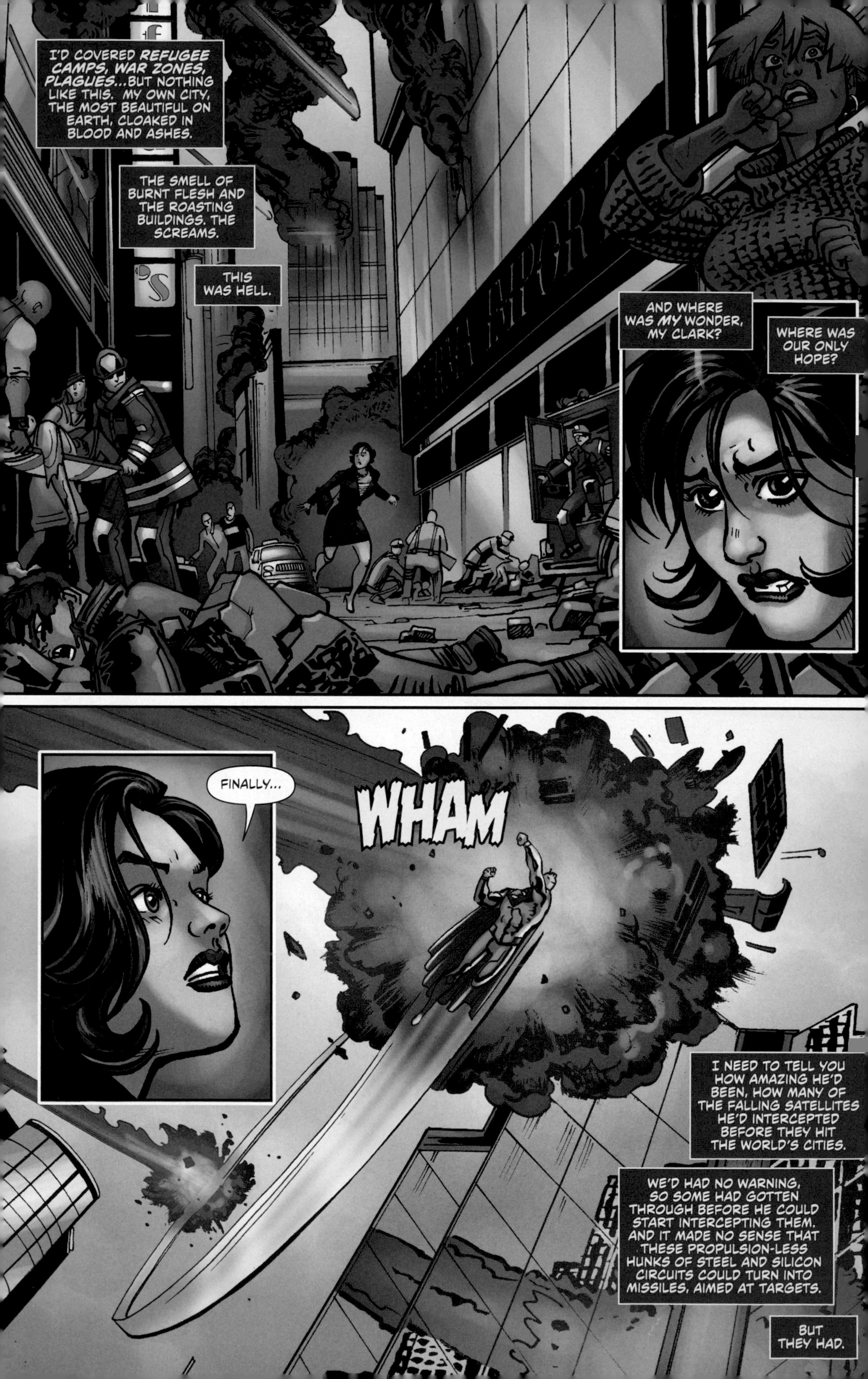
I'D COVERED REFUGEE CAMPS, WAR ZONES, PLAGUES...BUT NOTHING LIKE THIS. MY OWN CITY, THE MOST BEAUTIFUL ON EARTH, CLOAKED IN BLOOD AND ASHES.
THE SMELL OF BURNT FLESH AND THE ROASTING BUILDINGS. THE SCREAMS.
THIS WAS HELL.
AND WHERE WAS MY WONDER, MY CLARK?
WHERE WAS OUR ONLY HOPE?
FINALLY...
WHAM
I NEED TO TELL YOU HOW AMAZING HE'D BEEN, HOW MANY OF THE FALLING SATELLITES HE'D INTERCEPTED BEFORE THEY HIT THE WORLD'S CITIES.
WE'D HAD NO WARNING, SO SOME HAD GOTTEN THROUGH BEFORE HE COULD START INTERCEPTING THEM. AND IT MADE NO SENSE THAT THESE PROPULSION-LESS HUNKS OF STEEL AND SILICON CIRCUITS COULD TURN INTO MISSILES, AIMED AT TARGETS.
BUT THEY HAD.

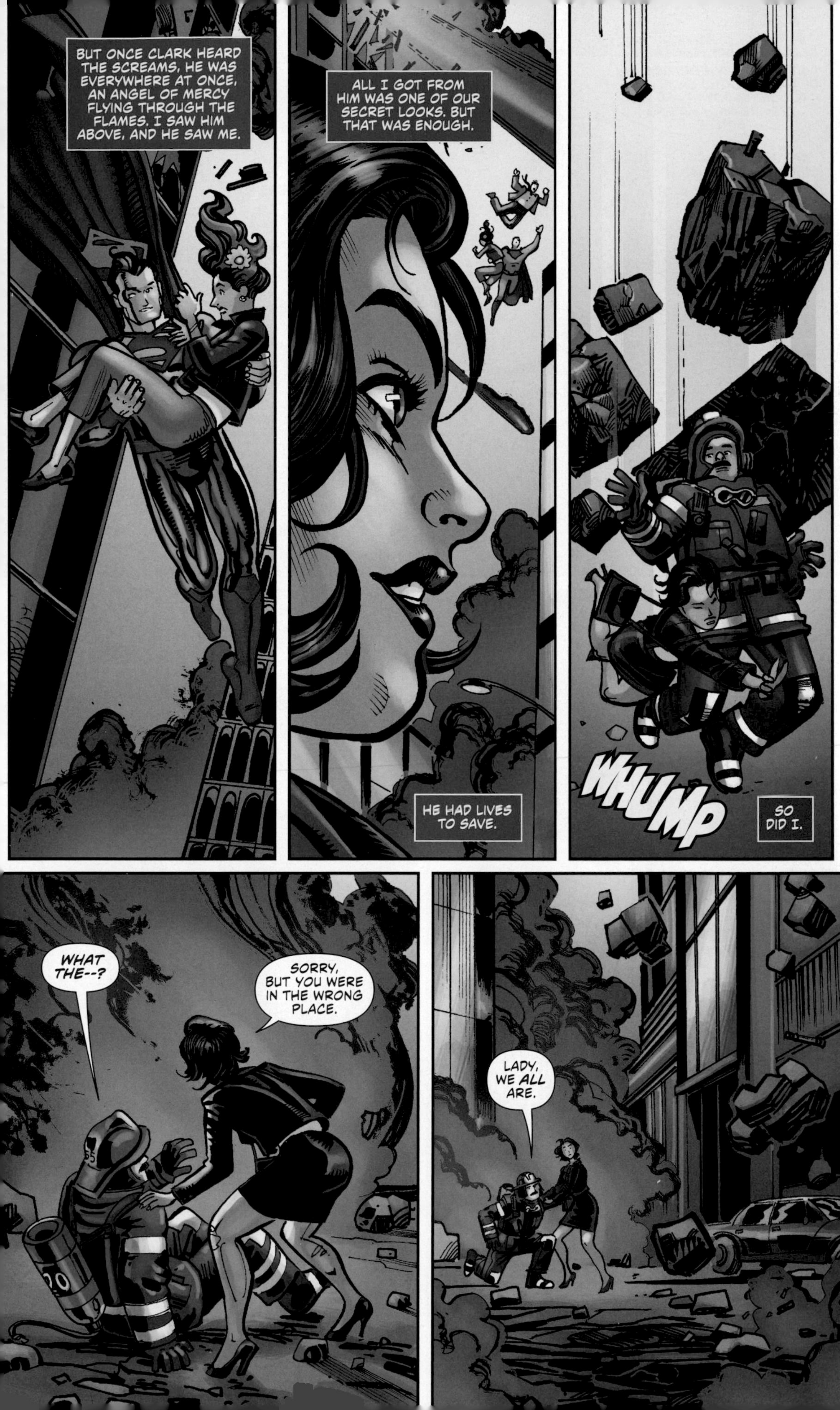
BUT ONCE CLARK HEARD THE SCREAMS, HE WAS EVERYWHERE AT ONCE, AN ANGEL OF MERCY FLYING THROUGH THE FLAMES. I SAW HIM ABOVE, AND HE SAW ME.
ALL I GOT FROM HIM WAS ONE OF OUR SECRET LOOKS. BUT THAT WAS ENOUGH.
HE HAD LIVES TO SAVE.
WHUMP
SO DID I.
WHAT THE--?
SORRY, BUT YOU WERE IN THE WRONG PLACE.
LADY, WE ALL ARE.

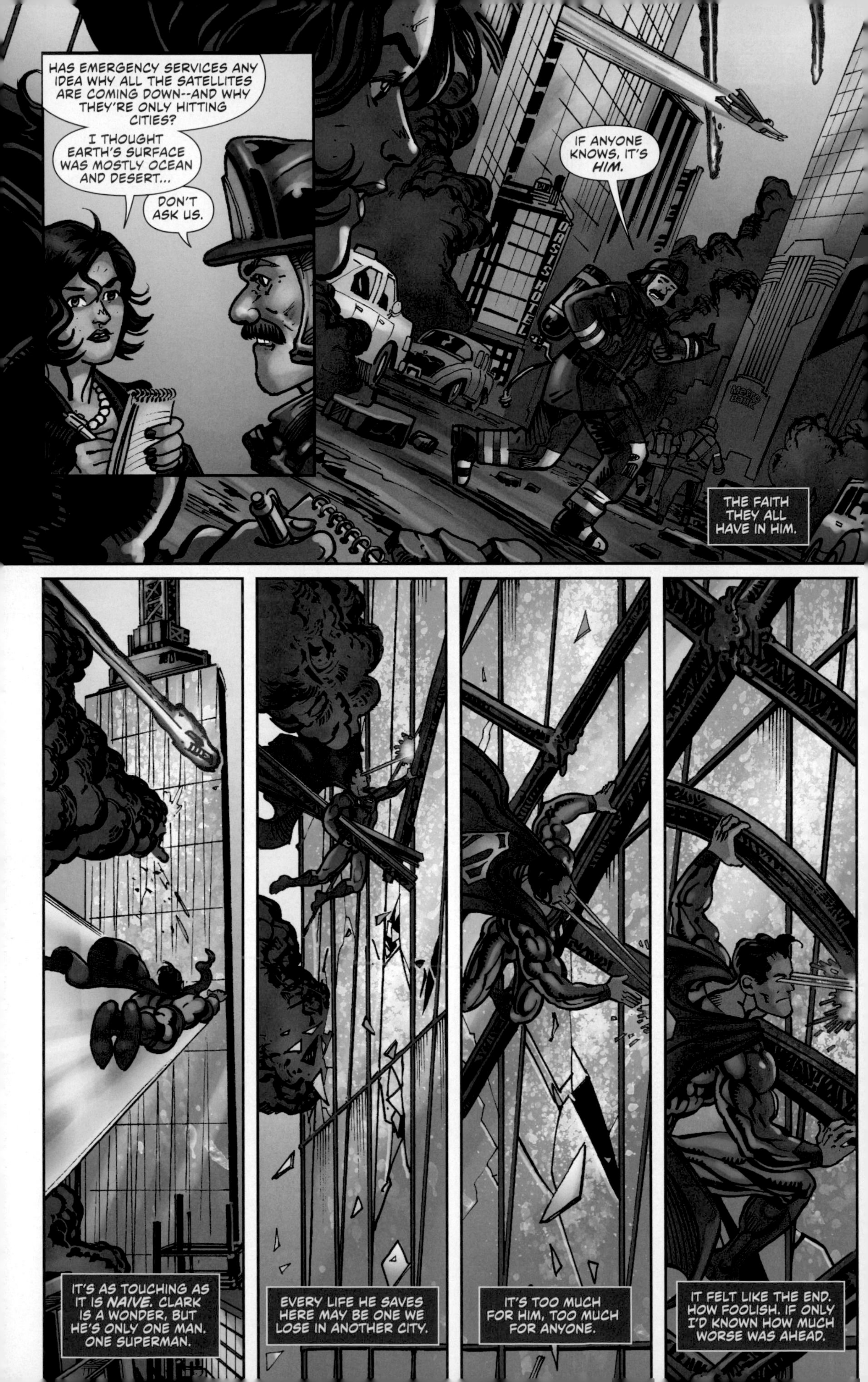
HAS EMERGENCY SERVICES ANY IDEA WHY ALL THE SATELLITES ARE COMING DOWN--AND WHY THEY'RE ONLY HITTING CITIES?
I THOUGHT EARTH'S SURFACE WAS MOSTLY OCEAN AND DESERT...
DON'T ASK US.
IF ANYONE KNOWS, IT'S *HIM.*
OASIS HOTEL
Metro Bank
THE FAITH THEY ALL HAVE IN HIM.
IT'S AS TOUCHING AS IT IS *NAIVE.* CLARK IS A WONDER, BUT HE'S ONLY ONE MAN. ONE SUPERMAN.
EVERY LIFE HE SAVES HERE MAY BE ONE WE LOSE IN ANOTHER CITY.
IT'S TOO MUCH FOR HIM, TOO MUCH FOR ANYONE.
IT FELT LIKE THE END. HOW FOOLISH. IF ONLY I'D KNOWN HOW MUCH WORSE WAS AHEAD.

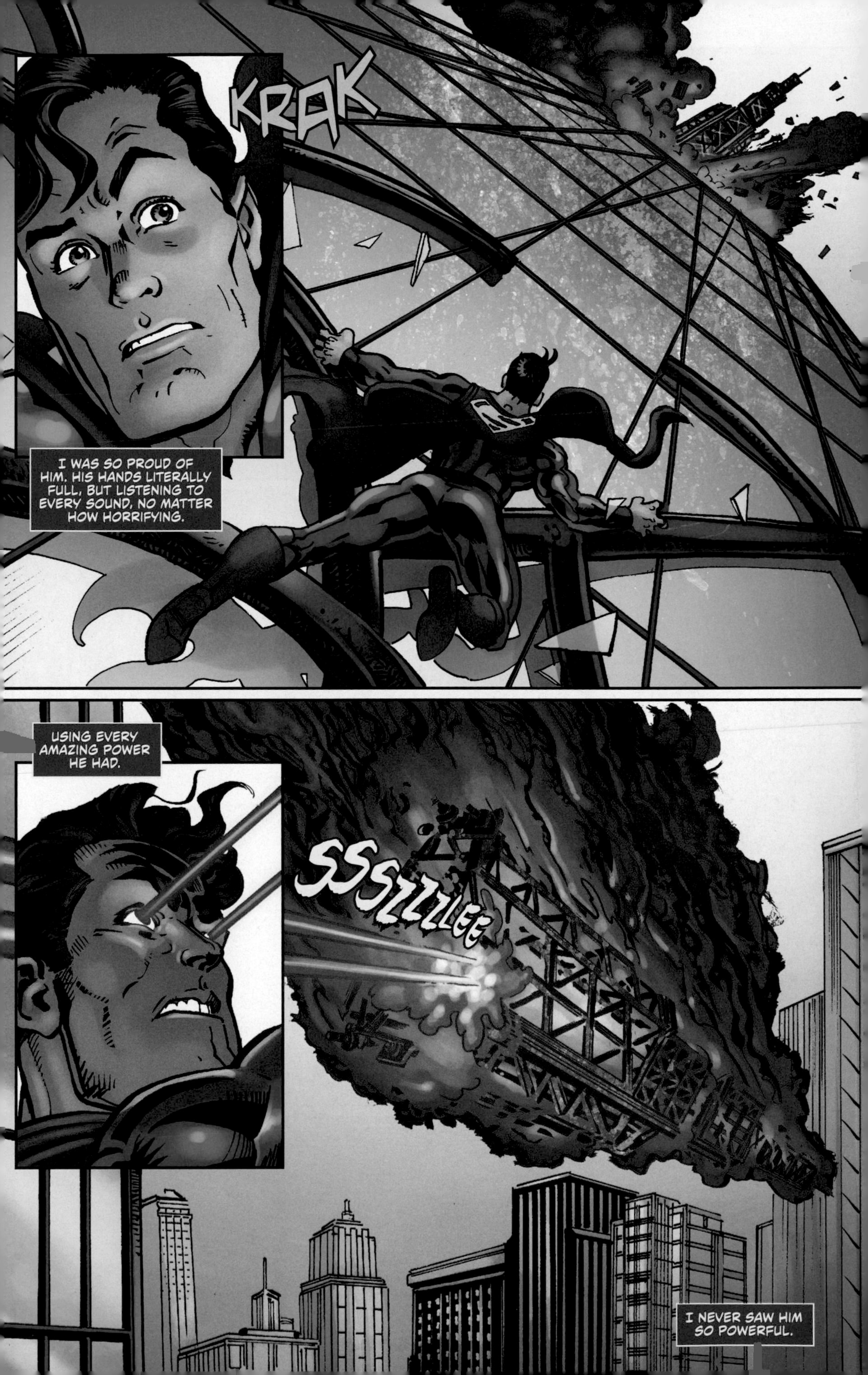
KRAK
I WAS SO PROUD OF HIM. HIS HANDS LITERALLY FULL, BUT LISTENING TO EVERY SOUND, NO MATTER HOW HORRIFYING.
USING EVERY AMAZING POWER HE HAD.
SSSZZZZLEE
I NEVER SAW HIM SO POWERFUL.

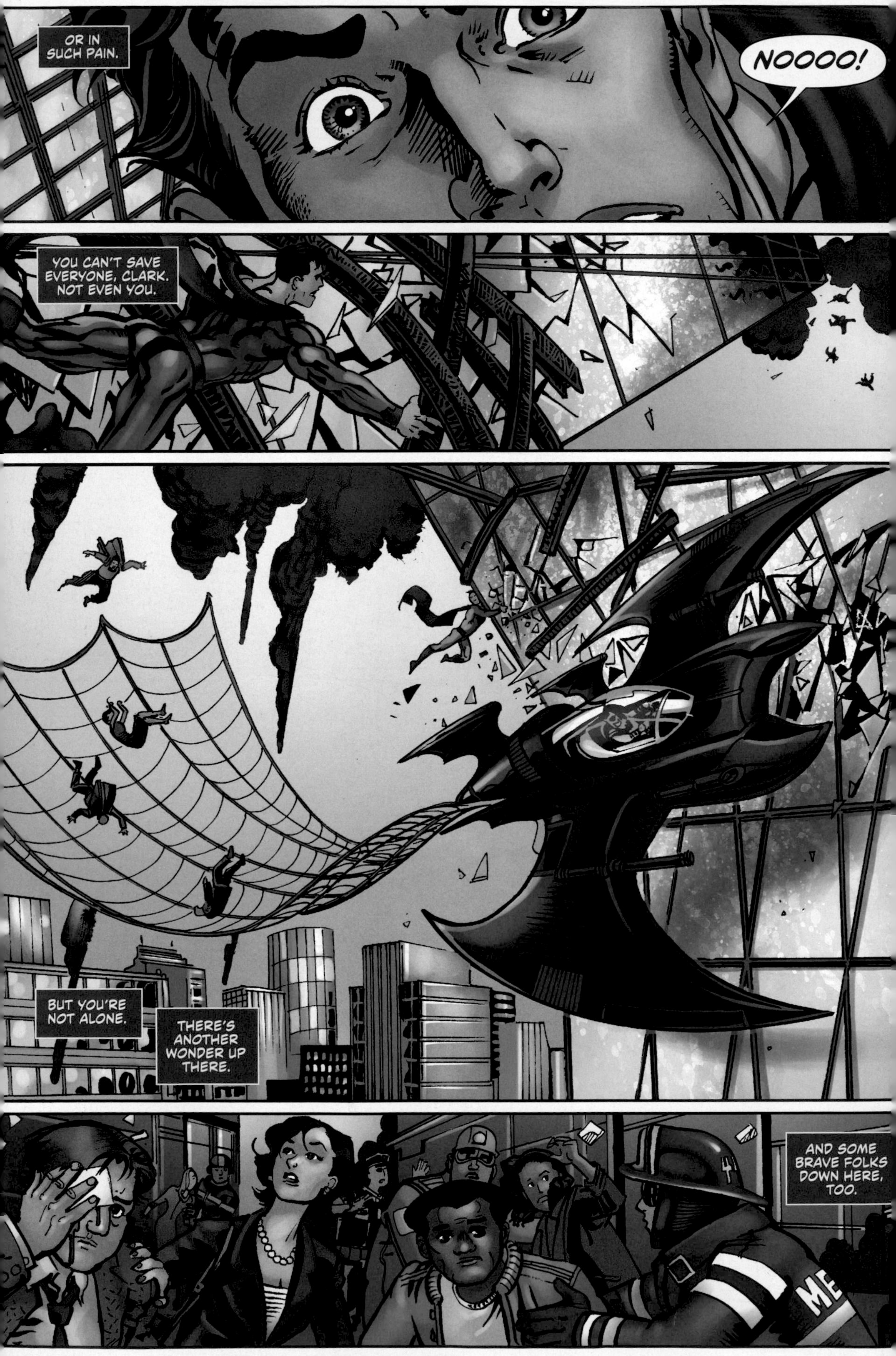
OR IN SUCH PAIN.
NOOOO!
YOU CAN'T SAVE EVERYONE, CLARK. NOT EVEN YOU.
BUT YOU'RE NOT ALONE.
THERE'S ANOTHER WONDER UP THERE.
AND SOME BRAVE FOLKS DOWN HERE, TOO.

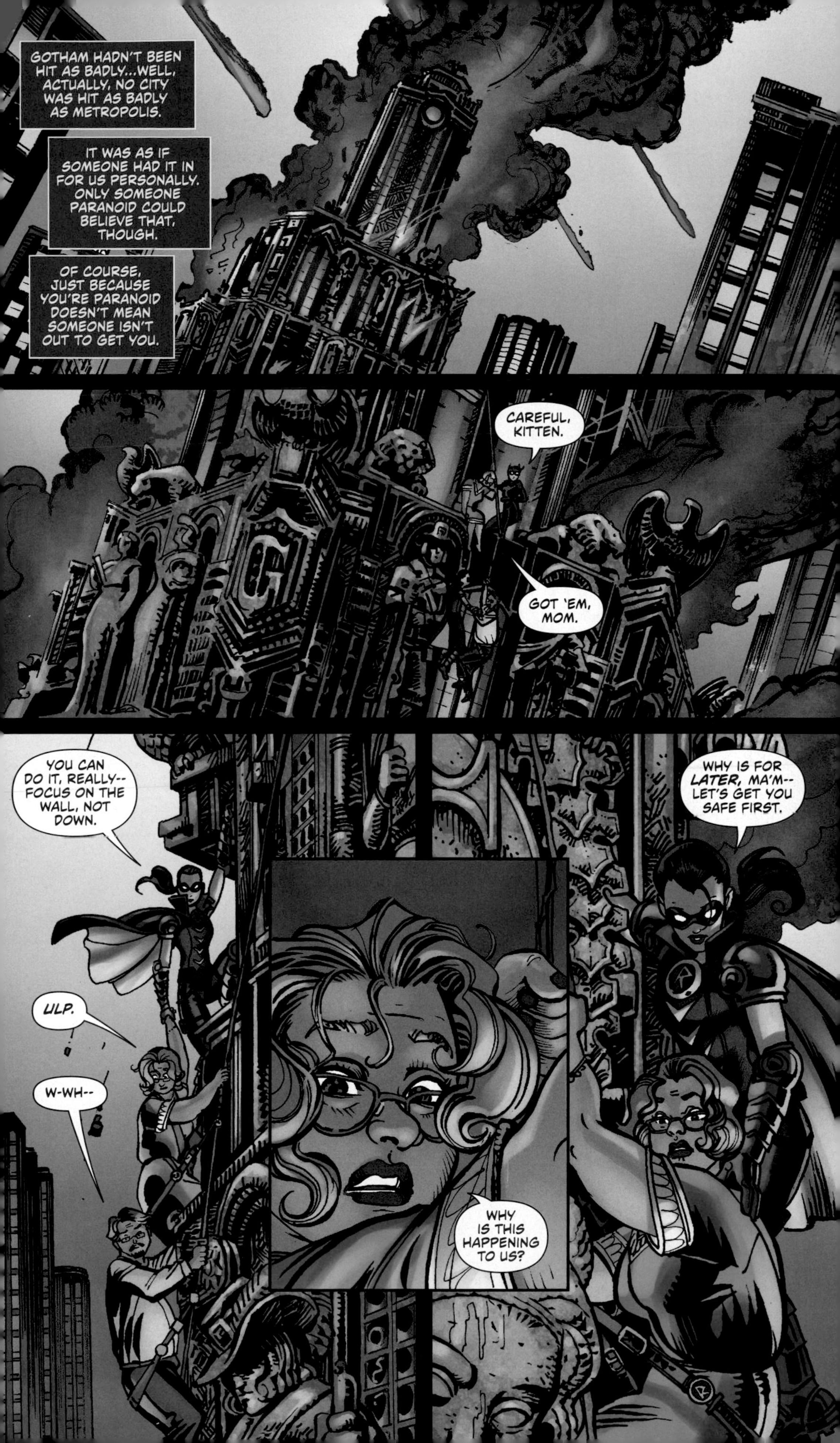
GOTHAM HADN'T BEEN HIT AS BADLY...WELL, ACTUALLY, NO CITY WAS HIT AS BADLY AS METROPOLIS.
IT WAS AS IF SOMEONE HAD IT IN FOR US PERSONALLY. ONLY SOMEONE PARANOID COULD BELIEVE THAT, THOUGH.
OF COURSE, JUST BECAUSE YOU'RE PARANOID DOESN'T MEAN SOMEONE ISN'T OUT TO GET YOU.
CAREFUL, KITTEN.
GOT 'EM, MOM.
YOU CAN DO IT, REALLY-- FOCUS ON THE WALL, NOT DOWN.
ULP.
W-WH--
WHY IS FOR LATER, MA'M-- LET'S GET YOU SAFE FIRST.
WHY IS THIS HAPPENING TO US?

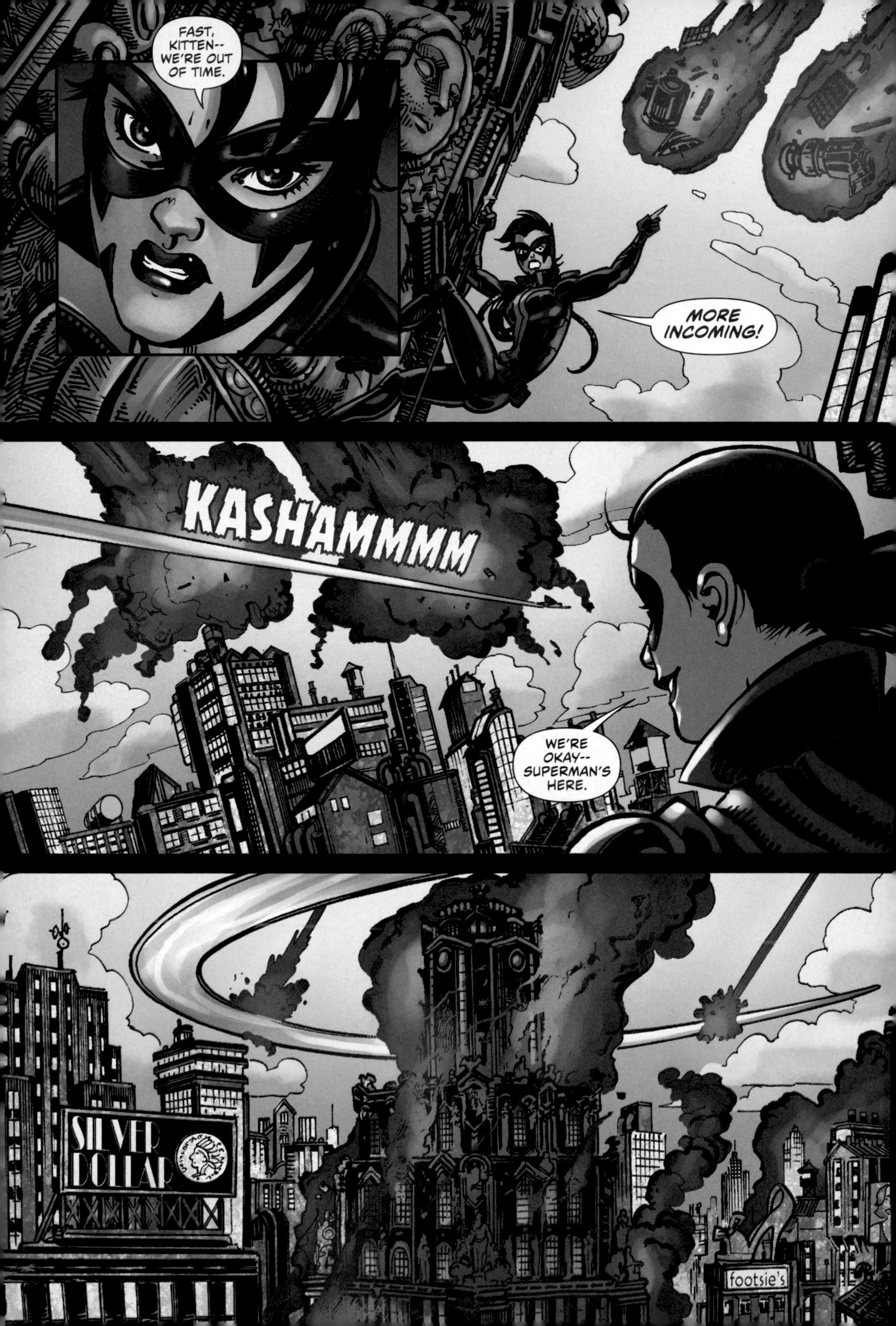
FAST, KITTEN-- WE'RE OUT OF TIME.
MORE INCOMING!
KASHAMMMM
WE'RE OKAY-- SUPERMAN'S HERE.
SILVER DOLLAR
footsie's

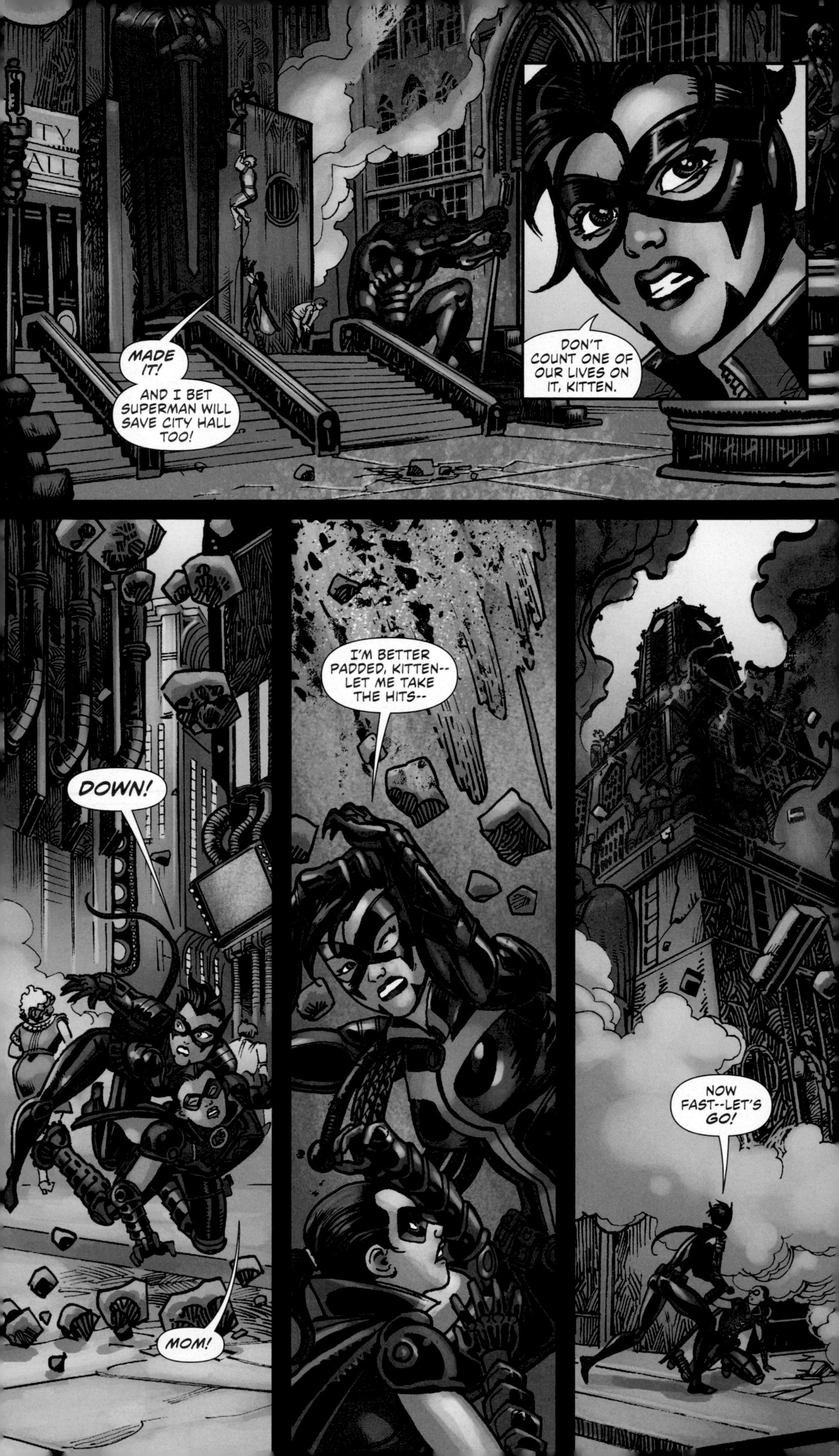
CITY HALL
MADE IT!
AND I BET SUPERMAN WILL SAVE CITY HALL TOO!
DON'T COUNT ONE OF OUR LIVES ON IT, KITTEN.
DOWN!
MOM!
I'M BETTER PADDED, KITTEN-- LET ME TAKE THE HITS--
NOW FAST--LET'S GO!

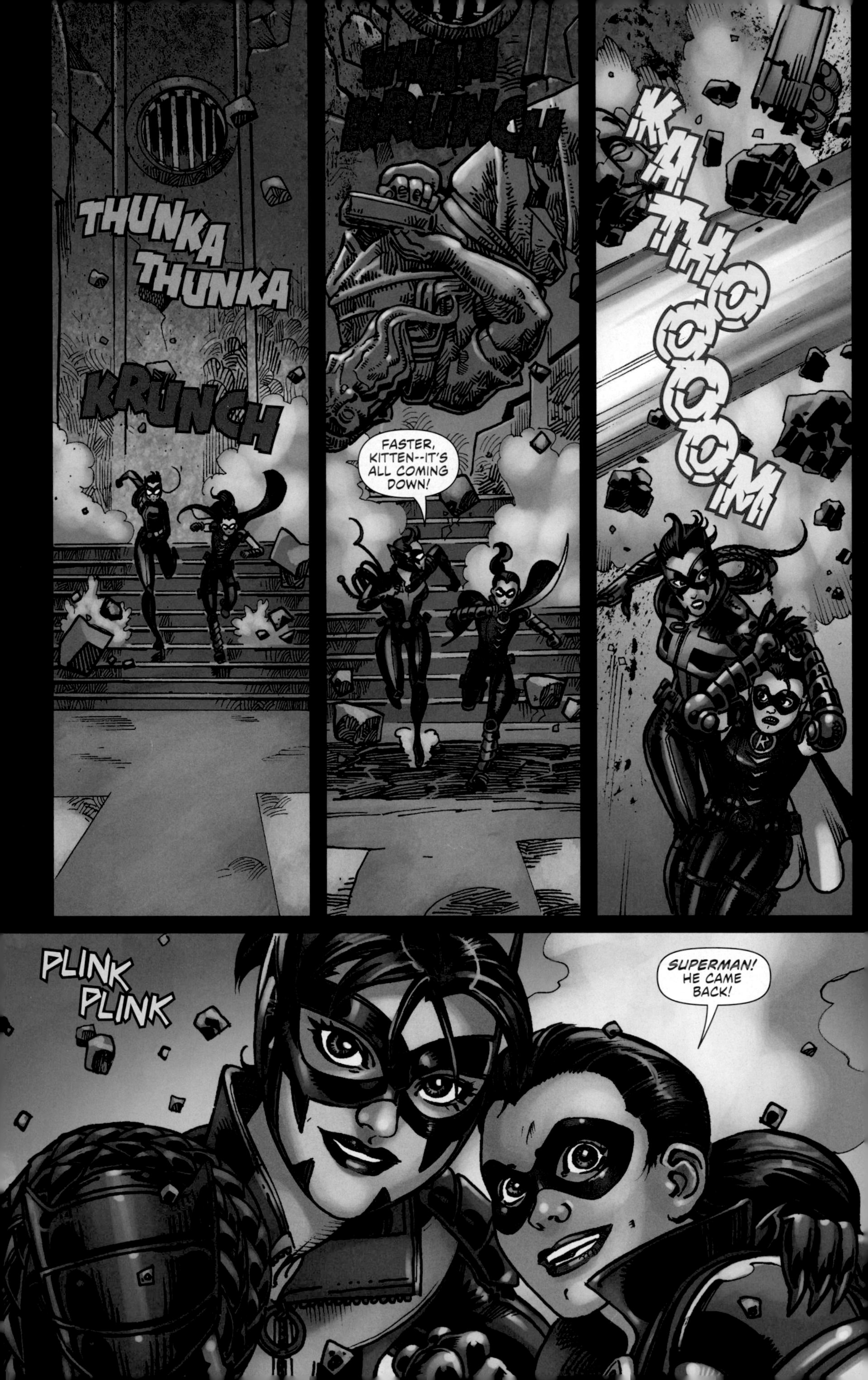
THUNKA THUNKA
KRUNCH
KRUNCH
FASTER, KITTEN--IT'S ALL COMING DOWN!
KA-THOOOOOM
PLINK PLINK
SUPERMAN! HE CAME BACK!

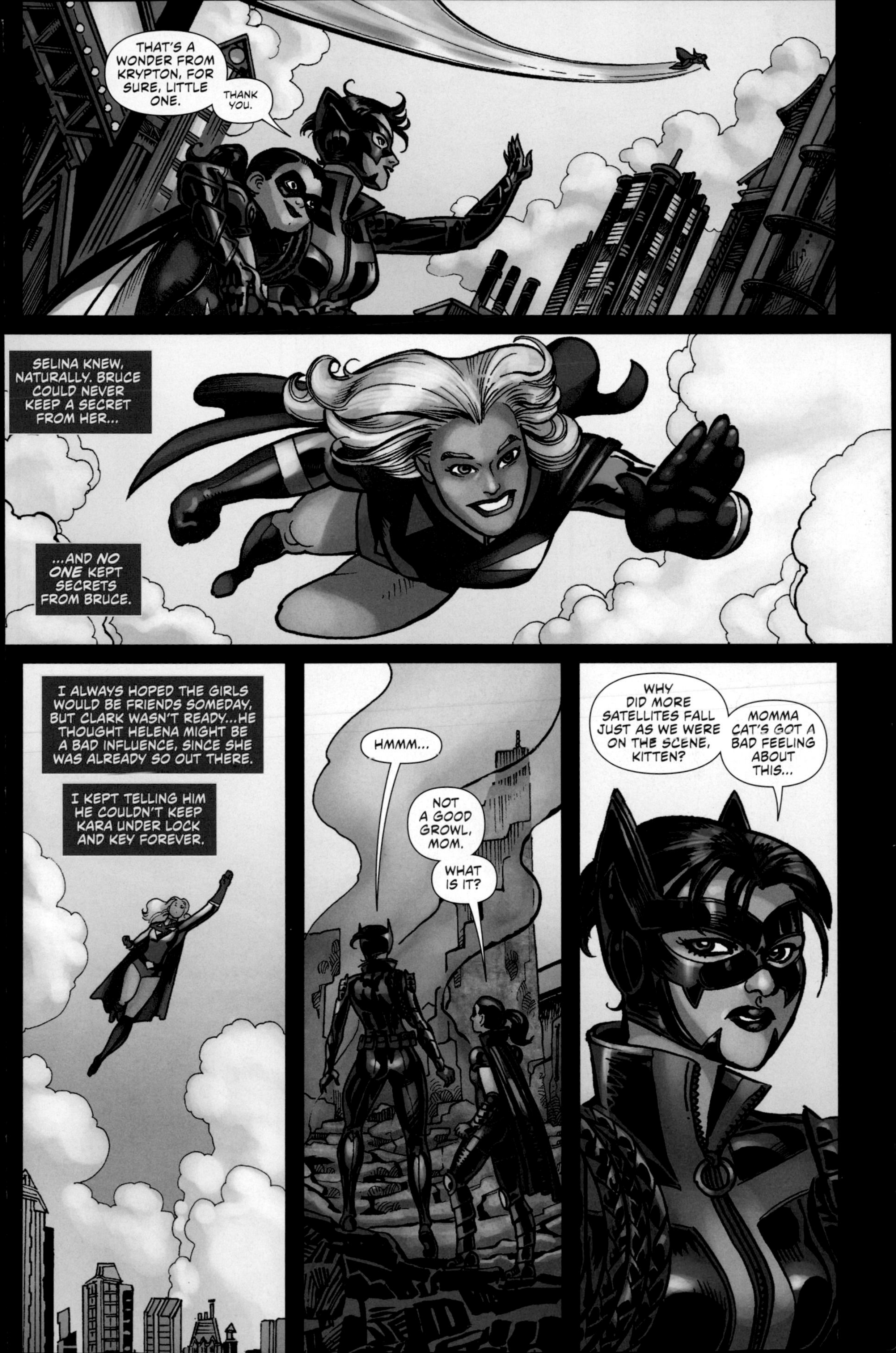
THAT'S A WONDER FROM KRYPTON, FOR SURE, LITTLE ONE.
THANK YOU.
SELINA KNEW, NATURALLY. BRUCE COULD NEVER KEEP A SECRET FROM HER...
...AND NO ONE KEPT SECRETS FROM BRUCE.
I ALWAYS HOPED THE GIRLS WOULD BE FRIENDS SOMEDAY, BUT CLARK WASN'T READY...HE THOUGHT HELENA MIGHT BE A BAD INFLUENCE, SINCE SHE WAS ALREADY SO OUT THERE.
I KEPT TELLING HIM HE COULDN'T KEEP KARA UNDER LOCK AND KEY FOREVER.
HMMM...
NOT A GOOD GROWL, MOM.
WHAT IS IT?
WHY DID MORE SATELLITES FALL JUST AS WE WERE ON THE SCENE, KITTEN?
MOMMA CAT'S GOT A BAD FEELING ABOUT THIS...

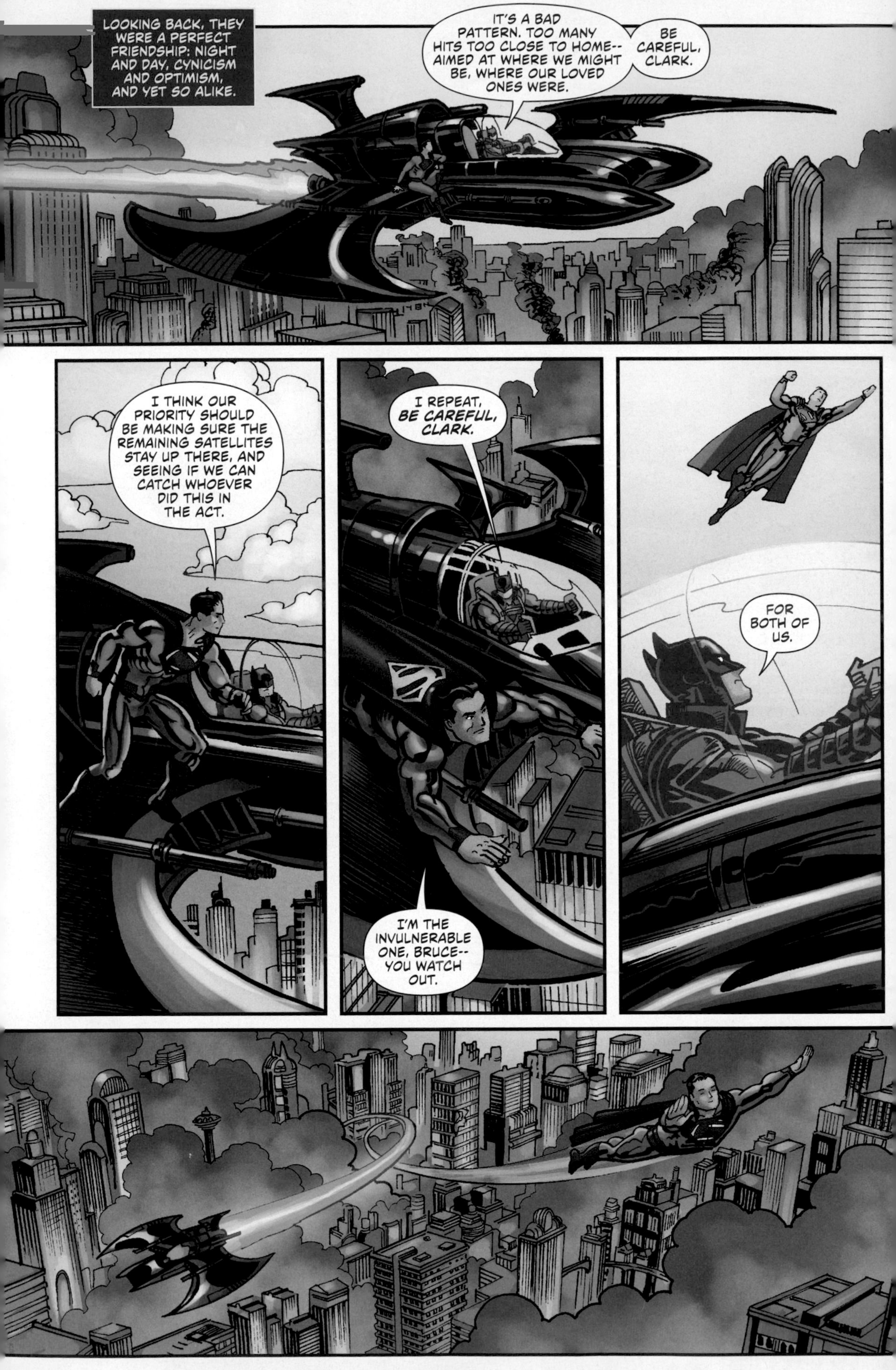
LOOKING BACK, THEY WERE A PERFECT FRIENDSHIP: NIGHT AND DAY, CYNICISM AND OPTIMISM, AND YET SO ALIKE.
IT'S A BAD PATTERN. TOO MANY HITS TOO CLOSE TO HOME-- AIMED AT WHERE WE MIGHT BE, WHERE OUR LOVED ONES WERE.
BE CAREFUL, CLARK.
I THINK OUR PRIORITY SHOULD BE MAKING SURE THE REMAINING SATELLITES STAY UP THERE, AND SEEING IF WE CAN CATCH WHOEVER DID THIS IN THE ACT.
I REPEAT, *BE CAREFUL, CLARK.*
I'M THE INVULNERABLE ONE, BRUCE-- YOU WATCH OUT.
FOR BOTH OF US.

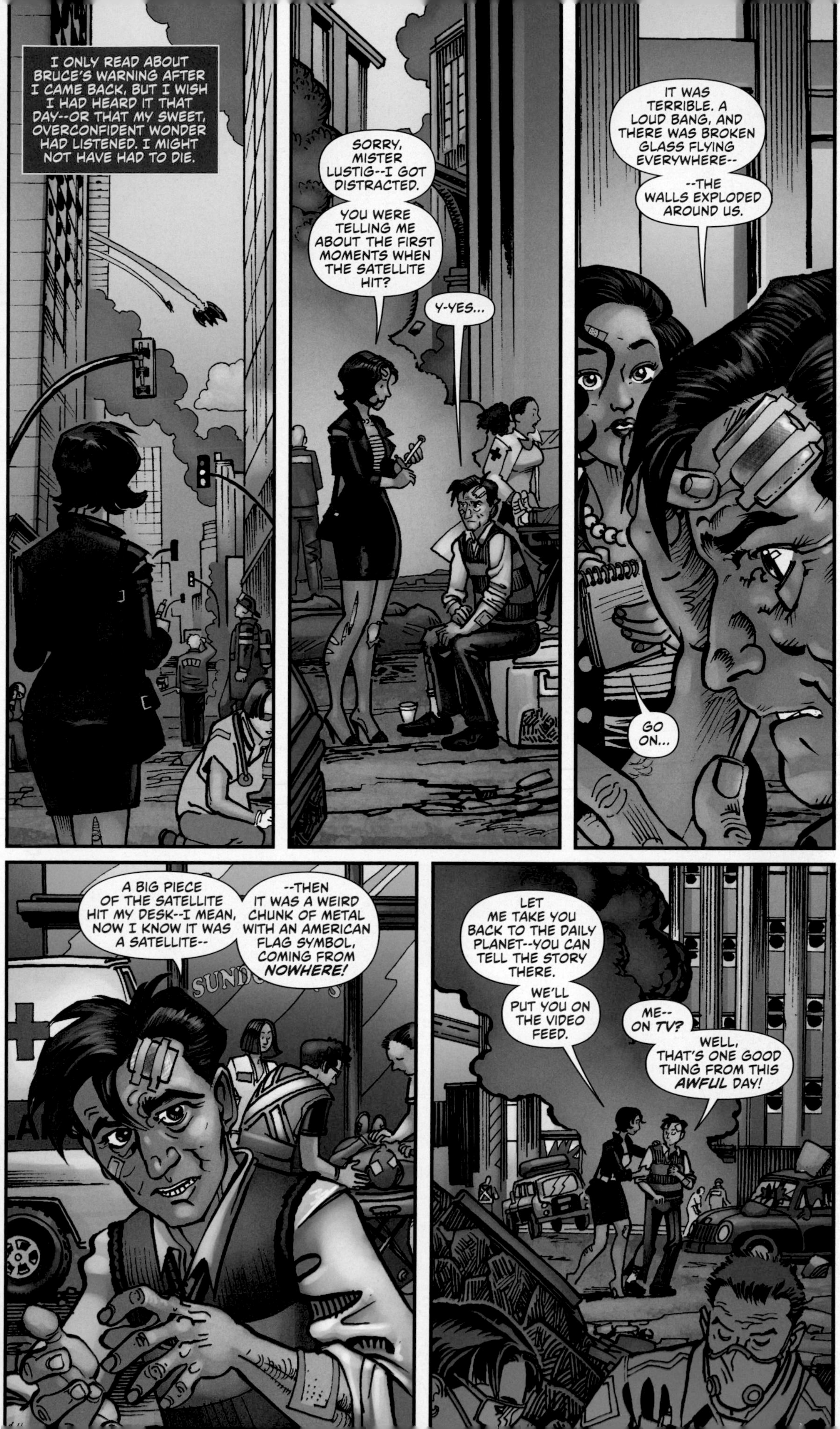
I ONLY READ ABOUT BRUCE'S WARNING AFTER I CAME BACK, BUT I WISH I HAD HEARD IT THAT DAY--OR THAT MY SWEET, OVERCONFIDENT WONDER HAD LISTENED. I MIGHT NOT HAVE HAD TO DIE.
SORRY, MISTER LUSTIG--I GOT DISTRACTED.
YOU WERE TELLING ME ABOUT THE FIRST MOMENTS WHEN THE SATELLITE HIT?
Y-YES...
IT WAS TERRIBLE. A LOUD BANG, AND THERE WAS BROKEN GLASS FLYING EVERYWHERE--
--THE WALLS EXPLODED AROUND US.
GO ON...
A BIG PIECE OF THE SATELLITE HIT MY DESK--I MEAN, NOW I KNOW IT WAS A SATELLITE--
--THEN IT WAS A WEIRD CHUNK OF METAL WITH AN AMERICAN FLAG SYMBOL, COMING FROM *NOWHERE!*
LET ME TAKE YOU BACK TO THE DAILY PLANET--YOU CAN TELL THE STORY THERE.
WE'LL PUT YOU ON THE VIDEO FEED.
ME-- ON *TV?*
WELL, THAT'S ONE GOOD THING FROM THIS *AWFUL* DAY!

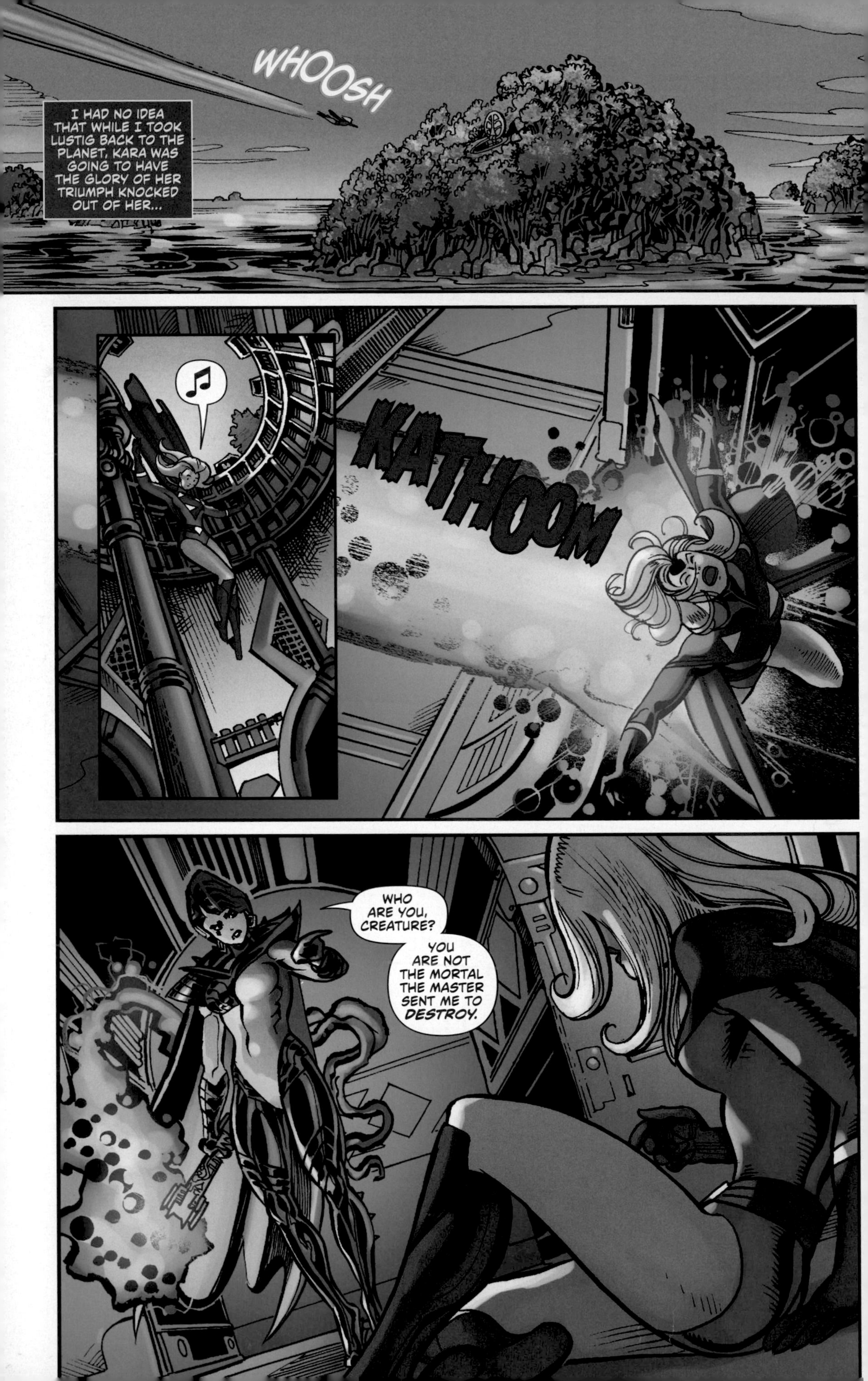
WHOOSH
I HAD NO IDEA THAT WHILE I TOOK LUSTIG BACK TO THE PLANET, KARA WAS GOING TO HAVE THE GLORY OF HER TRIUMPH KNOCKED OUT OF HER...
♫
KATHOOM
WHO ARE YOU, CREATURE?
YOU ARE NOT THE MORTAL THE MASTER SENT ME TO DESTROY.

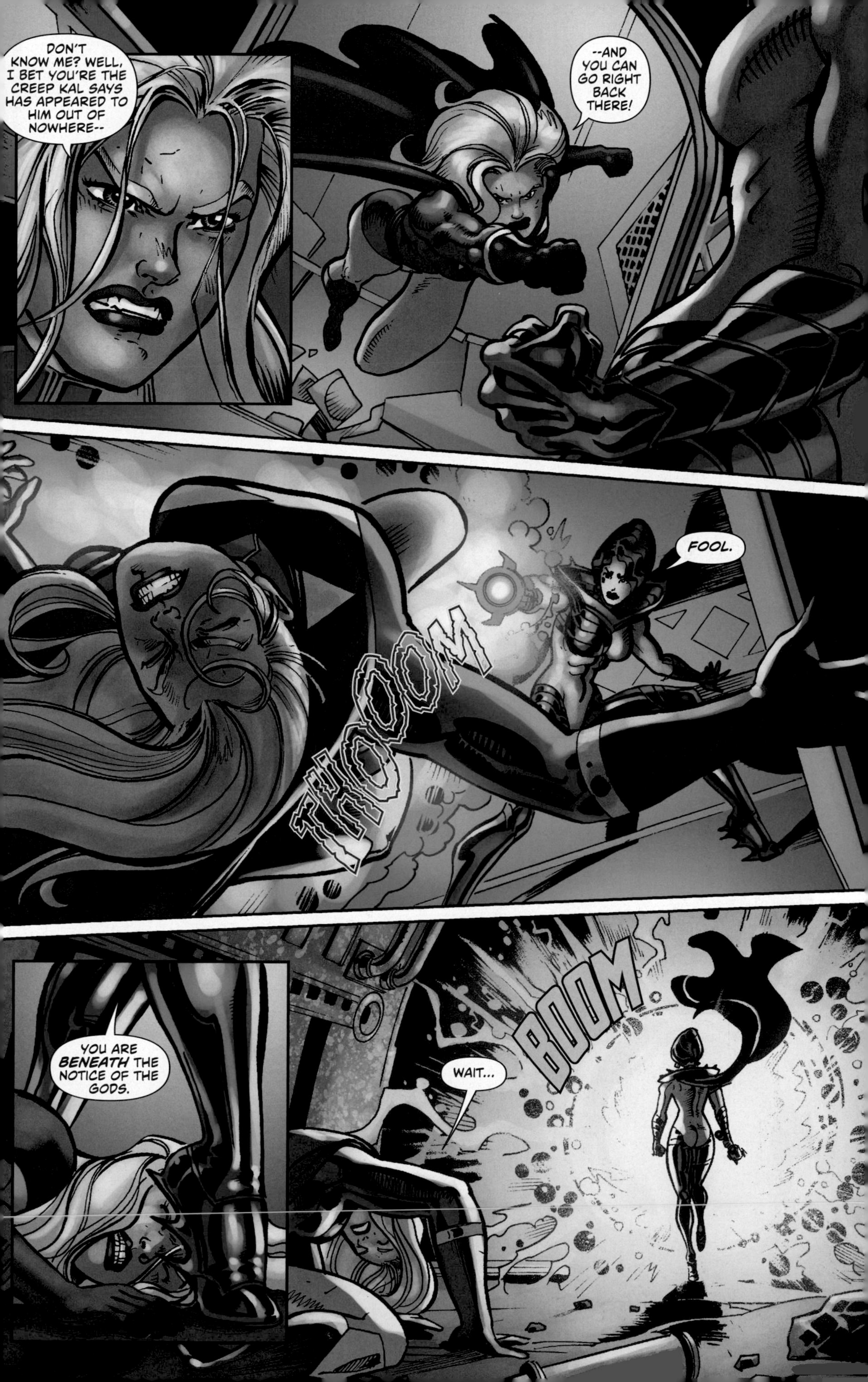
DON'T KNOW ME? WELL, I BET YOU'RE THE CREEP KAL SAYS HAS APPEARED TO HIM OUT OF NOWHERE--
--AND YOU CAN GO RIGHT BACK THERE!
FOOL.
THOOOM
YOU ARE BENEATH THE NOTICE OF THE GODS.
BOOM
WAIT...

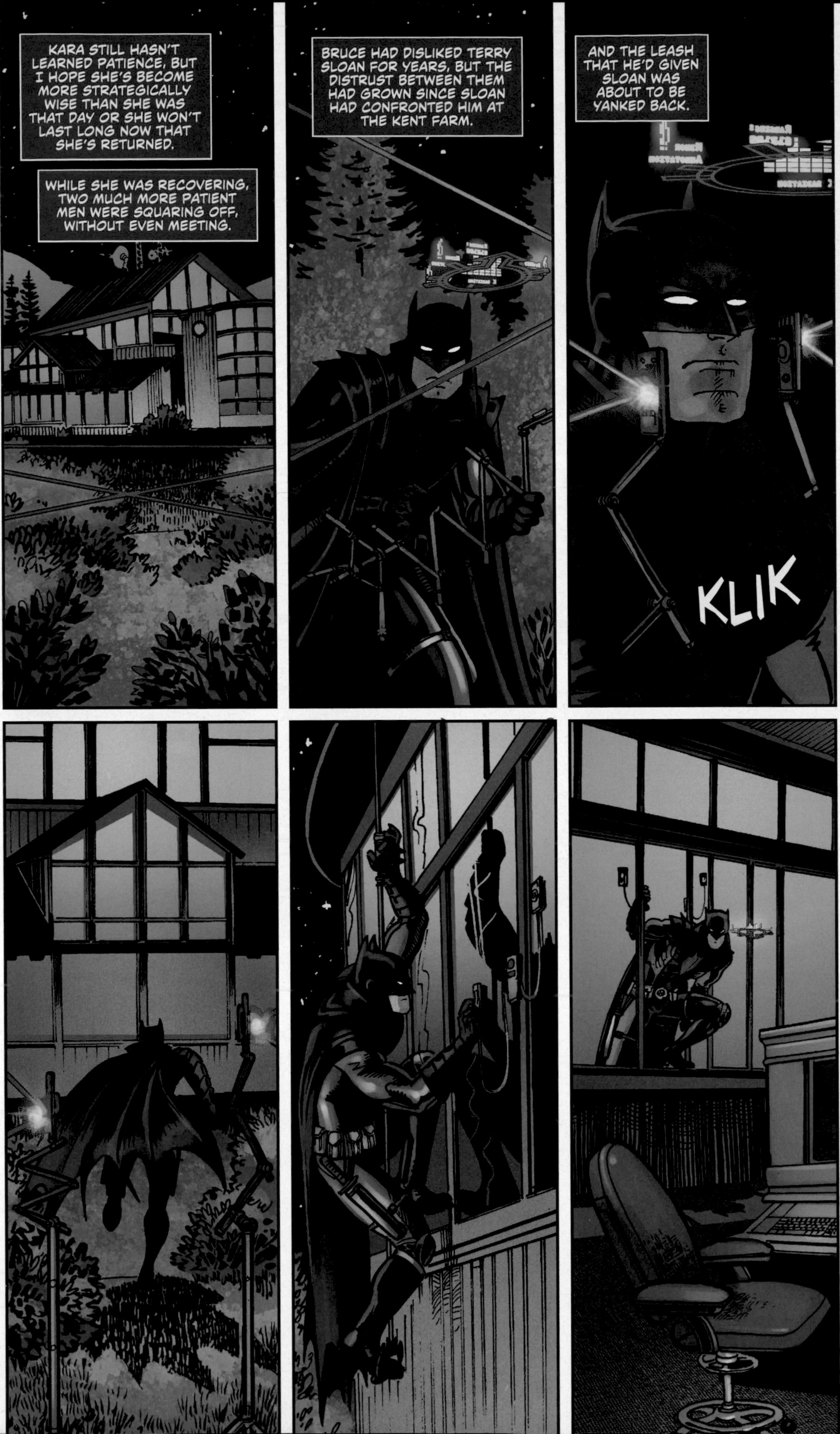
KARA STILL HASN'T LEARNED PATIENCE, BUT I HOPE SHE'S BECOME MORE STRATEGICALLY WISE THAN SHE WAS THAT DAY OR SHE WON'T LAST LONG NOW THAT SHE'S RETURNED.
WHILE SHE WAS RECOVERING, TWO MUCH MORE PATIENT MEN WERE SQUARING OFF, WITHOUT EVEN MEETING.
BRUCE HAD DISLIKED TERRY SLOAN FOR YEARS, BUT THE DISTRUST BETWEEN THEM HAD GROWN SINCE SLOAN HAD CONFRONTED HIM AT THE KENT FARM.
AND THE LEASH THAT HE'D GIVEN SLOAN WAS ABOUT TO BE YANKED BACK.
KLIK

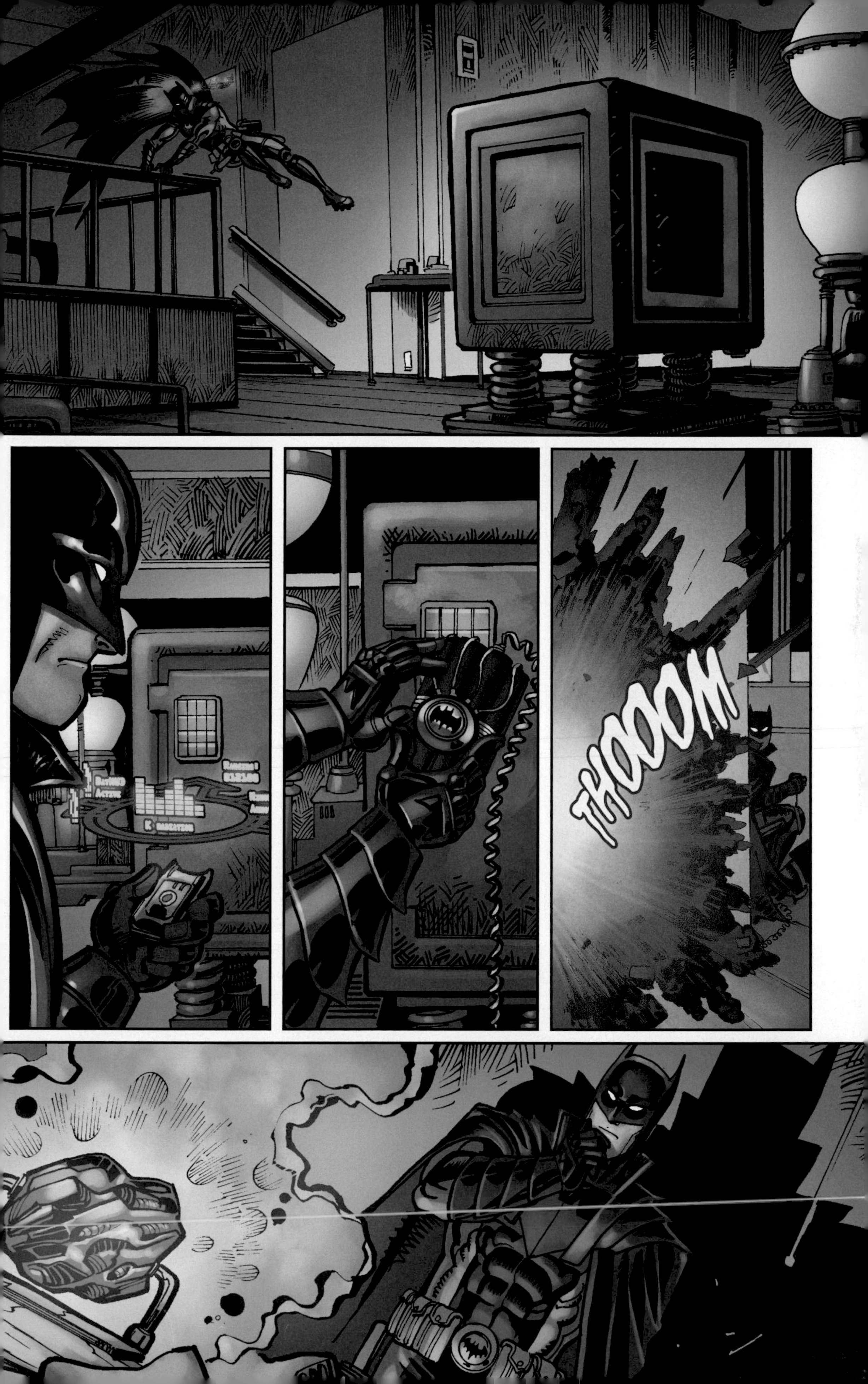
ACTIVE
THOOOM

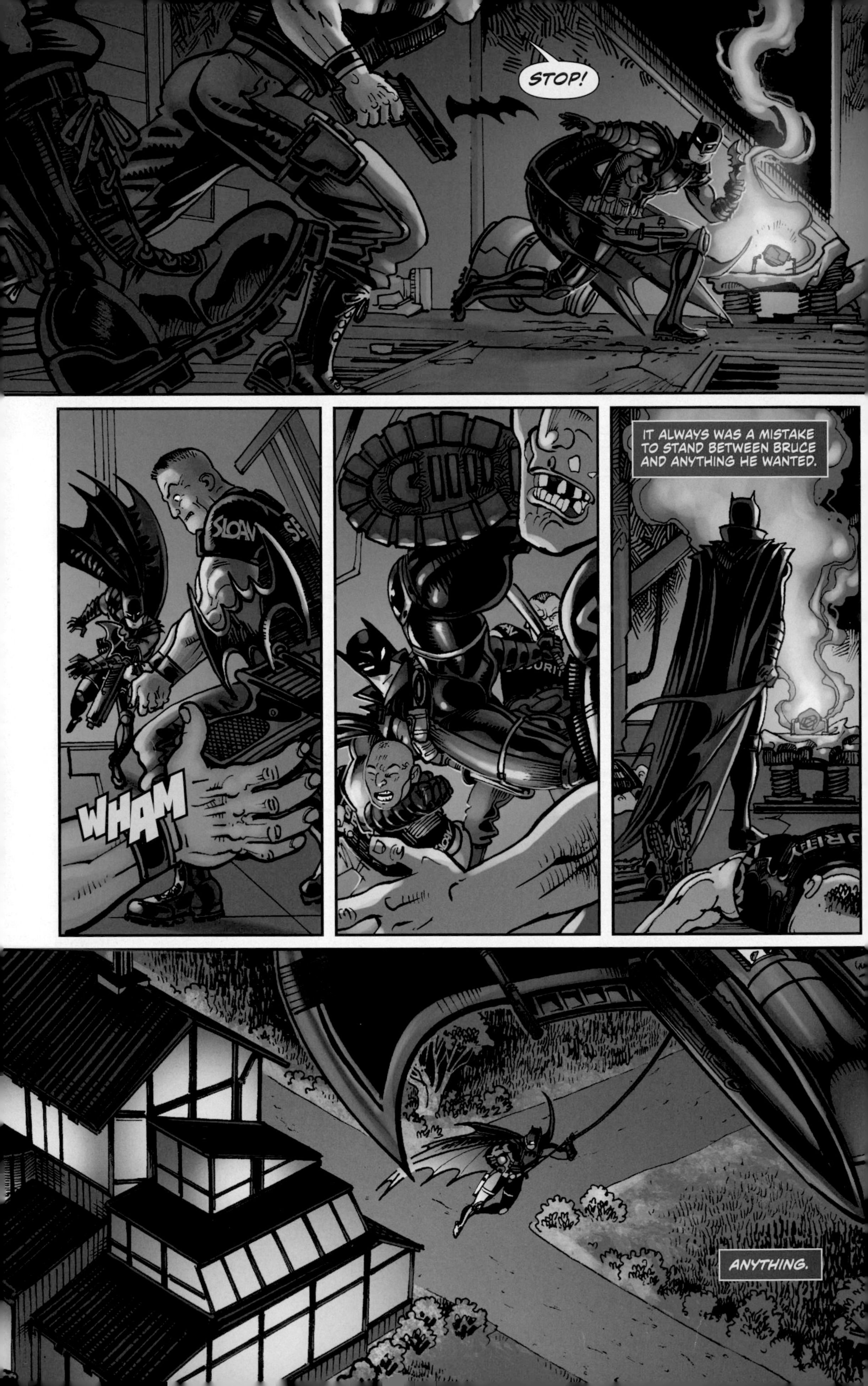
STOP!
WHAM
IT ALWAYS WAS A MISTAKE TO STAND BETWEEN BRUCE AND ANYTHING HE WANTED.
ANYTHING.

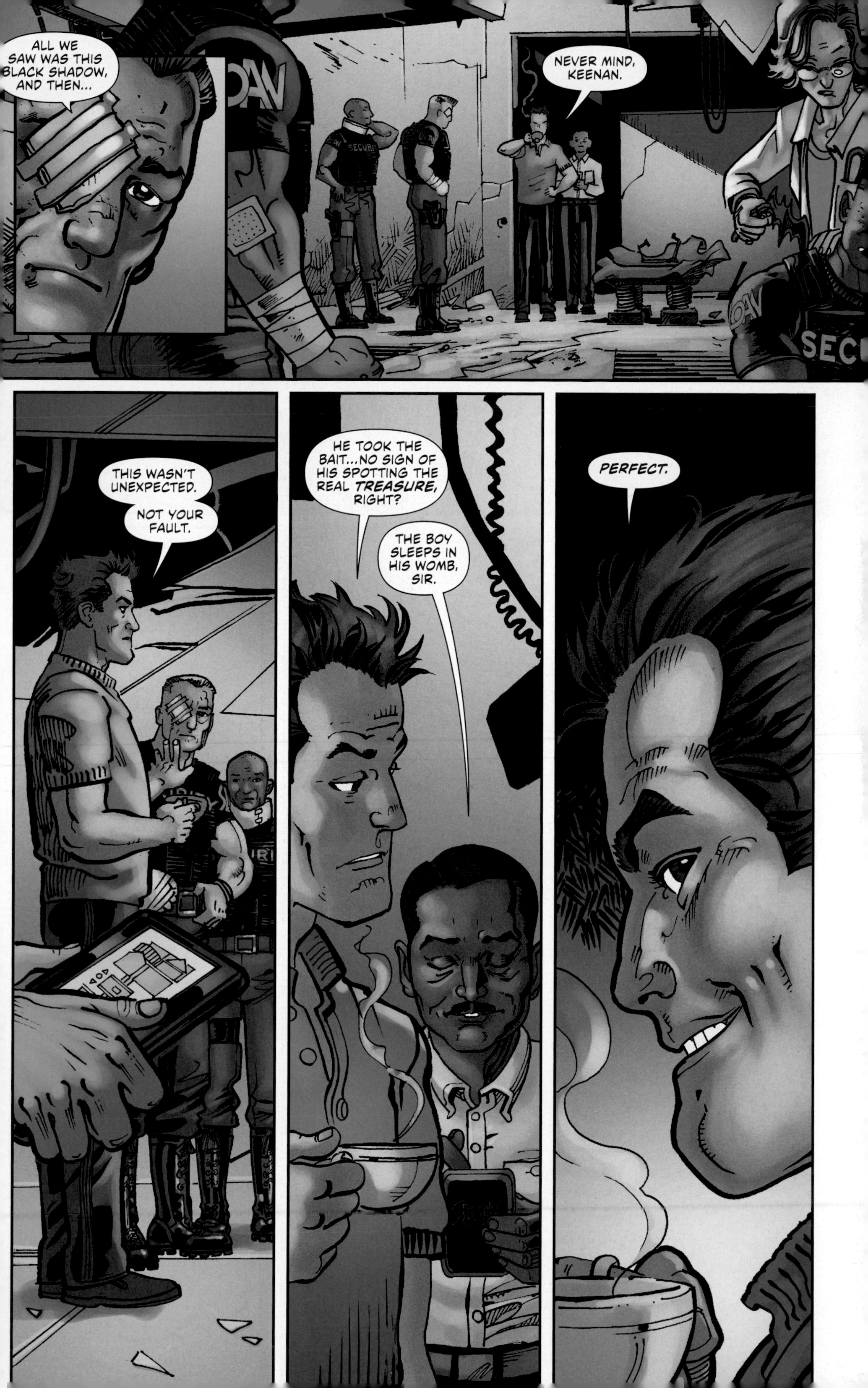
ALL WE SAW WAS THIS BLACK SHADOW, AND THEN...
NEVER MIND, KEENAN.
THIS WASN'T UNEXPECTED.
NOT YOUR FAULT.
HE TOOK THE BAIT...NO SIGN OF HIS SPOTTING THE REAL TREASURE, RIGHT?
THE BOY SLEEPS IN HIS WOMB, SIR.
PERFECT.

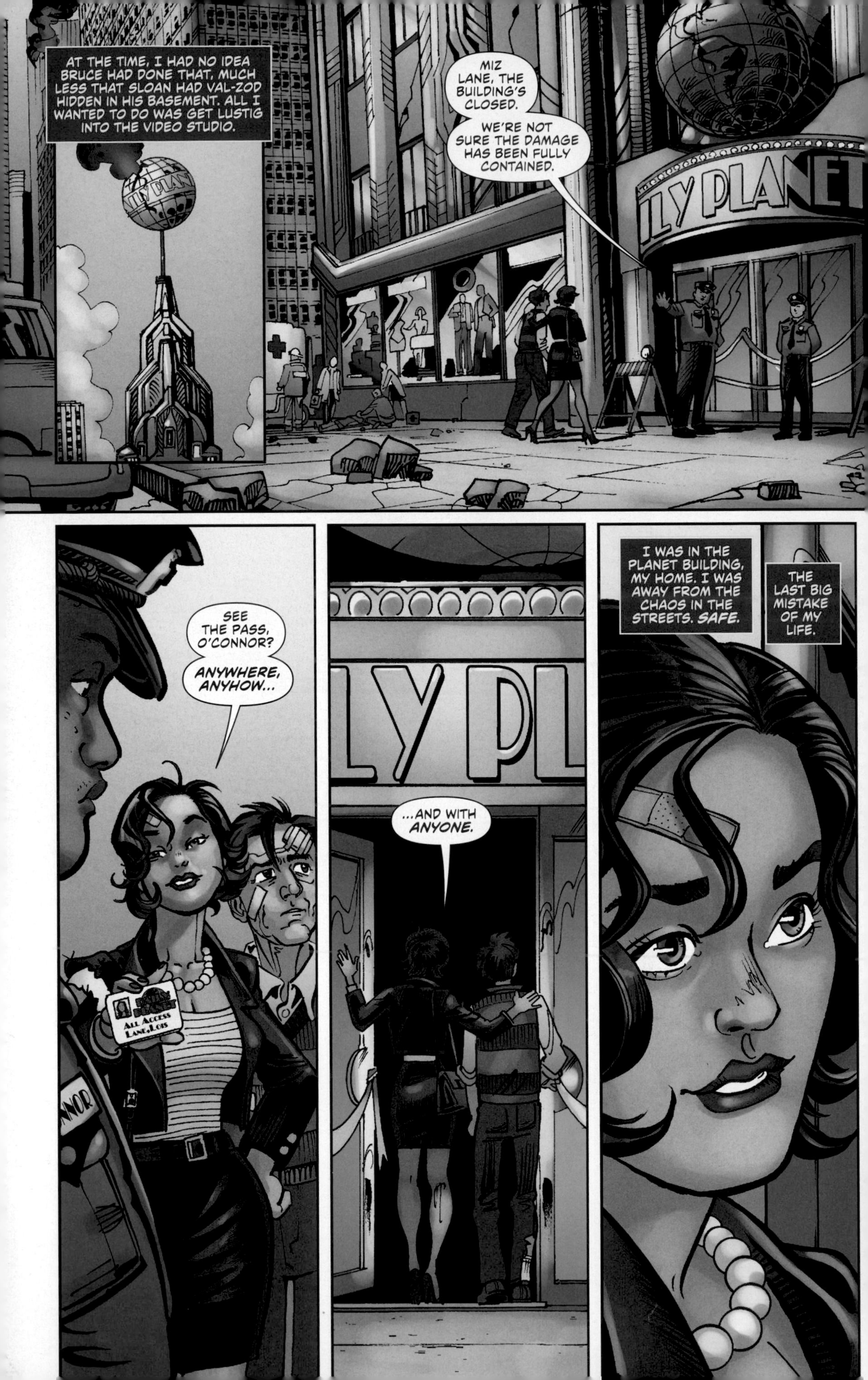
AT THE TIME, I HAD NO IDEA BRUCE HAD DONE THAT, MUCH LESS THAT SLOAN HAD VAL-ZOD HIDDEN IN HIS BASEMENT. ALL I WANTED TO DO WAS GET LUSTIG INTO THE VIDEO STUDIO.
MIZ LANE, THE BUILDING'S CLOSED.
WE'RE NOT SURE THE DAMAGE HAS BEEN FULLY CONTAINED.
SEE THE PASS, O'CONNOR?
ANYWHERE, ANYHOW...
ALL ACCESS
LANE, LOIS
...AND WITH *ANYONE.*
I WAS IN THE PLANET BUILDING, MY HOME. I WAS AWAY FROM THE CHAOS IN THE STREETS. *SAFE.*
THE LAST BIG MISTAKE OF MY LIFE.

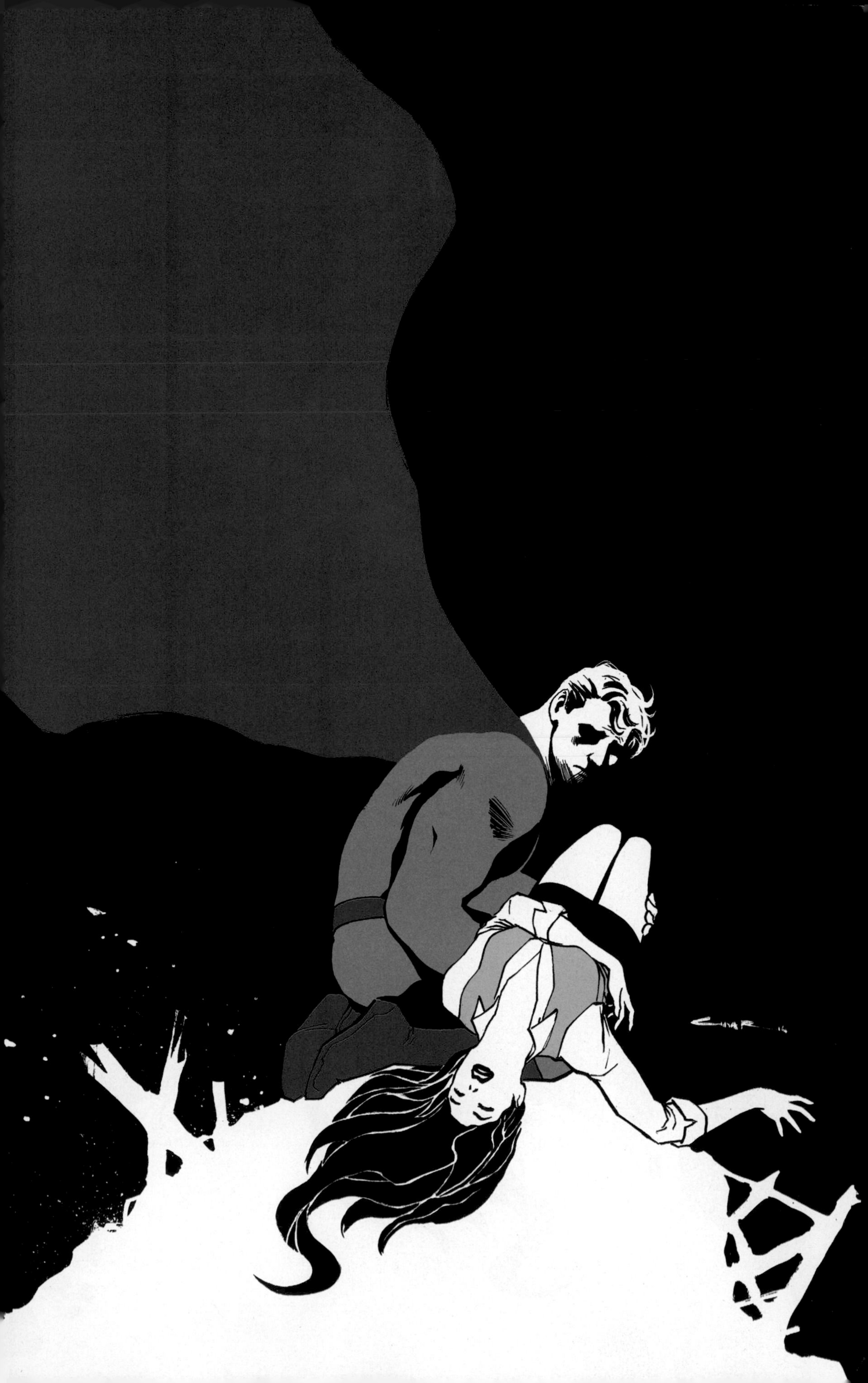

PART SIX: DOOMS

PAUL LEVITZ writer **JED DOUGHERTY** artist **CHRIS SOTOMAYOR** colorist
TRAVIS LANHAM letterer cover art by **YILDIRAY CINAR**

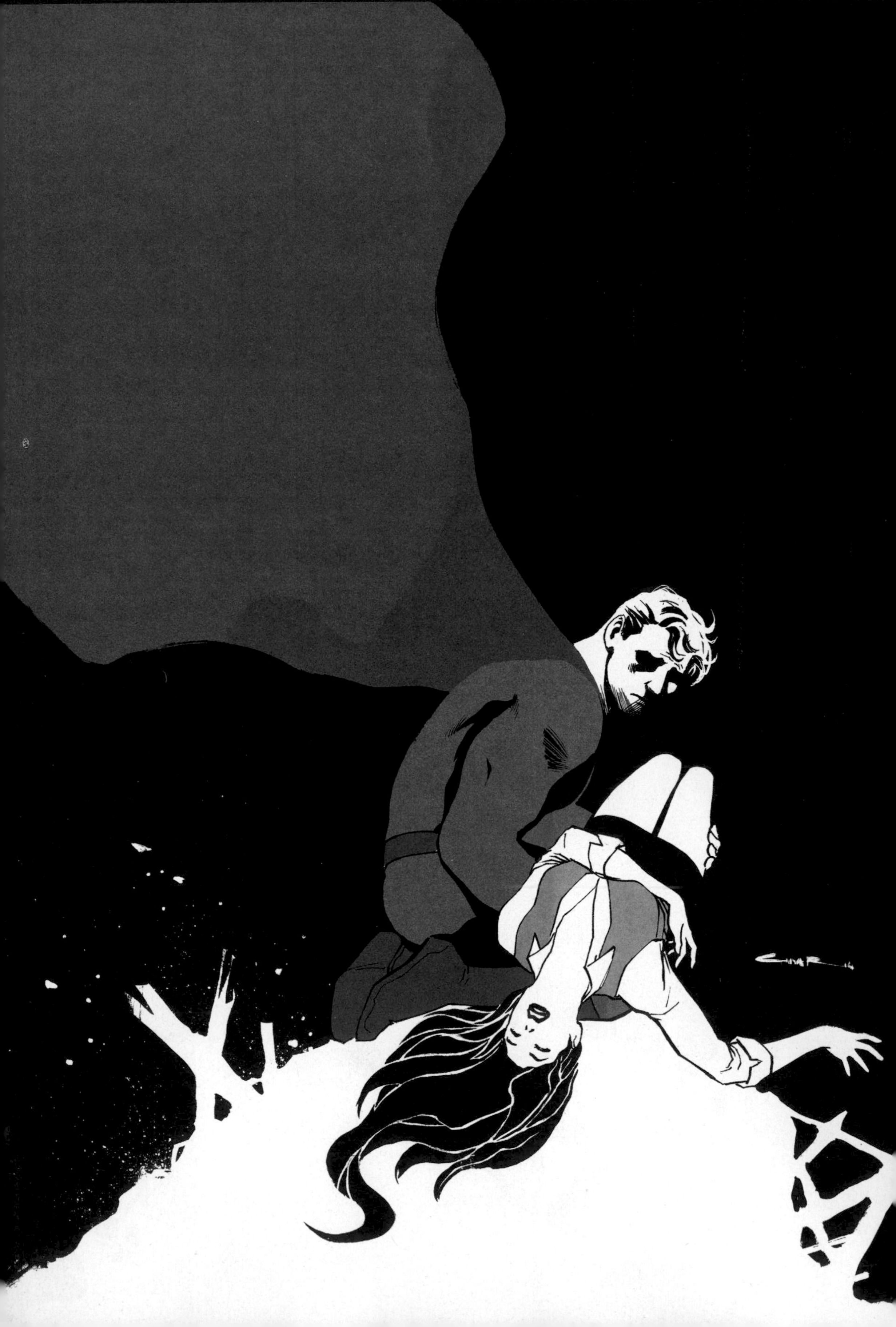

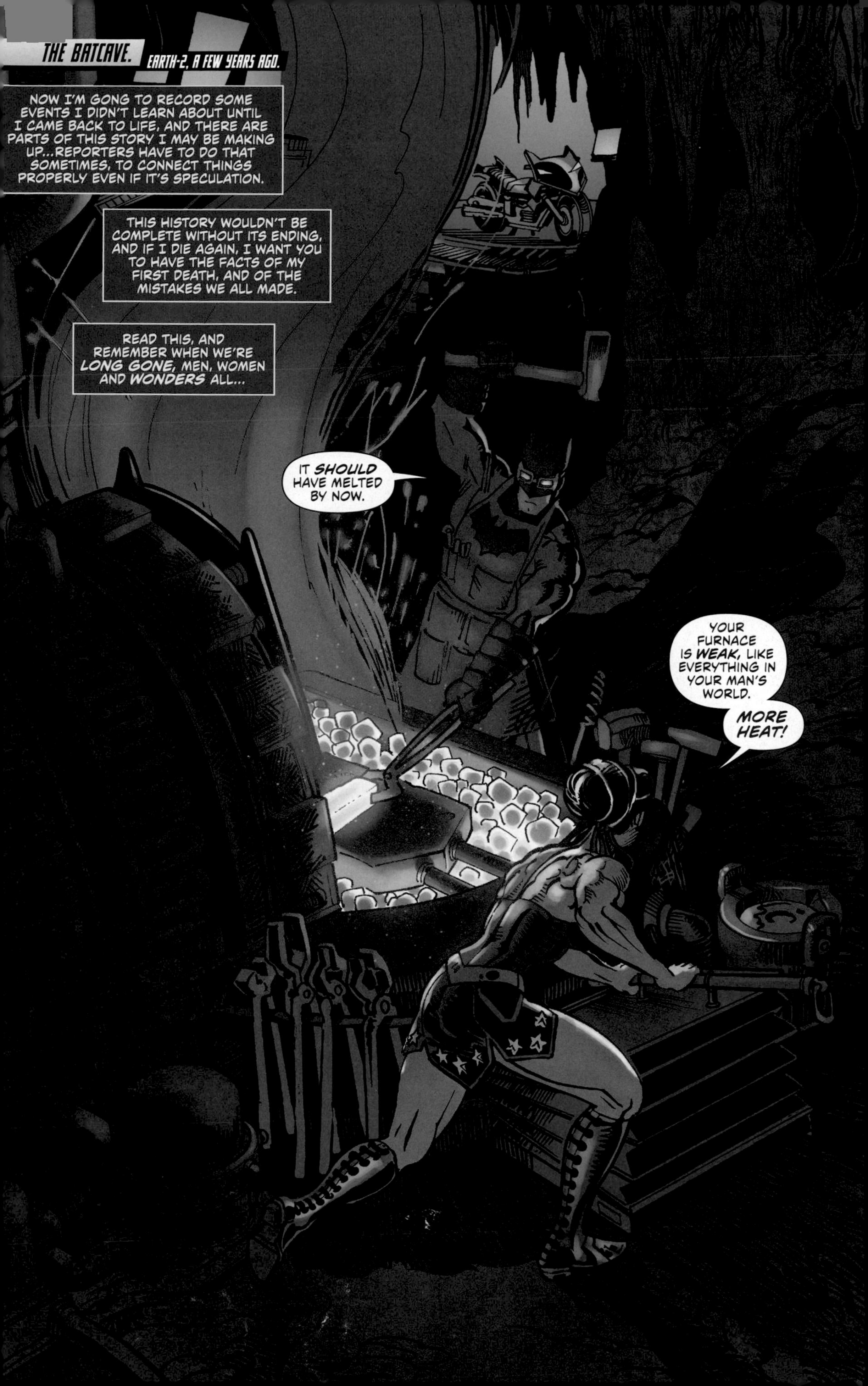
THE BATCAVE.
EARTH-2, A FEW YEARS AGO.
NOW I'M GONG TO RECORD SOME EVENTS I DIDN'T LEARN ABOUT UNTIL I CAME BACK TO LIFE, AND THERE ARE PARTS OF THIS STORY I MAY BE MAKING UP...REPORTERS HAVE TO DO THAT SOMETIMES, TO CONNECT THINGS PROPERLY EVEN IF IT'S SPECULATION.
THIS HISTORY WOULDN'T BE COMPLETE WITHOUT ITS ENDING, AND IF I DIE AGAIN, I WANT YOU TO HAVE THE FACTS OF MY FIRST DEATH, AND OF THE MISTAKES WE ALL MADE.
READ THIS, AND REMEMBER WHEN WE'RE LONG GONE, MEN, WOMEN AND WONDERS ALL...
IT SHOULD HAVE MELTED BY NOW.
YOUR FURNACE IS WEAK, LIKE EVERYTHING IN YOUR MAN'S WORLD.
MORE HEAT!

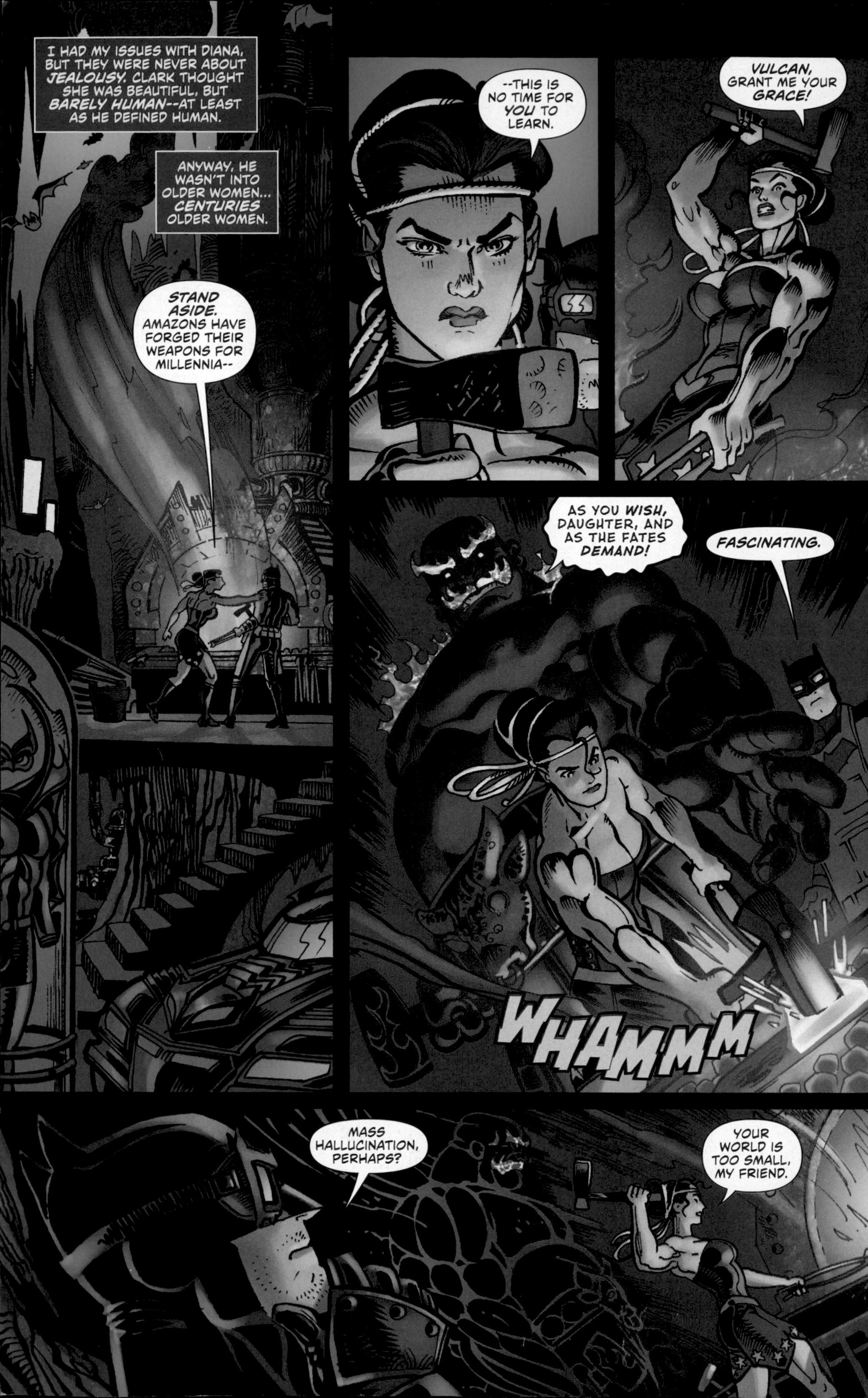
I HAD MY ISSUES WITH DIANA, BUT THEY WERE NEVER ABOUT JEALOUSY. CLARK THOUGHT SHE WAS BEAUTIFUL, BUT BARELY HUMAN--AT LEAST AS HE DEFINED HUMAN.
ANYWAY, HE WASN'T INTO OLDER WOMEN... CENTURIES OLDER WOMEN.
STAND ASIDE. AMAZONS HAVE FORGED THEIR WEAPONS FOR MILLENNIA--
--THIS IS NO TIME FOR YOU TO LEARN.
VULCAN, GRANT ME YOUR GRACE!
AS YOU WISH, DAUGHTER, AND AS THE FATES DEMAND!
FASCINATING.
WHAMMMM
MASS HALLUCINATION, PERHAPS?
YOUR WORLD IS TOO SMALL, MY FRIEND.

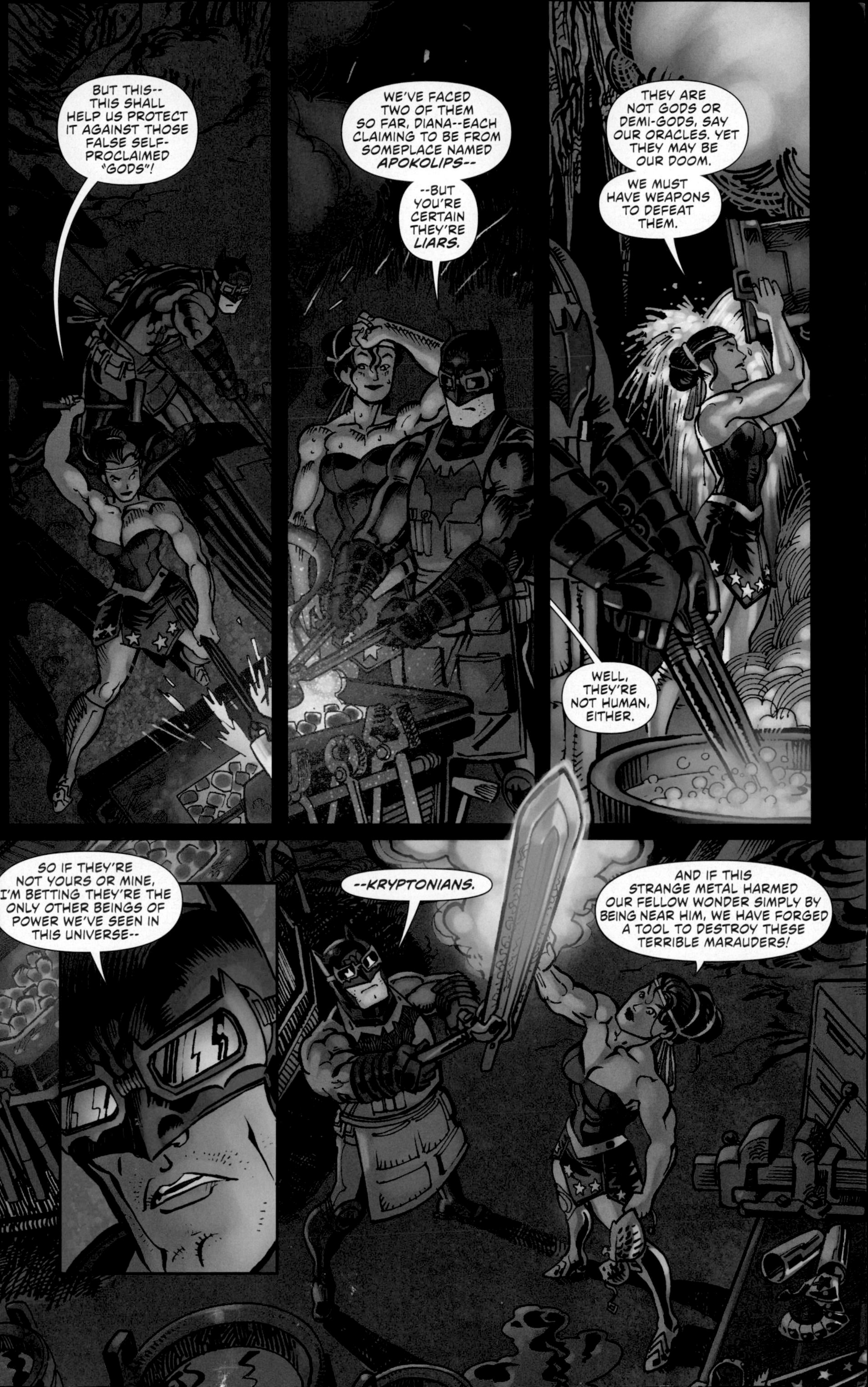
BUT THIS-- THIS SHALL HELP US PROTECT IT AGAINST THOSE FALSE SELF-PROCLAIMED "GODS"!
WE'VE FACED TWO OF THEM SO FAR, DIANA--EACH CLAIMING TO BE FROM SOMEPLACE NAMED APOKOLIPS--
--BUT YOU'RE CERTAIN THEY'RE LIARS.
THEY ARE NOT GODS OR DEMI-GODS, SAY OUR ORACLES. YET THEY MAY BE OUR DOOM.
WE MUST HAVE WEAPONS TO DEFEAT THEM.
WELL, THEY'RE NOT HUMAN, EITHER.
SO IF THEY'RE NOT YOURS OR MINE, I'M BETTING THEY'RE THE ONLY OTHER BEINGS OF POWER WE'VE SEEN IN THIS UNIVERSE--
--KRYPTONIANS.
AND IF THIS STRANGE METAL HARMED OUR FELLOW WONDER SIMPLY BY BEING NEAR HIM, WE HAVE FORGED A TOOL TO DESTROY THESE TERRIBLE MARAUDERS!

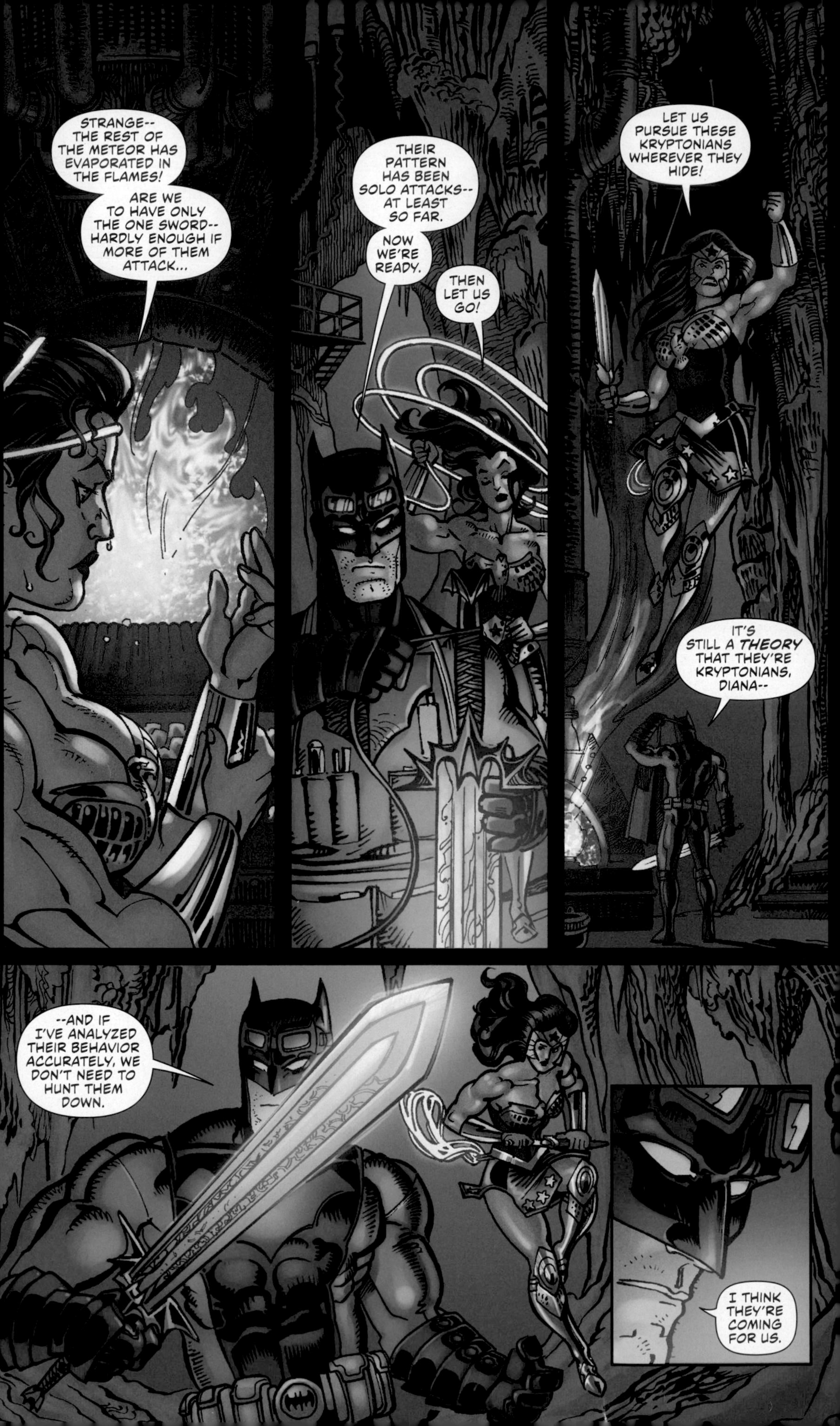
STRANGE-- THE REST OF THE METEOR HAS EVAPORATED IN THE FLAMES!
ARE WE TO HAVE ONLY THE ONE SWORD-- HARDLY ENOUGH IF MORE OF THEM ATTACK...
THEIR PATTERN HAS BEEN SOLO ATTACKS-- AT LEAST SO FAR.
NOW WE'RE READY.
THEN LET US GO!
LET US PURSUE THESE KRYPTONIANS WHEREVER THEY HIDE!
IT'S STILL A THEORY THAT THEY'RE KRYPTONIANS, DIANA--
--AND IF I'VE ANALYZED THEIR BEHAVIOR ACCURATELY, WE DON'T NEED TO HUNT THEM DOWN.
I THINK THEY'RE COMING FOR US.

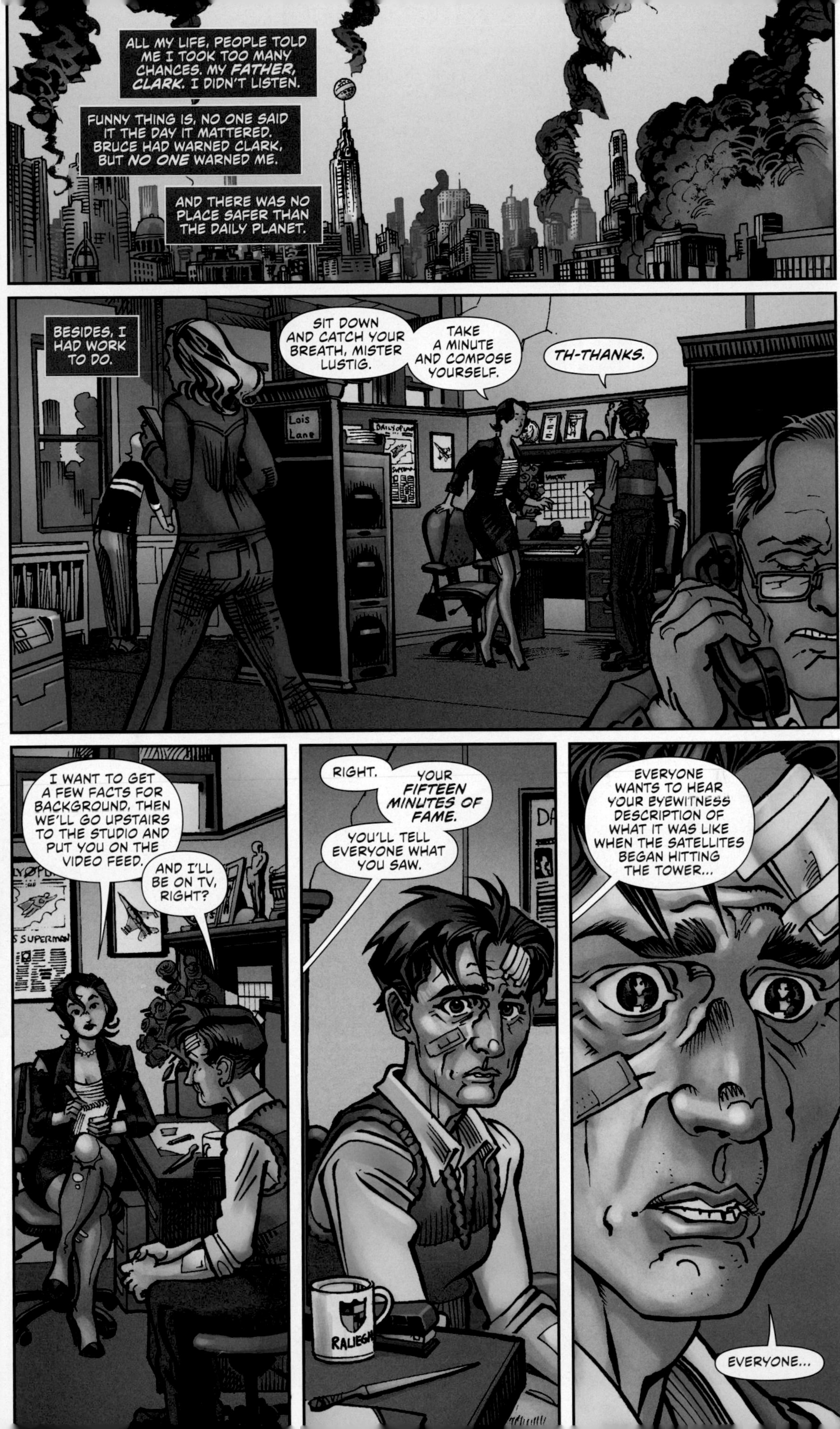
ALL MY LIFE, PEOPLE TOLD ME I TOOK TOO MANY CHANCES. MY *FATHER, CLARK.* I DIDN'T LISTEN.
FUNNY THING IS, NO ONE SAID IT THE DAY IT MATTERED. BRUCE HAD WARNED CLARK, BUT *NO ONE* WARNED ME.
AND THERE WAS NO PLACE SAFER THAN THE DAILY PLANET.
BESIDES, I HAD WORK TO DO.
SIT DOWN AND CATCH YOUR BREATH, MISTER LUSTIG.
TAKE A MINUTE AND COMPOSE YOURSELF.
TH-THANKS.
Lois Lane
I WANT TO GET A FEW FACTS FOR BACKGROUND, THEN WE'LL GO UPSTAIRS TO THE STUDIO AND PUT YOU ON THE VIDEO FEED.
AND I'LL BE ON TV, RIGHT?
RIGHT.
YOUR *FIFTEEN MINUTES OF FAME.*
YOU'LL TELL EVERYONE WHAT YOU SAW.
RALIEGH
EVERYONE WANTS TO HEAR YOUR EYEWITNESS DESCRIPTION OF WHAT IT WAS LIKE WHEN THE SATELLITES BEGAN HITTING THE TOWER...
EVERYONE...

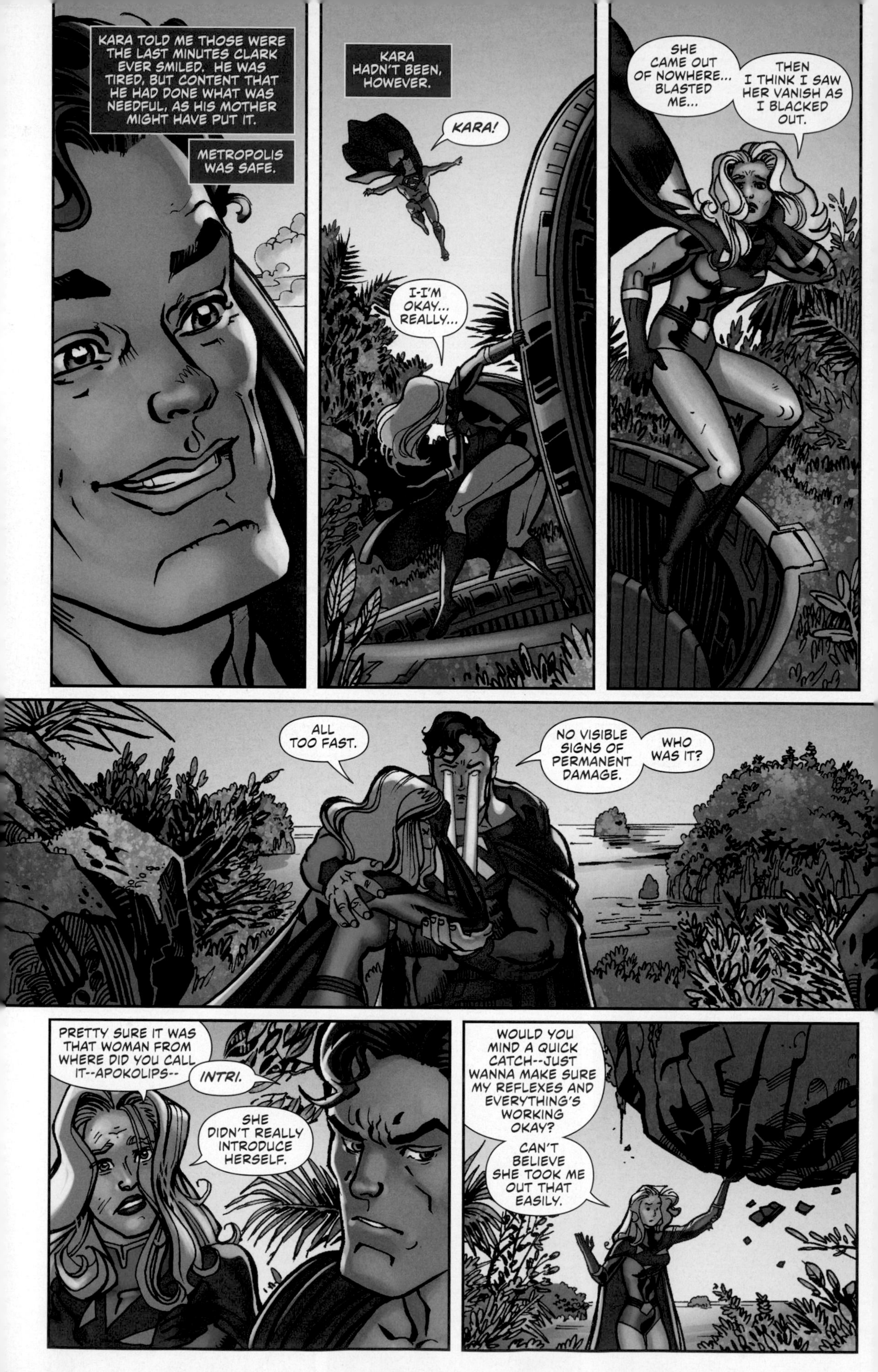
KARA TOLD ME THOSE WERE THE LAST MINUTES CLARK EVER SMILED. HE WAS TIRED, BUT CONTENT THAT HE HAD DONE WHAT WAS NEEDFUL, AS HIS MOTHER MIGHT HAVE PUT IT.
METROPOLIS WAS SAFE.
KARA HADN'T BEEN, HOWEVER.
KARA!
I-I'M OKAY... REALLY...
SHE CAME OUT OF NOWHERE... BLASTED ME...
THEN I THINK I SAW HER VANISH AS I BLACKED OUT.
ALL TOO FAST.
NO VISIBLE SIGNS OF PERMANENT DAMAGE.
WHO WAS IT?
PRETTY SURE IT WAS THAT WOMAN FROM WHERE DID YOU CALL IT--APOKOLIPS--
INTRI.
SHE DIDN'T REALLY INTRODUCE HERSELF.
WOULD YOU MIND A QUICK CATCH--JUST WANNA MAKE SURE MY REFLEXES AND EVERYTHING'S WORKING OKAY?
CAN'T BELIEVE SHE TOOK ME OUT THAT EASILY.

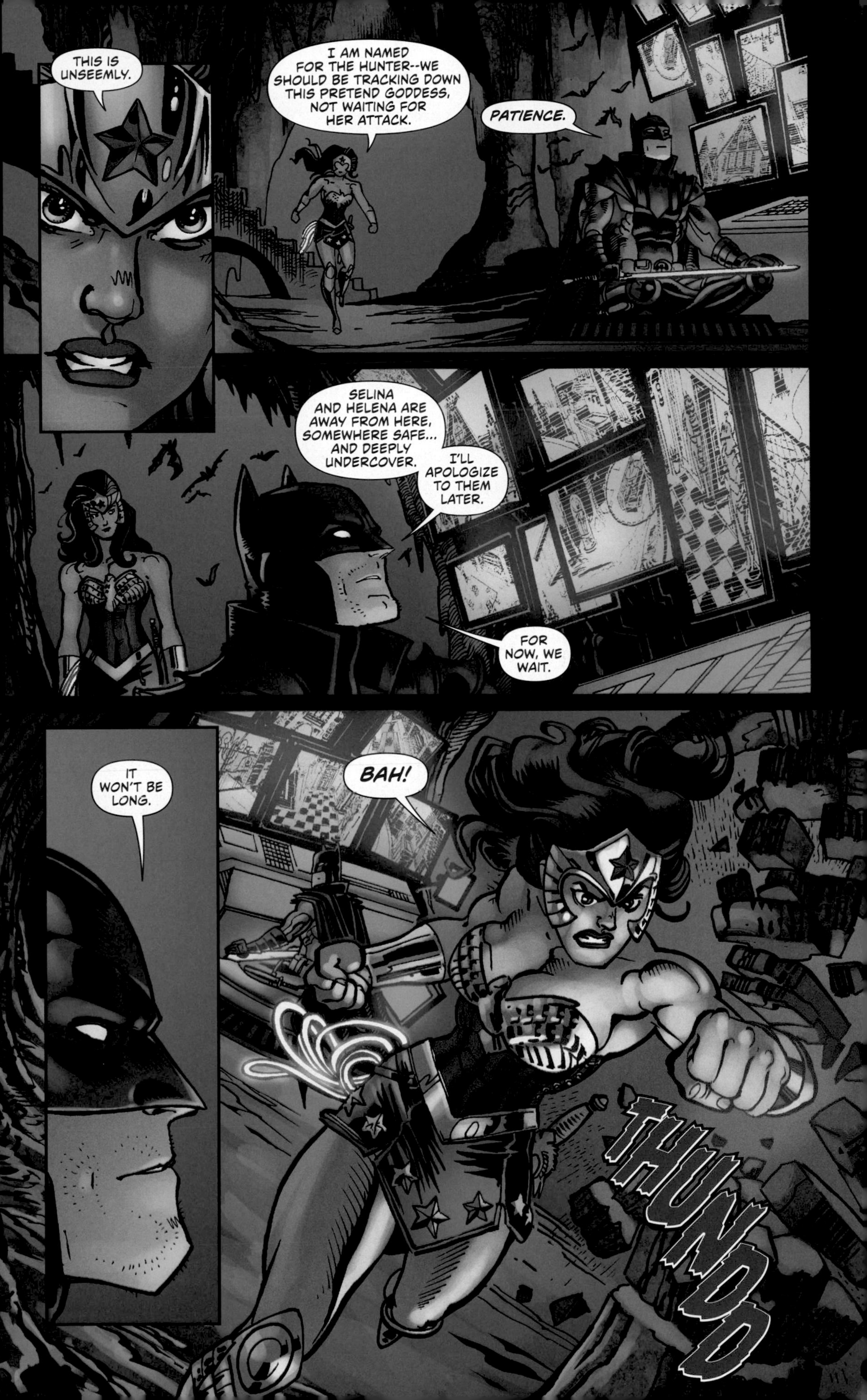

THIS IS UNSEEMLY.
I AM NAMED FOR THE HUNTER--WE SHOULD BE TRACKING DOWN THIS PRETEND GODDESS, NOT WAITING FOR HER ATTACK.
PATIENCE.
SELINA AND HELENA ARE AWAY FROM HERE, SOMEWHERE SAFE... AND DEEPLY UNDERCOVER.
I'LL APOLOGIZE TO THEM LATER.
FOR NOW, WE WAIT.
IT WON'T BE LONG.
BAH!
THUNDD

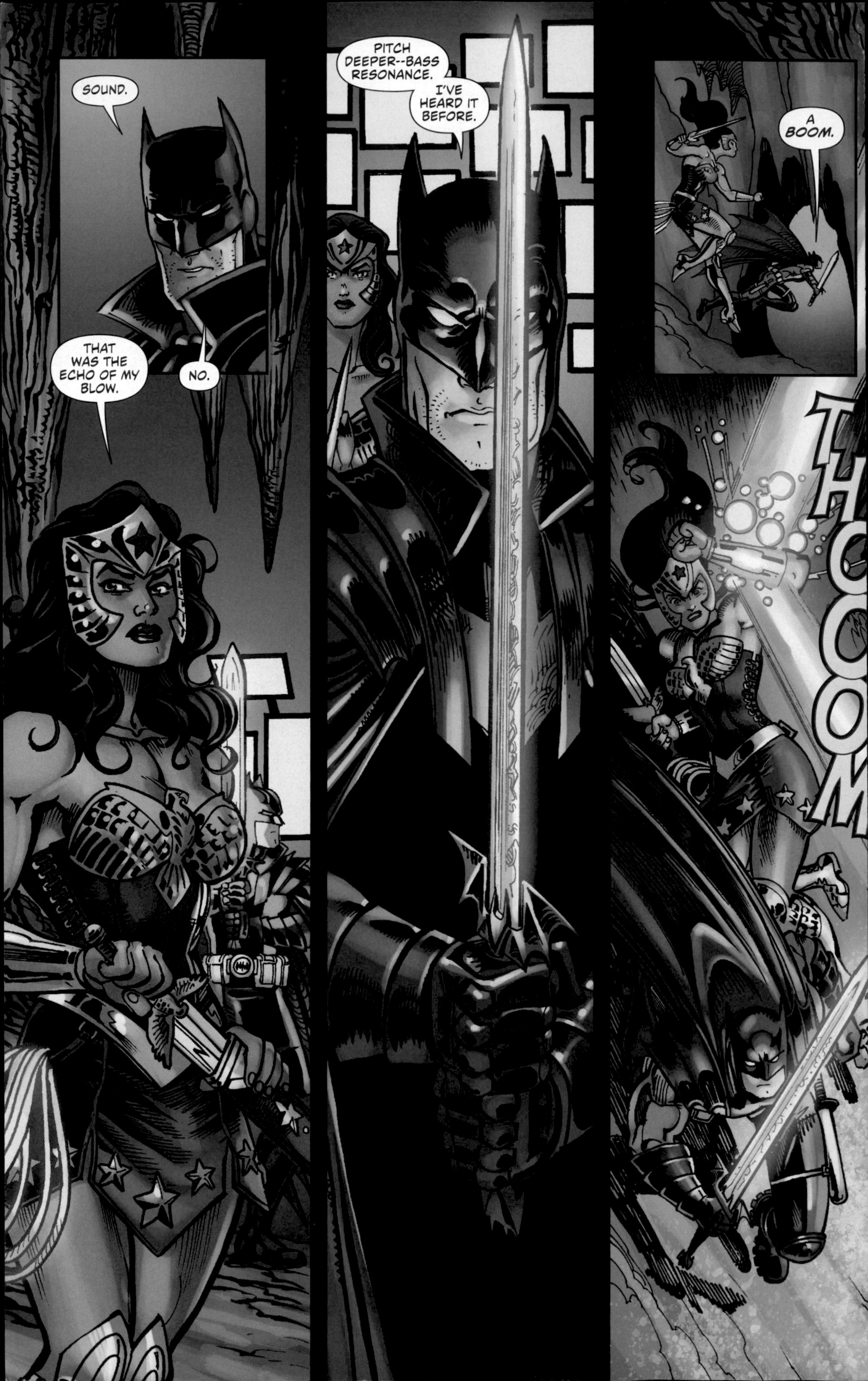
SOUND.
NO.
THAT WAS THE ECHO OF MY BLOW.
PITCH DEEPER--BASS RESONANCE.
I'VE HEARD IT BEFORE.
A BOOM.
THOOOM

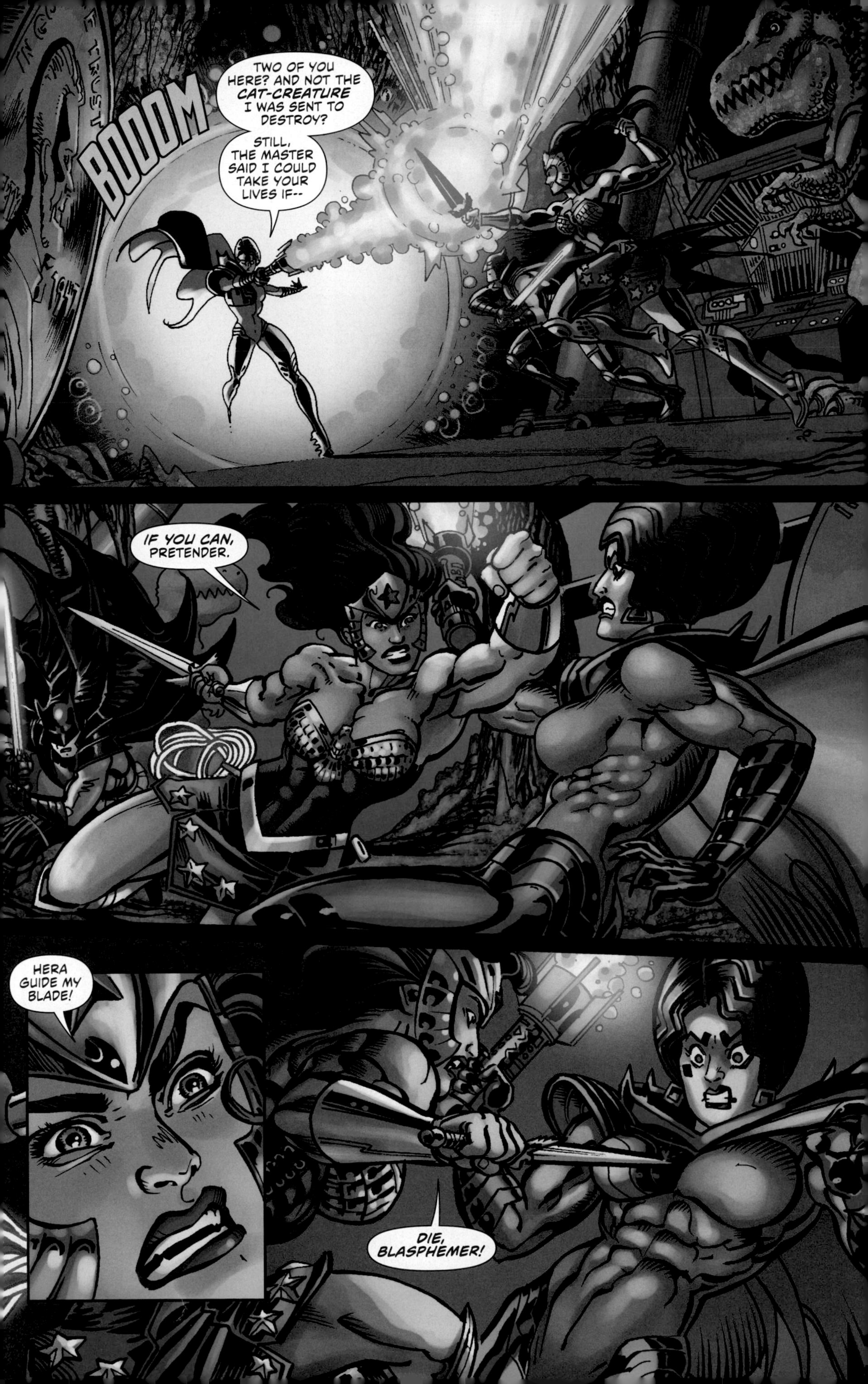
BOOOM
TWO OF YOU HERE? AND NOT THE CAT-CREATURE I WAS SENT TO DESTROY?
STILL, THE MASTER SAID I COULD TAKE YOUR LIVES IF--
IF YOU CAN, PRETENDER.
HERA GUIDE MY BLADE!
DIE, BLASPHEMER!

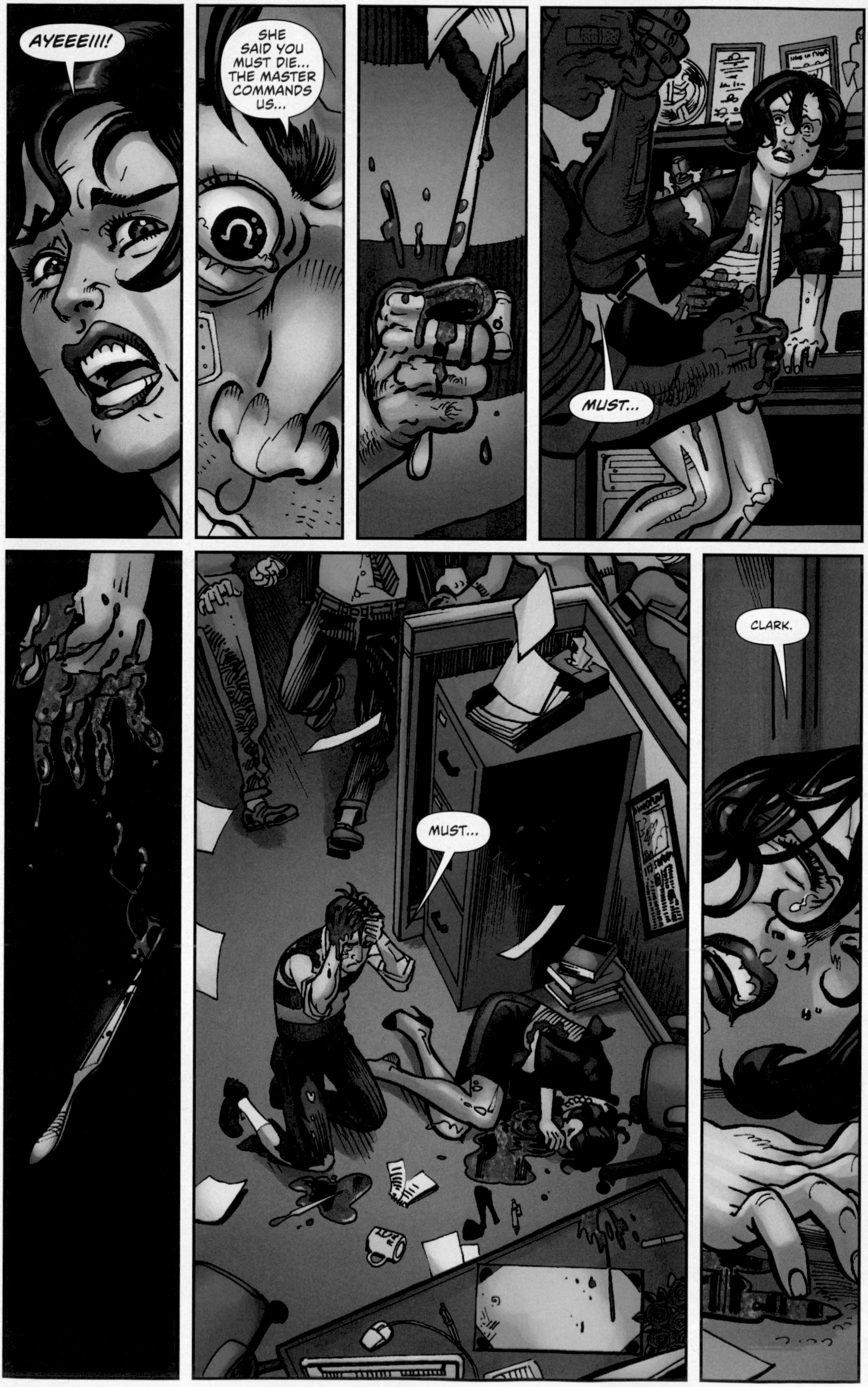
AYEEEIII!
SHE SAID YOU MUST DIE... THE MASTER COMMANDS US...
MUST...
MUST...
CLARK.

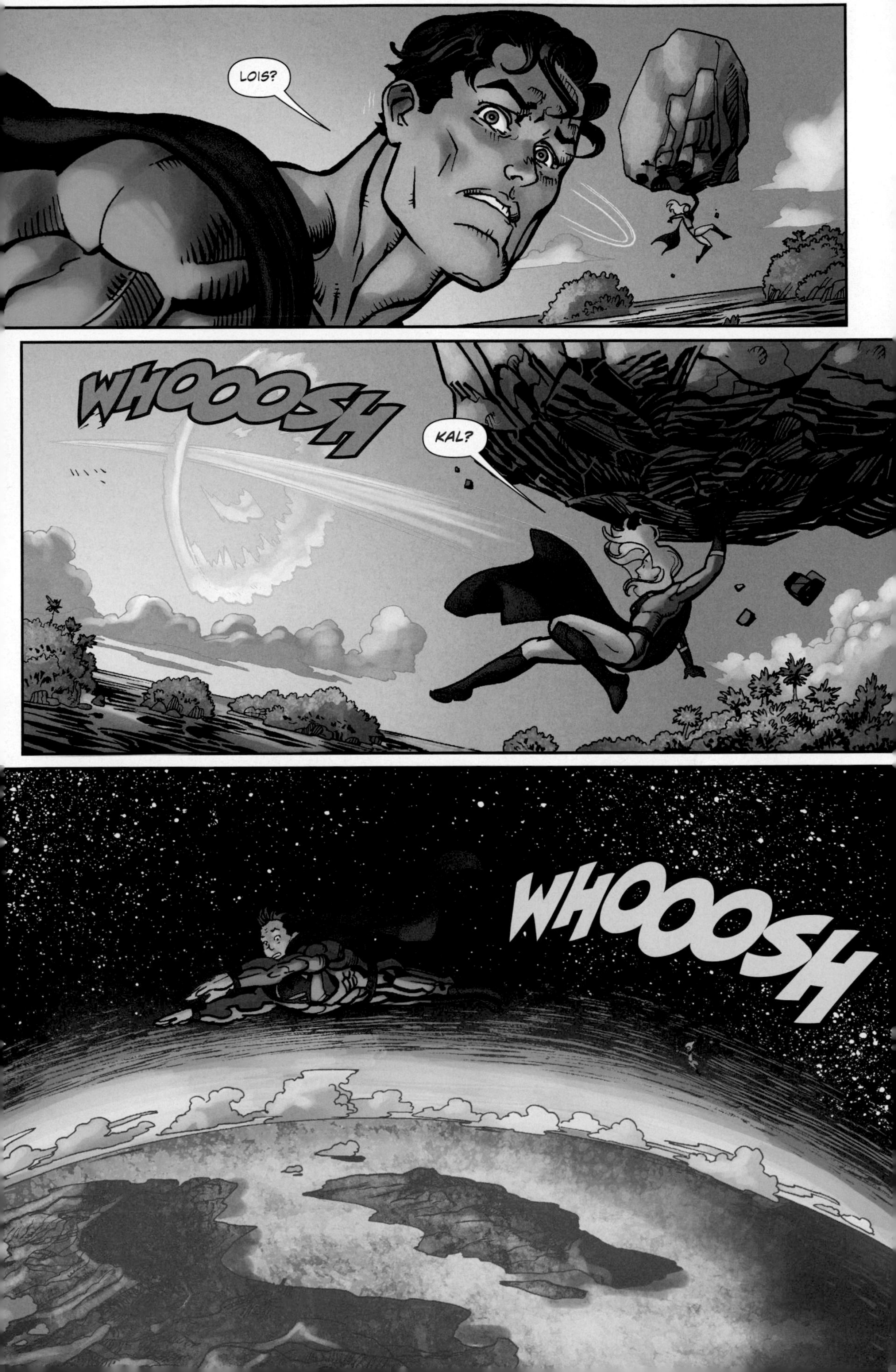
LOIS?
WHOOOSH
KAL?
WHOOOSH

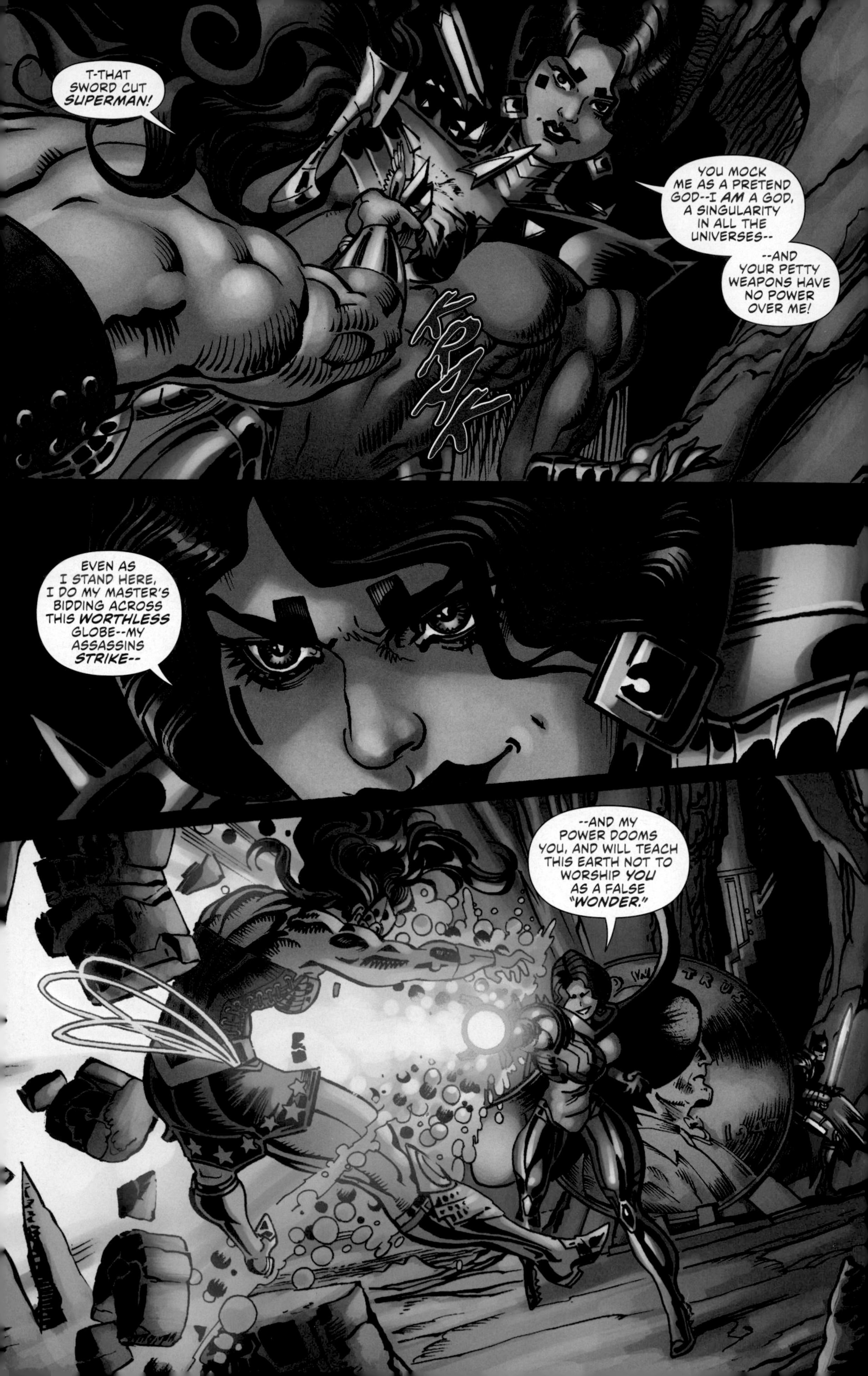
T-THAT SWORD CUT SUPERMAN!
YOU MOCK ME AS A PRETEND GOD--I AM A GOD, A SINGULARITY IN ALL THE UNIVERSES--
--AND YOUR PETTY WEAPONS HAVE NO POWER OVER ME!
KRAK
EVEN AS I STAND HERE, I DO MY MASTER'S BIDDING ACROSS THIS WORTHLESS GLOBE--MY ASSASSINS STRIKE--
--AND MY POWER DOOMS YOU, AND WILL TEACH THIS EARTH NOT TO WORSHIP YOU AS A FALSE "WONDER."

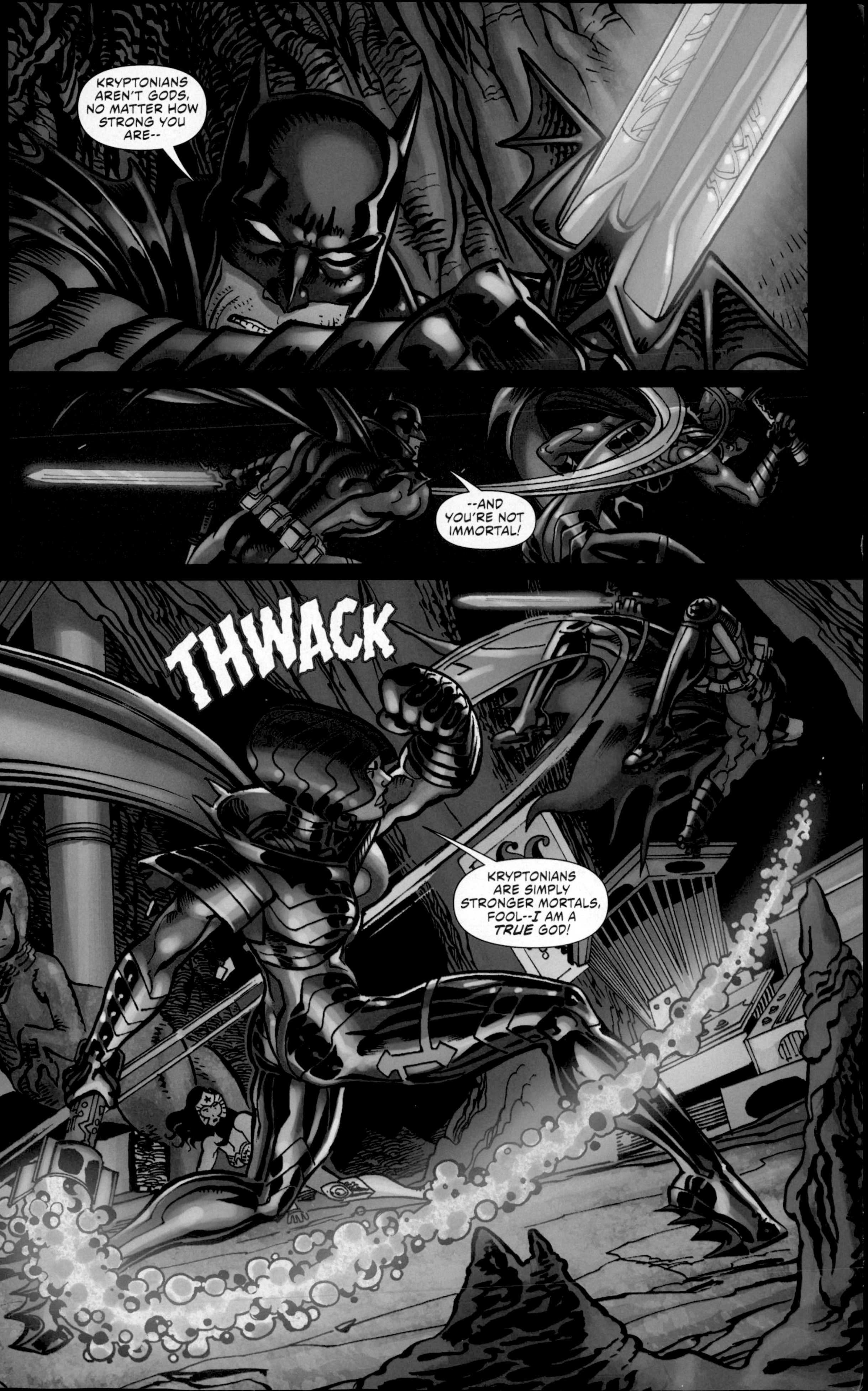
KRYPTONIANS AREN'T GODS, NO MATTER HOW STRONG YOU ARE--
--AND YOU'RE NOT IMMORTAL!
THWACK
KRYPTONIANS ARE SIMPLY STRONGER MORTALS, FOOL--I AM A TRUE GOD!

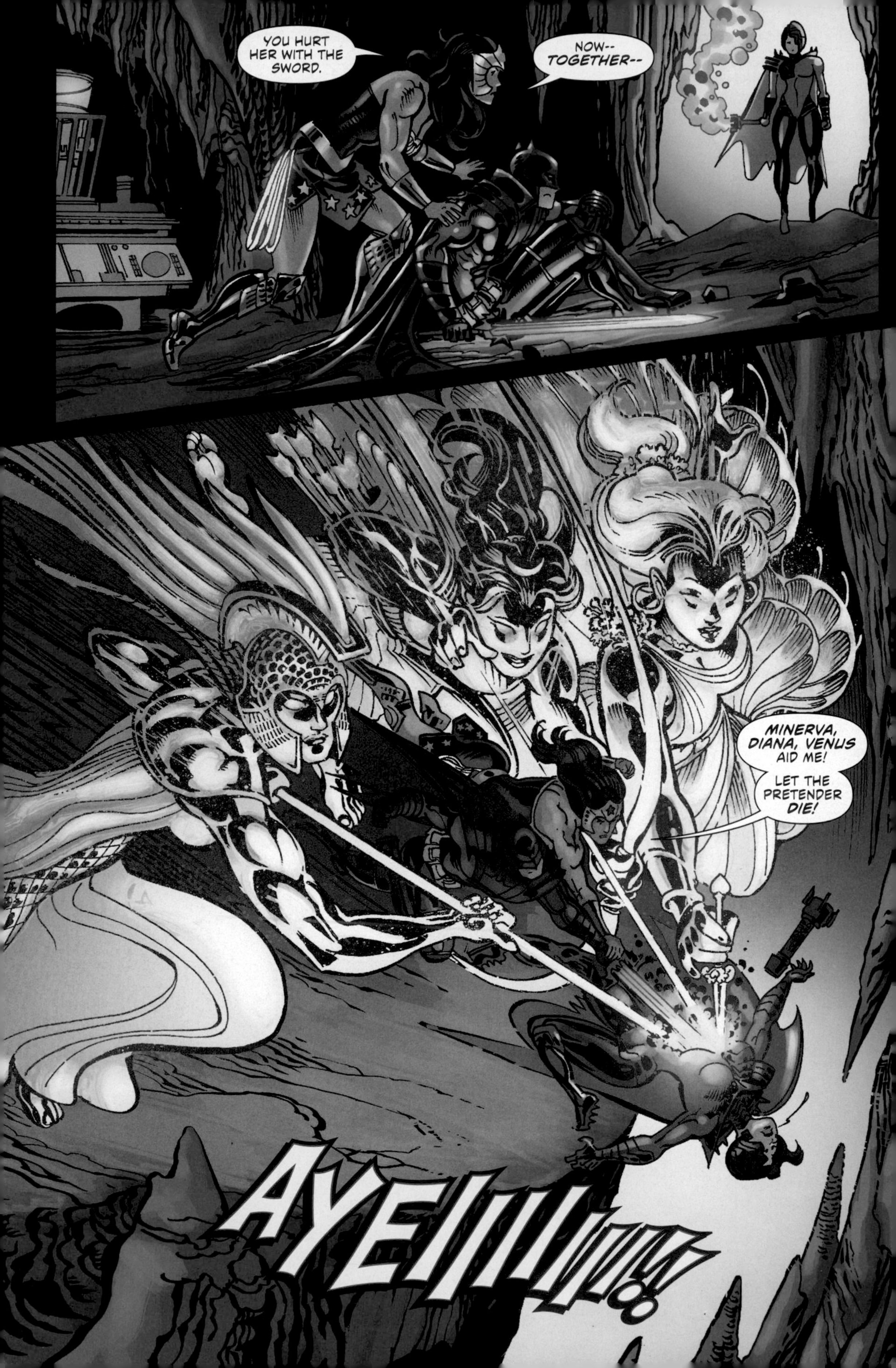

YOU HURT HER WITH THE SWORD.
NOW-- TOGETHER--
MINERVA, DIANA, VENUS AID ME!
LET THE PRETENDER DIE!
AYEIIIII!!

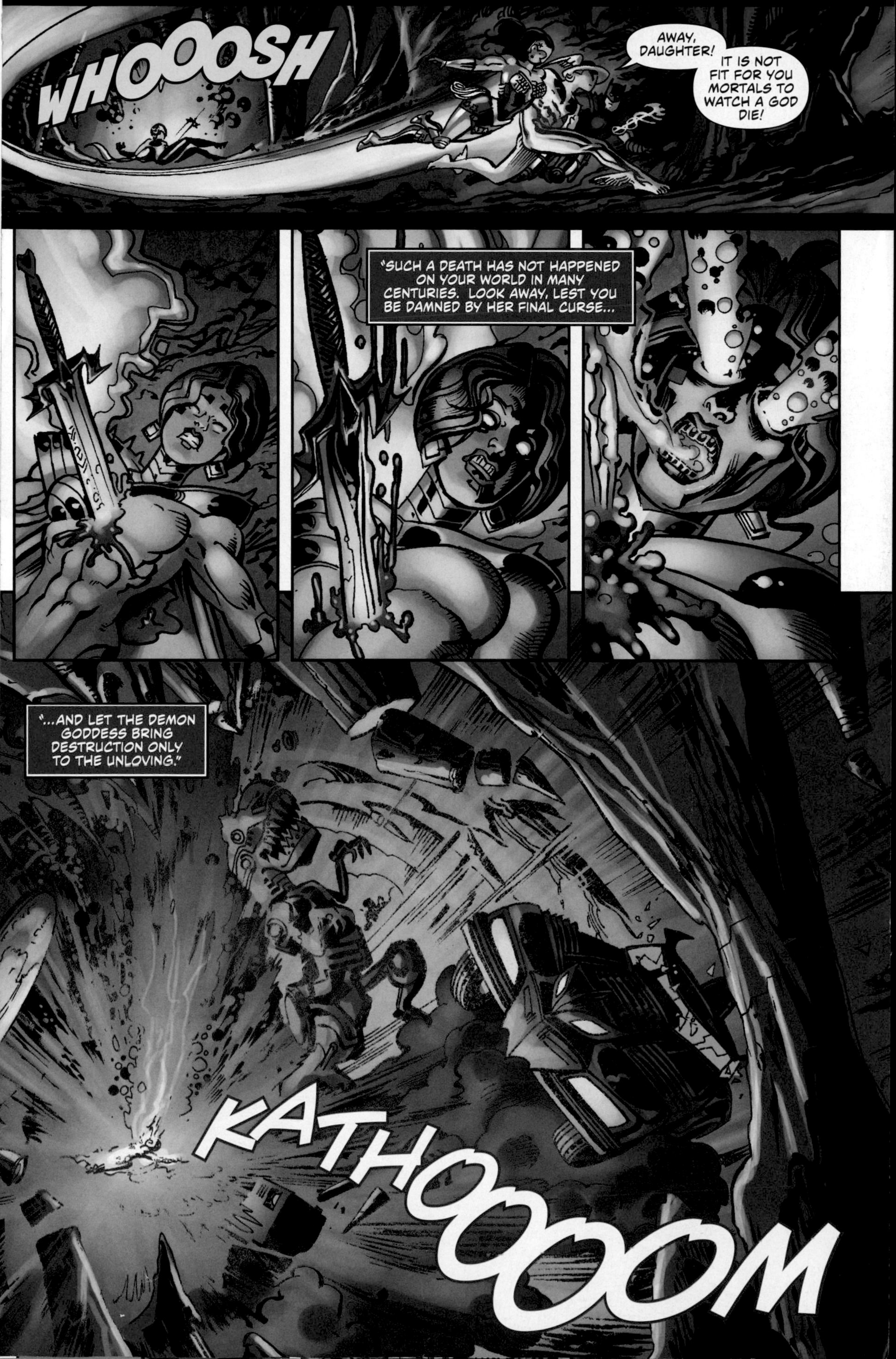
WHOOOSH
AWAY, DAUGHTER!
IT IS NOT FIT FOR YOU MORTALS TO WATCH A GOD DIE!
"SUCH A DEATH HAS NOT HAPPENED ON YOUR WORLD IN MANY CENTURIES. LOOK AWAY, LEST YOU BE DAMNED BY HER FINAL CURSE...
"...AND LET THE DEMON GODDESS BRING DESTRUCTION ONLY TO THE UNLOVING."
KATHOOOOOM

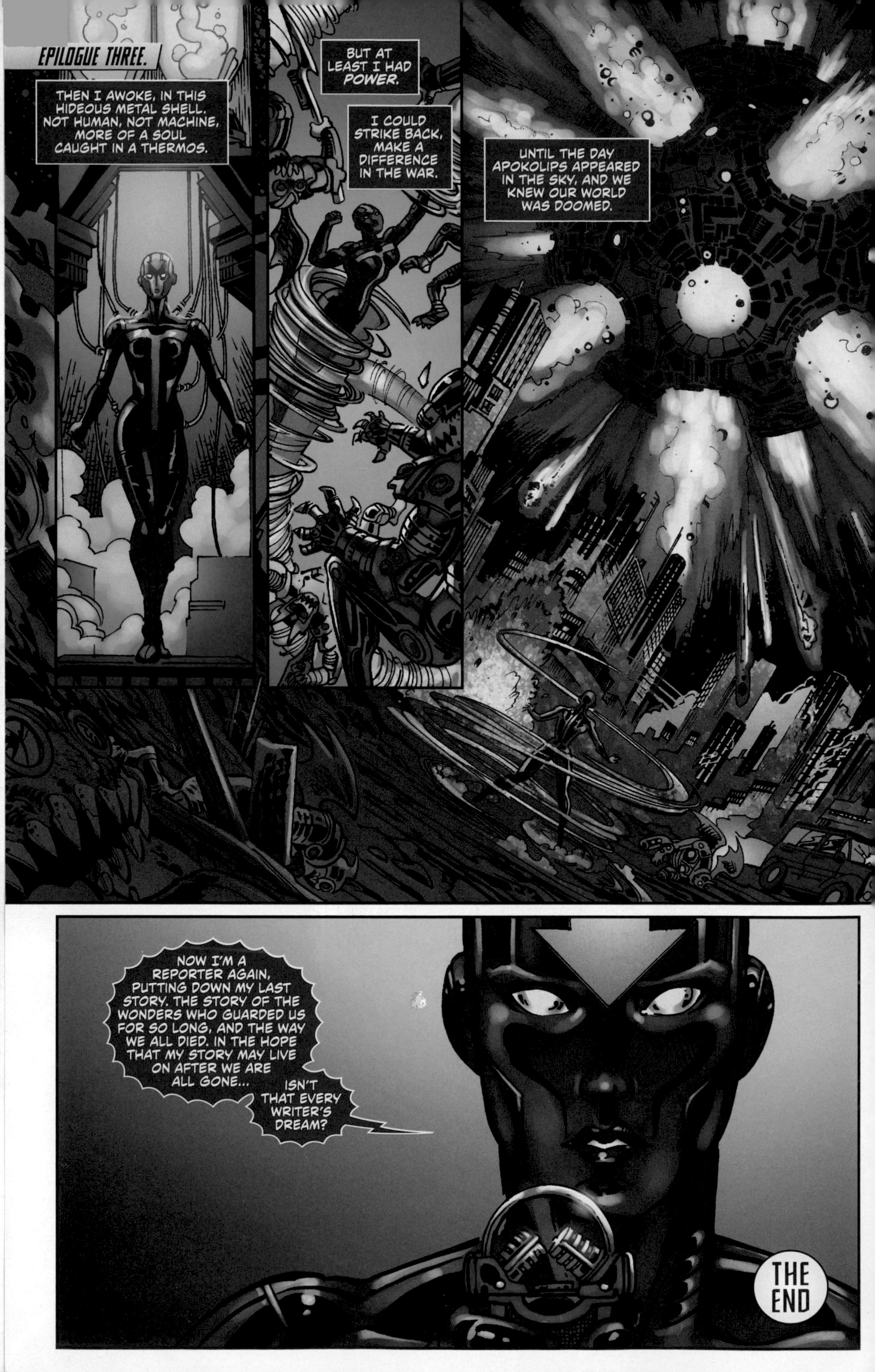
EPILOGUE THREE.
THEN I AWOKE, IN THIS HIDEOUS METAL SHELL. NOT HUMAN, NOT MACHINE, MORE OF A SOUL CAUGHT IN A THERMOS.
BUT AT LEAST I HAD POWER.
I COULD STRIKE BACK, MAKE A DIFFERENCE IN THE WAR.
UNTIL THE DAY APOKOLIPS APPEARED IN THE SKY, AND WE KNEW OUR WORLD WAS DOOMED.
NOW I'M A REPORTER AGAIN, PUTTING DOWN MY LAST STORY. THE STORY OF THE WONDERS WHO GUARDED US FOR SO LONG, AND THE WAY WE ALL DIED. IN THE HOPE THAT MY STORY MAY LIVE ON AFTER WE ARE ALL GONE...
ISN'T THAT EVERY WRITER'S DREAM?
THE END

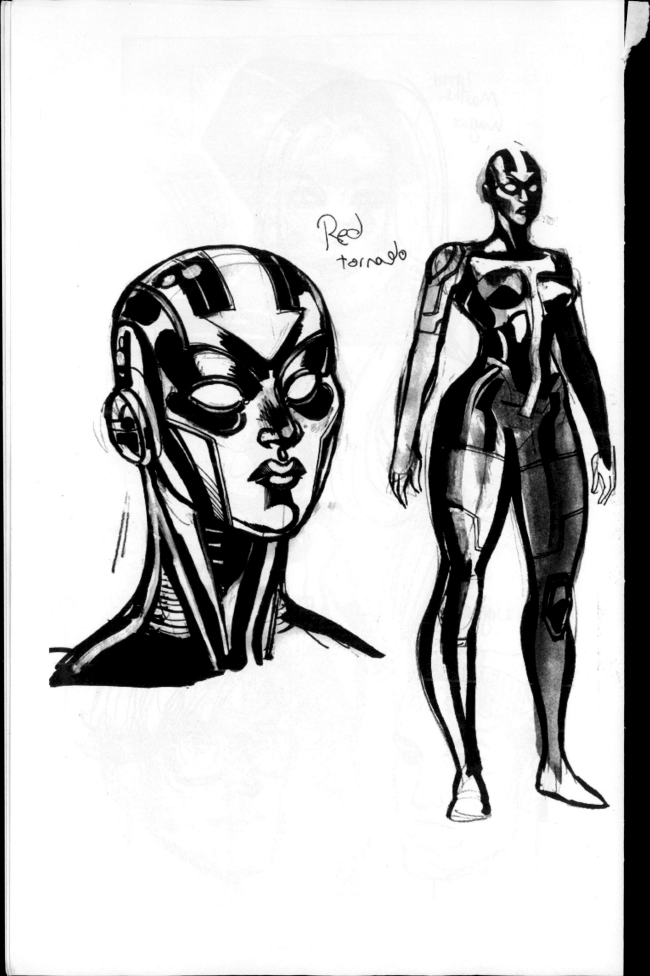

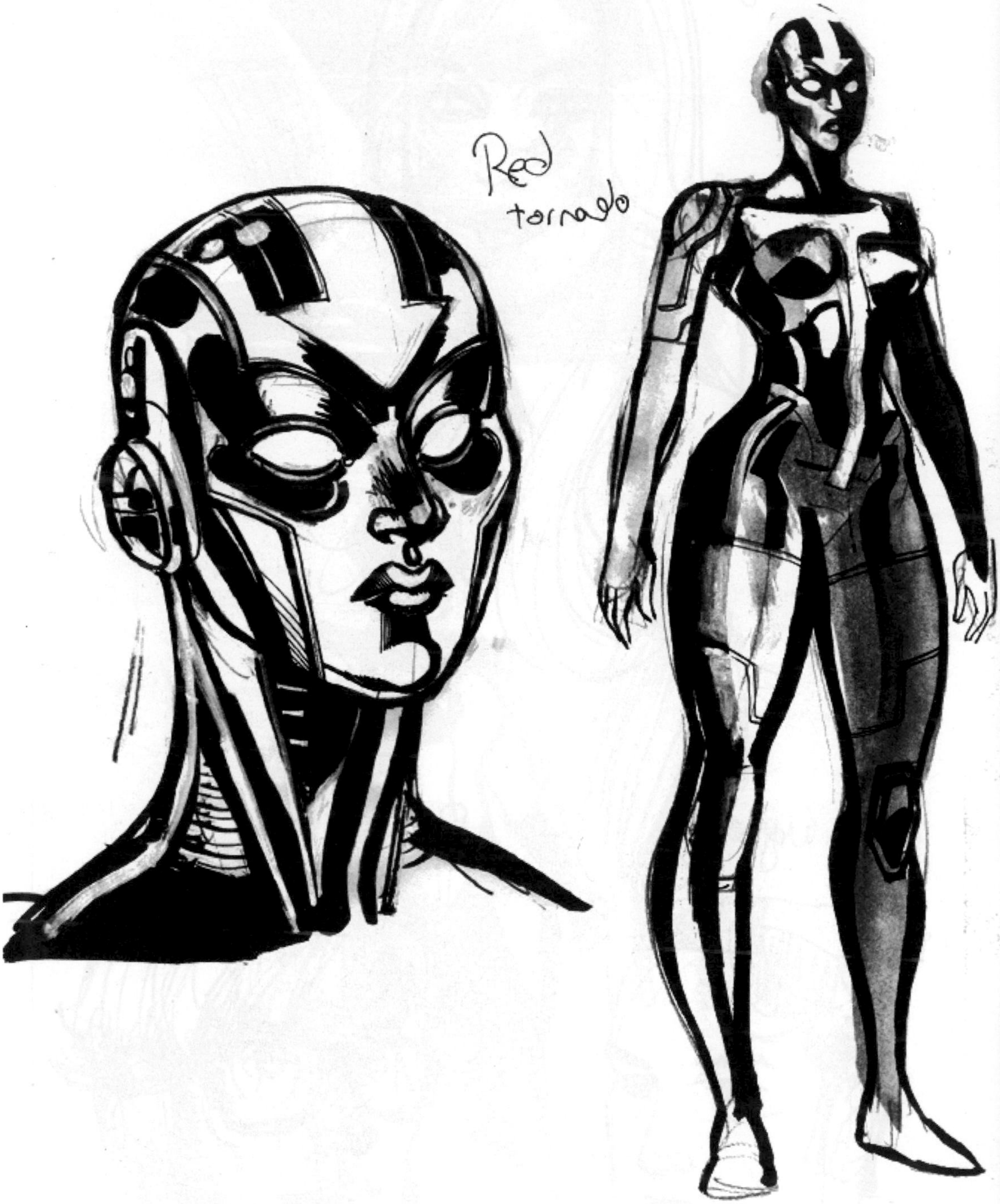
Red
tornado